W9-AWI-623

Replace pandemonium with peace!

Whether it's playtime, mealtime, or bedtime when your kids act up, this book will show you solutions based on the experiences of parents just like you, and a method of creating controlled conflict—which eventually leads to no conflict at all. Discover:

- How Larry taught his two-year-old son to behave properly around the family's expensive stereo equipment—without setting up any physical barriers

- How in *thirty minutes*, four-year-old Jesse learned that his usual strategies for getting attention—like whining, arguing, defying, and yelling—were no longer effective

- How Melanie dealt with the antics of her son Aedan, a four-year-old grocery store–bolter, who would dart off and chase whatever caught his eye

- How frustrated parents Lori and Wayne—who actually had son Kyle's hearing tested because he was so unresponsive—taught him to tune out the video games and respectfully tune into their requests

- How Corrine, battle-scarred mom of three under the age of five, dramatically transformed chaotic and dangerous minivan excursions with the kids into safe, even pleasant family outings.

Want your kids to be successful adults? Then teach them the skills of cooperation today by . . .

Drawing the Line

Drawing the Line

Ten Steps to Constructive Discipline— and Achieving a Great Relationship with Your Kids

Michael J. Weiss, PhD, and
Sheldon H. Wagner, PhD,

with Susan Goldberg

WARNER BOOKS

NEW YORK   BOSTON

If you purchase this book without a cover you should be aware that this book may have been stolen property and reported as "unsold and destroyed" to the publisher. In such case neither the author nor the publisher has received any payment for this "stripped book."

Copyright © 2006 by TJB Developmental Media, LLC

All rights reserved.

Warner Books

Time Warner Book Group
1271 Avenue of the Americas
New York, NY 10020
Visit our Web site at www.twbookmark.com.

Printed in the United States of America

First Edition: February 2006
10   9   8   7   6   5   4   3   2   1

Library of Congress Cataloging-in-Publication Data
Weiss, Michael J. (Michael Joseph).
Drawing the line : ten steps to constructive discipline—and achieving
a great relationship with your kids / Michael Weiss and Sheldon Wagner
with Susan Goldberg. — 1st ed.
p.   cm.
ISBN-13: 978-0-446-69500-8
ISBN-10: 0-446-69500-9
1. Discipline of children.   2. Behavior modification.   3. Parent and child.
4. Parenting.   I. Wagner, Sheldon (Sheldon H.), 1954–   II. Goldberg, Susan.
III. Title.
HQ770.4.W44 2006
649'.64—dc22   2005022273

This book is dedicated to the memory of
Ruth Laine Goldberg,
an extraordinary parent.

Contents

Introduction

I'll never forget the first time it happened. I was sitting in a restaurant, having dinner with a couple of friends—who, incidentally, happened to be our film editors—when a woman, a complete stranger, came up to our table and tapped me on the shoulder. "You're the doctor with the ponytail!" she said.

I stared at her for a moment, confused. My hand strayed to the back of my head. The ponytail—one of the last physical remnants of my misspent youth—was there, yes.

"Uh . . . ," I said, looking at her quizzically.

"You're Dr. Michael Weiss, right? I love your TV show! My daughter sleeps through the night because of you!"

Over the next several years, I got used to being stopped on the street, at the mall, in restaurants. Always, it was a version of the same experience: Parents would confirm that I was indeed that "guy with the ponytail on that TV show," and then they'd tell me just how their lives—and their kids' behavior—had changed from watching it. "My boys don't fight nearly as much," they'd say, or "I've stopped dreading mealtimes now," or, "Toilet training my youngest was so much easier than it was for the other two."

The show they were referring to was *Real Families*, a half-hour cable TV show that my partner (and co-author of this book), Sheldon Wagner, and I had created in the mid-1990s. Its premise was about as simple as it got: The two of us, child psychologists, went into the homes of real kids with real behavior problems and helped their parents learn effective, compassionate ways of dealing with their behavior.

Simple, yes. But, as we were to discover, our show proved revolutionary to literally thousands of parents around the world.

"He's Just Not Like This at Home . . ."

For us, there was nothing revolutionary about what we were doing. As part of my clinical practice, I'd been going into people's homes for the past twenty years, a practice that began when I was a graduate student at Tufts University, working with a fantastic supervisor, Dr. Philip Zelazo (now a professor of psychology at McGill University in Montreal, Canada).

Phil was studying kids with delayed development, and I was working with him on his studies, observing and testing the participating kids. Over and over, we'd see these kids in our offices and in the lab, and over and over their parents would say the same thing: "You know, he's really not like this at home."

The first dozen times or so I heard it, I chalked it up to parental anxiety. But—and perhaps *this* is revolutionary—it finally occurred to me that maybe we *should* listen to children's parents. Maybe it would make sense that kids would behave one way at home and differently in an unfamiliar, clinical setting. Maybe it would benefit both our research and our skills as psychologists and therapists to go into actual homes and see how children—and their parents— behaved when they were in familiar surroundings.

I'll never forget the first day I spent an hour with a child in his own home. At the end, I turned and said to his mom, "You know, he's really not like this in the lab!" And this poor kid's mother just nodded. What she should have said was, *Well, duh! And why weren't you here five months ago?*

In an instant, I realized something so simple that it should have been obvious (and yet it wasn't—and still isn't—obvious to so many of my colleagues, who work out of incredibly well-equipped, high-tech university laboratories and plush offices): *If you want to see what's really going on in a family, you have to become part of it.* Rather than making kids and parents come to us, we had to go to them, and observe and listen to them in their own spaces. Then, and only then, could we intervene. And for many of these kids, kids who were at significant risk, intervention was critical: We had to get in early, and intensively—at home and in the classroom—in order to make a difference.

Drawing the Line

And so began the era of the home visit. This was the late 1970s. Phil had been going into clients' homes for a while, but now I also became a champion of the concept. In 1984, Phil and I both moved to McGill University. There, over the next ten years, I really honed the concept of the home visit and perfected the art of what I now call Drawing the Line. By the time I moved back to the United States, to work at Harvard's prestigious Children's Hospital in Boston, I could go into any home, with any kid, and make that kid explode on demand.

Yes, you read right: explode on demand. I would walk into these homes—homes usually of kids with significant developmental delays and/or behavior problems, kids whose parents were often at their wit's end—and tell those parents, "I'm going to pose a challenge to your child. I'll bet you a hundred dollars that, within the next hour, I can set up a simple scenario that will push all your kid's buttons. And I'll bet you that by the end of that hour, your child not only will have taken a significant step forward in terms of development, but also will actually like me, too."

Now the parents' curiosity was piqued. "Okay," they'd say, "be our guest."

Then I'd say, "The thing is, your kid's not going to like this. There's probably going to be some screaming and crying going on at first. Do you mind if I have your daughter screaming her guts out in the next ten minutes or so? If you can bear with me, I promise we'll find a way that this can work—for you and for her."

At this point, some people, a small percentage, said no. "I hear enough yelling as it is," they'd tell me, and I'd be shown the door. I was thrown out of some of the finest homes in North America. And that was fine—those parents knew their limits, and I respected those limits.

Most parents, however, let me go on. They wanted to see what I would do next, whether or not they liked it. Others figured that they heard so much screaming and crying in their homes on a regular basis, another hour's worth wouldn't make a difference—especially if it led to a significant developmental change. "Go ahead," they'd tell me. "Let's see what happens."

And what happened was always the same. With the kids with behavior problems—kids who just wouldn't listen to their parents, who wouldn't give Mom or Dad a moment's peace—I would typically set up a very simple situation. "Your mom and dad and I are going to sit in the kitchen and have a big, long grown-up conversation," I'd tell the kids. "We need you to stay in the living room and play with your toys. Can you do that for me?"

Well, as a matter of fact, most of these kids couldn't do that. For them, it was a setup for defiance. You could just see them thinking it: *This guy with the ponytail says that I can't come into the kitchen to see my mom? No way.* Within minutes, most kids crossed the line—that clear-as-day line where the carpeting in the living room ended and the kitchen tiles began. And then I would insist that they stay on their side of the line. And then, like clockwork, they would explode—screaming, crying, throwing monster tantrums, even, in a few memorable situations, threatening to throw up. All because I'd asked them to—no, *made* them—stay five feet away from their parents and not interrupt the adults' conversation.

Over the next ten, fifteen, sixty minutes, we'd play out the scenario over and over. I'd use a variety of techniques—techniques we'll describe in detail in the following chapters—to not only *make* kids respect the new boundaries, but get them to *want* to respect the new boundaries as well.

The parents had front-row seats for the entire exchange. They'd sit (sometimes on their hands) at the kitchen table and watch it all—watch their darling offspring go utterly berserk, and watch me be the biggest son-of-a-gun their kids had ever encountered in my insistence that the kids respect that line between the two rooms. Their responses alternated between "What a nice guy!" and "What a brute!" and then eventually came around to, "Did you see what he got our kid to do? I didn't know she was capable of that."

Initially, most parents were kind of horrified—at how determined and mechanical I was, at just how hysterical their kids could get, at how noisy and chaotic it all seemed. The horror would be replaced with astonishment, and then relief as their kids finally "got" it. Even more astonishing to parents was the fact that their kids actually *liked* me: By the end of that hour, I'd generally be on the living room floor with the kids, playing happily with them and making them giggle. Shy toddlers would cuddle with me and bring me their teddy bears.

Once parents could see with their own eyes, in their own homes, that their own kids were indeed capable of cooperation, they were eager to learn how to Draw the Line on their own terms. They knew how I did it. And once they understood the basic techniques I had used, they could adapt those techniques to suit their own comfort levels and family sensibilities. Very quickly, they developed a command of Drawing the Line.

First, we worked in the privacy of kids' homes. Whether it was kids who didn't listen or delayed toilet training, refusals to eat or go to sleep, sibling battles, rudeness, whining, what have you, I helped parents figure out the patterns that promoted problem behaviors (and those patterns are remarkably consistent from family to family, household to household). Then I showed them how to change or replace those patterns to promote more appropriate behavior—and household peace.

As parents became more adept at home, we took the same philosophies outside: to the car, to the mall, to church or synagogue services, to the park, to school. I began consulting to school boards, both for typical and for special-education classrooms. Again and again, parents and teachers were at first a tiny bit (or a lot) horrified, then astonished, then thrilled.

FROM DRAWING THE LINE TO *REAL FAMILIES*

My employers at my new job, however, were less than thrilled. I had left my mentor, Phil Zelazo, and McGill University, and found a job as a clinical fellow at the Children's Hospital Boston and Harvard University School of Medicine. Harvard University! Imagine how happy my mother was: She could now talk about "my son, the doctor, at Harvard."

Little did I realize that the job title was code for "low-paid-bottom-of-the-barrel faculty member." I was about to be bitterly disappointed. As far as my boss saw things, I never showed up to work. Even though I logged more hours with kids and families than anyone else in the institution, the fact that I never seemed to be in the building rankled my supervisor. Plus, I outright refused to administer IQ tests, which was the principal job for the psychologists in our department. Why would I sit around giving kids misleading and meaningless tests, I figured, when I could be doing intervention full-time?

So I quit. I quit Harvard. I quit the Children's Hospital—two moves that most career counselors would have found questionable, at best. My parents worried. My friends and colleagues worried. Heck, even I was worried: Would I be able to find work?

As it turned out, I didn't need to worry. When I left the Children's Hospital, I had more work than I could handle. All the families I had worked with came with me. They, too, didn't want to sit around while their kids took IQ test after IQ test and still trashed the house. They wanted results. And Drawing the Line got results. But these families were my most ardent supporters not because of the party tricks I could get kids to do, but because their kids liked me, too.

Through word of mouth, I attracted more and more clients, until finally I couldn't handle the amount of work I had. A mutual friend introduced me to Sheldon Wagner. We were the odd couple of psychology, as different as night and day—me the hippie-wannabe holdover with the ponytail, Sheldon much more buttoned-down conservative; me ready to get rough-and-tumble with kids on the playroom floor, to fly by the seat of my pants, Sheldon with a much more theoretical, academic approach that was rooted in his thorough understanding of the research and literature on developmental psychology. He was the yin to my yang, and we got along great. By the early 1990s, we were managing a staff of forty, consulting to almost two hundred school boards, and had worked with, literally, thousands of kids.

We loved the work. But we were also getting frustrated—with just how often we had to repeat ourselves, to both our staff and our clients. Over and over, we found ourselves telling people the same things: how to Draw the Line. How the correct *timing* is essential when it comes to dealing with kids' behavior. How, when, and how much to *talk* to kids who are acting up—and why less talk is best in the heat of the moment. *Where* parents and caregivers should position themselves in relation to the kids. The incredible value of *rewards*, and the virtues of *penalizing* inappropriate behavior. The absolute need to *respond* to kids, to love them unconditionally, and to display that love and *warmth*—while also demanding high standards of behavior through high levels of *control*. How to *practice* new behaviors, and how to slowly *wean* kids from parental support. Why a *permissive* style of parenting is such a dead end, as is an *authoritarian* model that bullies kids into behaving.

We knew that if we could spend less time repeating ourselves, we could devote more time to working with kids and taking them farther and farther. Sheldon and I brainstormed ways to get past the repetition, until finally we hit upon the idea of making a series of educational videos to illustrate our points.

It would have ended there if not for two very wise friends of mine, Irina and Tom O'Hara, who said, "Educational videos? Who's going to watch those? If you're going to make educational videos, why not go all the way and put it on television?"

We were just naive enough—and just lucky enough—to take their advice to heart. We would make a show based on our clinical practice: those hundreds upon hundreds of psychological house calls to families. The premise was simple: We'd find families with typical kids and typical behavior problems—your garden-variety listening, eating, sleeping, cooperating, fighting, bullying, tantrum-throwing, toileting problems. We'd go in and Draw the Line, on camera. And in the process, we'd teach viewers (as well as our staff and clients) that set of principles and techniques we'd been honing all these years.

Everyone thought we were crazy. "People like you don't make television shows," we were told. "Who wants to watch a couple of psychologists deal with bratty children?" Further, the pundits told us—in what would become one of the most ironic statements to ever come out of a TV executive's mouth—that, as far as television was concerned, reality was a dead end. "No one cares about reality," said everyone I talked to. "Trust us: No one wants to watch real people on television."

Despite everyone's misgivings—including some of our own—we raised the money to produce a pilot, and we bought half an hour of airtime in Ottawa, Ontario, Canada. The first episode of *Real Families* aired on an evening in December 1997, right after the evening news. And much to our astonishment, we matched the ratings of the national news. We had an audience. People wanted to watch us in action.

"CAN YOU COME TO OUR HOUSE?"

In fact, people wanted us to come to their homes and work with their kids. At first, we found families through clients and friends. By the time we aired as a daily show a year later, families found us. We were deluged with requests from desperate parents, people who were willing to go on international television with their family's difficulties and dirty laundry in order to get some help. "You know, we're not the type of people who would normally do this," parents told us over and over. "We're not real attention seekers. But we need you."

We took our film crews into homes around North America, and Drew the Line, on camera, with kids and parents. Over and over, we set up controlled periods of conflict with the kids. We pushed their buttons to get them to behave badly, so we could teach them how to behave well.

We visited single moms and two-parent homes, only children and broods of five and six, all kinds of cultural and religious backgrounds. Some families had a ton of money, others very little. Some were college and university educated, while others didn't have a high school diploma. Over seemingly endless cups of coffee at kitchen tables, we found that, despite these surface differences, most parents were in pretty much the same boat: They felt inadequate. They didn't understand how and why their kids could behave the way they did. They felt exhausted, and sometimes ashamed. They told us of their guilt, their frustration, their anger and depression when it came to dealing with their kids. These were loving, caring parents who wanted to provide their kids with every advantage in the book. But they felt thwarted. Their kids were hellions. And they didn't know what to do.

So we showed them. We taught them the basics of Drawing the Line, and we watched, again and again, as kids responded and as parents began to pick up the skills and tricks to creating cooperative children. It worked, over and over again. Why? Well, much of our success was based on the fact that child development has a certain universality in it. What drives behavior—good or not—is also based on fairly universal rules. If you understand what those rules are, you can work with them to change kids' behavior. And we did.

Within a year, the show was airing daily on networks in Canada. Then the United Kingdom got wind of it, and it spread to England, Ireland, and Australia. We became a household name in Belgium. Japanese networks picked it up, then Chinese, then Mexican. The

Israelis loved us. And then *Real Families* began airing in the United
States on the Oxygen Network.

I got used to people stopping me on the streets. People told me of
Real Families playgroups and parties, where parents got together in
groups to watch and discuss the shows. Parents from all over the
world phoned in and e-mailed us. Some just wanted to let us know
how much they enjoyed the show. (A small but significant percentage told us in no uncertain terms how much they hated it, and what
a brute I was for "torturing" small children and making them cry and
scream. To them I say, "What am I doing? I'm asking the kids to stay
five feet away and play.")

But most wanted advice—if not a personal consultation, then at
least an e-mail response on how to deal with their kids' behavior.
They wanted us to come over—to move in, even. We fielded hundreds of phone calls, and generated a stack of e-mails thicker than a
New York phone book of requests, and the question that came up
again and again was this: "Do Dr. Weiss and Dr. Wagner have a
book?"

This, finally, is that book. Here, in one place, we explain all the
tricks of our trade: how to Draw the Line with your kids—in your
way, in your house. Since we probably can't make it to your home
for a house call, we can offer you the knowledge, information,
strategies, and, hopefully, the confidence to take matters into your
own hands and learn how to create or reclaim a great relationship
with your kids, solving some of the most stubborn behavior problems around in the process. Most of all, I hope this book becomes
an important stepping-stone in your bid to have fun with the kids—
because that's what it's all about.

In this book, we'll take you through a ten-step program that will
teach you how to Draw the Line with your kids. Here's what you can
expect:

- In chapter 1, an exploration of the theory behind our hands-on
  work, and a compelling explanation of why it's so important to
  have high expectations for kids' behavior—along with a warm,

loving style of parenting. Simply put, the skills that your child learns from birth to age five are the foundation for his or her success as an adult.

- An explanation, in chapter 2, of our tried-and-true strategy of Drawing the Line, or learning how to set up manageable periods of conflict with your kids—when you're ready, on your terms. Although it seems counterintuitive, if you know how, where, when, and *why* your kids are most likely to act up, you also have the skills to deal with their inappropriate behavior effectively and teach them new, more mature, and more appropriate behavior. Over the course of the book, we'll help you create your own unique plan for Drawing the Line with your kids.

- In chapter 3, a look at *R.I.P.*, or *rewarding, ignoring,* and *penalizing*—three of a parent's most potent tools in understanding and effectively dealing with kids' behavior. With these three tools, parents can create an environment where all members of the family can *Relate in Peace*.

- An understanding of *timing, less talking,* and *proximity* makes all the difference in how you relate to kids. Chapter 4 explains why it's so important to nip unwanted behavior in the bud, by reacting immediately, keeping talk to a minimum, and getting close to the kids.

- In chapter 5, we explain how Practice Makes Parent and why it's so important to practice new behavioral skills with your kids. Just as your golf game, your piano skills, or your yoga won't improve without consistent practice, neither will your parenting skills, or the kids' behavior. We help you put your plan into action by taking you through *five real-life examples of how different families* Drew the Line. We'll go through plans for some of the most common parenting concerns, including bedtime, mealtime, toilet training, and sibling battles.

- In chapter 6, we'll show you how the parents in chapter 5 slowly faded out their support as their kids internalized their new, more mature, skills and behaviors.

- A blueprint for getting on the same page as your spouse, partner, or co-parent, chapter 7 shows how parents often polarize
  around their kids' behavior: One partner becomes increasingly
  permissive in response to the other's strictness, while the strict
  one feels the need to become even more hard-line in response
  to his or her mate . . . and so on. By recognizing each other's
  tendencies and *developing a joint parental plan*, parents can stop
  polarizing and start parenting more effectively.
- Chapter 8, Parent Traps, sums up our personal hit list of some
  of the most common—and potentially most damaging—
  parenting errors out there. Here are our suggestions for what
  not to do, along with positive alternatives.
- In chapter 9, Parent Triumphs, we offer you our take on the
  most important things parents can do to raise healthy, loving,
  well-adjusted, and successful kids. If the goal of parenting is to
  create successful adults, we think that parents who can, for the
  most part, avoid the traps and embrace the triumphs are well
  on their way to achieving that goal.

OUR KIDS SCREAM, TOO

We'd like to launch you into this book with one important disclo-
sure: We, the three co-authors of this book, have kids, too. Whether
you're the shrink or the client, the same issues come up. Our kids all
cried as babies. Our kids have toddler tantrums. They don't like to
try new foods, have trouble sleeping through the night, and battle
with their siblings. Like everyone else, we get tired and frustrated.
We have arguments with our spouses. Generally, we're just as
capable as every other parent out there of messing up. We Drew the
Line with our own kids, and we made our share of mistakes. And—
amid the frustrations and mistakes—we learned a lot about the
imperfections that go along with being parents.

A Note to Parents of Kids with Developmental Delays

Most of the techniques in this book came out of our work with children who had serious developmental delays or behavioral problems. These were the kids we saw daily in university and hospital laboratories, kids for whom early and intense intervention was crucial.

The kids on the *Real Families* television show, in contrast, are generally typical kids—kids without any diagnosis beyond "Sometimes she acts like a brat and I don't know what to do." When it came down to Drawing the Line with these kids, the same principles applied. With typical kids, though, the process was often much more straightforward: If I could toilet train a violent, nonverbal, twelve-year-old with a diagnosis of autism spectrum disorder (and I could, and I did), then it was a piece of cake to get a typical—if stubborn—three-year-old to use the potty.

The strategies on the following pages will be useful for kids with delays and developmental disabilities. But with these kids, Drawing the Line will be only one part of a much more intensive, comprehensive education and therapeutic program that includes a complete medical evaluation and follow-up. If you're the parent of a child with a developmental disability, we hope you'll find the strategies outlined in this book useful. But please don't let them become a substitute for your child's complete program.

Despite what some of the experts and some of the books will tell you, no one is a perfect parent, and there is no one way of being a parent. In fact, it's in those moments where we mess up that we often gain one of parenting's most useful skills: humility. And in recognizing our humility, we also, sometimes, found a sense of humor

We've been there. We're getting through—and we hope that this book helps you get through that much faster, that much easier, that much better, and that it gives you that much more joy from your kids and lets you have that much more fun with them. Because, in the end, that's what it's all about.

Drawing
the Line

— 1 —

What Do You Want for Your Kids?

Want your kids to be successful adults?
Then teach them the skills of cooperation—today!

Think back, if you can, to the time before your first child arrived, during pregnancy or as you awaited the arrival of your adopted or foster child. Think about all the grand dreams you had for your future offspring. She was going to be president—if not of the country, then of a major corporation. He was going to be a basketball star, a famous artist, a doctor. She'd win the Nobel Peace Prize, be a poet, a parent, a paleontologist—something great.

Now take a look around your toy-strewn living room as you think about a particularly difficult day with said offspring. Maybe you were late getting out the door because little Johnny—the one who was going to be president—refused to get out of bed, get dressed, or eat anything for breakfast but the one cereal you were out of. Maybe you tried to go grocery shopping but had to leave the store because the two-year-old future paleontologist threw a monster tantrum when you wouldn't let her tear down the pasta display or buy her candy at the checkout line. Maybe the kids battled it out all day long, or the school phoned, or you fought with them over homework or TV or putting away toys, or you couldn't get anyone to bed on time, or . . .

At times like these, all those long-term goals and grand dreams can be forgotten as parents just struggle to get through the day without losing it. *President?* a worn-out parent thinks. *Who cares about being president? I just want her to eat her bloody peas.*

Well, here's the thing: The two aren't so far apart.

In other words, getting her to eat her peas today is one fairly crucial step along the road toward becoming president. The social and behavioral skills that kids acquire in childhood—skills such as cooperation, persistence, impulse control, politeness, proper hygiene, self-organization, and more—last a lifetime. Getting your kids to learn to taste different foods, get up on time and get ready for school on their own, clean up their toys, get along with their siblings, be charming in the grocery store, and go to sleep at a decent hour in their own beds will lay the foundation for a happy, healthy, successful adult life. Kids who have these skills are at a distinct advantage over their peers who don't, and that advantage lasts a lifetime. (Just have a look at the results of the famous "Marshmallow Test"—page 3.)

As you read ahead, keep in mind the ultimate goal for parents: to raise successful adults. Throughout the rest of this book, we'll be helping you teach your kids how to behave appropriately, to acquire those crucial social and behavioral skills so necessary to achieve that goal. Yes, it's true that kids who listen can make parents' lives easier. But this is about more than making parents' lives easier. It's about making kids' lives *better*—for the long term.

In this chapter, we'll explain why teaching children the skills of good behavior is so crucial to their success, not only throughout childhood but into the grown-up years as well. We'll discuss how parenting styles play a crucial role in helping kids learn these skills. And we'll take the first steps toward helping you Draw the Line— helping you identify your kids' target behaviors and their positive alternatives, and deciding what you'd like to tackle first. So read on.

Having Your Marshmallows and Eating Them, Too

What kids' ability to wait now tells us about their future success.

In the 1960s, Stanford University psychologist Dr. Walter Mischel and his colleagues began a now classic series of research studies that have come to be known as the "Marshmallow Tests."* Researchers gave four-year-old children a choice: "You can have one marshmallow, right now. But if you can wait fifteen minutes while I go run a quick errand, you can have two marshmallows when I come back. It's up to you."

The methods varied from study to study. Sometimes the treats were left within the kids' view, sometimes not. Some kids had to wait twenty minutes. Sometimes the researchers used different treats. And in some cases, the children were given strategies for waiting and getting their minds off the candy.

Overall, about a third of the kids just couldn't wait. They took the one marshmallow before the fifteen minutes were up, forfeiting their chance at the larger treat.

About two thirds of the kids, on the other hand, were willing to wait, even though it obviously pained many of them. Some used coping strategies to make the wait more bearable, such as singing, telling themselves stories, rocking, looking away, or—in one memorable case—falling asleep until the researcher returned.

Years later, Dr. Mischel tracked down the same group of kids as they graduated from high school, and tested them again for a range of personal and social markers of success. In adolescence, the differences between the "grab-the-marshmallow-now" preschoolers and their friends who were able to wait for the double reward were dramatic, and astonishing.

The ones who waited had better grades in school and higher SAT scores. They were more socially competent, self-reliant, assertive, confident, and personally effective. They coped better with problems and used reason rather than emotions when stressed or frustrated. They were more likely to embrace challenges, and to plan and pursue their goals instead of giving up when things got tough. They continued to control their impulses and delay gratification in pursuit of larger rewards. And more!

On the other hand, as adolescents, the former marshmallow grabbers didn't do as well as their counterparts who had waited all those years ago. The grabbers shied away from social contacts. They were more stubborn and less decisive, easily upset and put off by frustrations. They were more prone to jealousy, tended to think of themselves as "unworthy" or "bad," and were more likely to overreact to irritation and lose their temper. And—

after all those years—they still weren't able to delay gratification: They would settle for less in the short run rather than work for much more in the longer term.

So what does the Marshmallow Test tell us? It tells us that there's a crucial relationship between even very young children's abilities to be patient and wait—to *delay gratification*—and their success later on in life. Kids who can wait aren't passive little sheep who are too timid to grab what they want right away. Rather, they get what they want the hard way—they work for it. Their self-control translates into the self-reliance and self-discipline that will serve them well the rest of their lives.

On the other hand, children who have a hard time waiting are at risk. They know what they want right now, but they don't have the designs and persistence to know what they want in the future or how to get it.

As Daniel Goleman, the author of *Emotional Intelligence,* writes, "There is no psychological skill more fundamental than resisting impulses. It is the root of emotional self-control." Think about it: Time and time again, we're offered the opportunity to take something now or exert a little self-control and get something more for our efforts later. We'd like that extra slice of cake, but we don't eat it because we know our waistlines will thank us later. Similarly, we'd rather stay on the couch and watch TV, but we go to the gym, because exercise now pays off later when we don't have to battle heart disease or obesity. We save up money now to buy something bigger—like a bike, or a house—in the future. We manage time by doing our homework or housework now—and playing after—so that we don't have to catch up to a mountain of work later.

And we teach our kids the skills of delayed gratification and resisting their impulses now, while they're young, because the older they get, the more difficult it becomes for them to learn these skills. Our advice? Teach the kids how to wait and how to work hard for the things they want. They'll thank you for it later.

---

* Shoda, Y., W. Mischel, and P. K. Peake. "Predicting Adolescent Cognitive and Self Regulatory Competencies from Preschool Delay of Gratification." *Developmental Psychology* 26, no. 6 (1990): pp. 978–986.

"I Don't Want an Obedient Little Robot— But Some Cooperation Would Be Nice"

The fallout when kids can't listen: the erosion of self-image and its consequences.

"But I don't want to crush their spirits!"

That's what Rick, the father of three fantastic and rambunctious little boys, said when Michael showed up at his house. Rick and his wife, Corinne, found it difficult to go anywhere with the kids. If they weren't fighting in the car, the boys took off in three different directions the moment they were let loose in public. Rather than go on family outings and deal with Peter, Rhys, and Caleb's bolting, Rick and Corinne chose to stay home most of the time. They felt like prisoners in their own home. (In chapter 5, you'll read more about how Corinne worked with the boys on how to behave in the car.) And yet these parents were afraid—if they tried to rein in their high-energy boys, would they "break" the kids' spirits?

We hear from many parents like Rick and Corinne, parents who are unsure about setting limits or how much—or little—to "discipline" their kids. Today's parents are torn. They want their kids to behave well, but they fear turning them into complacent little robots. They've tried reasoning with their kids—but their kids don't seem all that reasonable mid-tantrum. They'd like their children to listen to them, but they don't want to "control" or "manipulate" them. They're worried that parental expectations for cooperation will squelch kids' freedom of thought, creativity, and spirit. They're nervous that they'll sacrifice their kids' self-esteem in the name of good behavior.

Well, we're here to tell you that kids can behave well *and* have great self-esteem. Kids can be polite and cooperative *and* still be creative and independent. Kids can learn to listen, to wait, and to control their impulses without becoming complacent little robots. In fact, the kids who have the skills to behave appropriately in any given situation are *more* likely to be creative, independent, and confident than their counterparts.

The Four Principles of Self-Management

As Michael told Rick: "Show me someone who's engaged in creative behavior—and that can be anyone from my favorite guitar player, B. B. King, to a kindergartner drawing at a table—and I'll show you a wellspring of self-control."

Kids don't gain self-esteem and independence from being allowed to do whatever they want, whenever they want. They get self-esteem over a multistep process that's all about learning how to negotiate the rules and boundaries:

- First, we teach kids the rules, so that they can learn *self-organization:* "Where does your stuff go? Where do you sit? How do you ask nicely? Are you allowed to touch that? It's time for bed."
- From self-organization, kids learn *self-awareness*. As they learn the rules, they become aware of their place and power in the world. "Oh, my stuff goes over there. Here's where I sit for story time. If I want something from Mom, I need to say 'please.' I'm not allowed to touch the power drill without Dad. I have to go to sleep now."
- Out of self-awareness comes *self-reliance:* "I know where that goes! I know where to sit! I can get what I need in the world! I can make stuff with Daddy! I can sleep in my own bed! I can do it myself!"
- From self-reliance come *self-esteem* and *independence:* "I did it! I did a good job! And hey, if I can do that, I bet I can do something harder. Oh, don't worry, Mom, I know how to do it on my own."

In the end, children who learn and internalize the rules of self-control ultimately have more freedom and creativity—and more opportunities and skills—than kids who have never heard the word *no*. By imposing reasonable limits, rules, and structure, parents like Rick and Corinne aren't squelching their kids' spirit, creativity, or independence. In fact, they're fostering it, by showing their kids how to channel that spirit, creativity, and independence into ever more sophisticated skills.

Let's take a look, for example, at another child: our friend Liam, who's two and a half years old. Like most kids his age, Liam is into everything—and what he's especially into is his dad, Larry's, stereo. Now, Larry is a bit of an audio-equipment junkie who has music playing whenever he's home. Next to Liam, his stereo is his pride and joy. Even though it's worth thousands of dollars, he's not about to put it away for the sake of baby-proofing the house. Instead, he's taken on the more challenging, but ultimately more rewarding, task of teaching Liam how to behave properly around the stereo.

How does Larry do this? Well, ever since Liam was able to crawl, he'd tend to make a beeline for the sound equipment. And why wouldn't he? After all, his dad was interested in it and spent a lot of time around it, so it was only natural that Liam should gravitate toward all those neat blinking lights, moving parts, and fun sounds, too. Given the chance, Larry knew, Liam would dismantle the stereo. So every time Liam got within touching distance of the system, Larry picked him up and moved him a few feet out of reach, saying firmly and clearly, "No, Liam, don't touch." When Liam didn't touch the stereo, his dad told him that he was doing a great job.

Liam, persistent kid that he is, kept trying. Dad, however, was a little more persistent. After a few weeks, the whole exercise became a game. Liam would approach the equipment and pretend to touch it, and then look at his dad and laugh. Clearly, he knew and understood that the stereo was off-limits. Yeah, sometimes he did get to it when his dad wasn't looking, but Larry just kept up the routine.

When Liam got to be a toddler, his parents could often hear him in the living room near the stereo. He'd stand next to it and say, "Nooo . . . don't touch!" It sounded as though he was mimicking

Larry. But in fact, he was inhibiting himself from touching—true self-control.

So what? Well, here's what. Now that Liam's older, he delights in the fact that his father *does* let him touch the stereo. He can turn on the power, open the machine, place the CD inside, hit the PLAY button—and groove to the music with his dad. Liam never mishandles the equipment. In fact, he treats it with reverence and care, imitating his father's every move. Why does his father let him touch it? Because Liam has learned care and respect for the equipment. Why does Liam delight in participating? Because his father made it clear that he had to earn the right to do something so responsible—and because he gets to spend time with his dad, who can tell him, honestly, that he's doing a great job. That's a genuine boost to his self-esteem.

Beyond ABC and 123: The *Real* Way to Tell if Kids Are Ready to Learn

When you ask parents what they think "school readiness" means, many talk about the three *R*'s—reading, writing, and 'rithmetic.

In fact, letters and numbers may not be nearly as important as parents think. The better indicators of a child's readiness to learn are social and behavioral. In the early 1990s, a group of child development experts that included the well-known pediatrician T. Berry Brazelton identified the seven critical *emotional* factors necessary for a child to enter the school environment with the tools to prosper:*

- **Confidence:** A confident child has a sense of control and mastery over his body, his behavior, and the world. He senses that he is more likely than not to succeed at what he undertakes, and that adults will be helpful.
- **Curiosity:** A curious child wants to find out about the world. She thinks that finding out about things is positive, fun, and pleasurable.
- **Intentionality:** A child who acts with intentionality wants to have an impact on the world, and he persists in his desire to have an impact. This relates to his sense of competence and being effective in the world.

- **Self-control:** A child who has self-control can modulate and control her own actions in age-appropriate ways. She has a sense of inner control.
- **Relatedness:** A child who can relate can engage with other people. He feels that he is understood by and can understand others.
- **Capacity to communicate:** A child with a well-developed capacity to communicate wants to and can verbally exchange ideas, feelings, and concepts with others. Her capacity for communication is related to her sense of trust in others and of pleasure in engaging with others, including adults.
- **Cooperativeness:** A cooperative child is able to balance his own needs with the needs of others.

"These characteristics," writes Brazelton, "equip children with a 'school literacy' more basic than knowledge of numbers and letters. It is the knowledge of how to learn."

The skills we admire in adults are the same skills that make children good learners. Learning how to learn begins in babyhood and continues throughout childhood. Parents who can teach their kids the above skills lay the foundation for lifelong success. In other words, get them ready for school, and you get them ready for the rest of their lives.

---

* National Center for Clinical Infant Programs (NCCIP). *Heart Start: The Emotional Foundations of School Readiness,* Zero to Three Monograph Series (Arlington, VA, 1992): p. 7.

This is a great example of learning self-control. At first, Larry enforced the rules. But after a while, *Liam* enforced them. He knew not to touch the stereo, even when no one was around to stop him. He's in charge of the situation. And the great thing is that his self-control has netted him new skills that translate into new opportunities for growth, creativity, and fun: Larry knows, for example, that he can take Liam out to concerts or into electronics shops without mayhem ensuing. What's more, Liam also knows how to transfer the skills he learned with Larry: He treats his baby brother with the same care and reverence he gives the stereo equipment.

Parents don't want little robots who will simply do what they're told, period. And neither do we. Rather, we want kids to internalize a code of conduct. We want kids to become moral people who can think for themselves, who are sensitive and respectful of others, and who like what they see in the mirror. These kinds of people have a positive sense of "self"—in other words, they have good self-esteem.

So feel confident in modeling and mandating appropriate behavior for your kids! Children who learn and internalize the rules of self-control ultimately have more freedom—and more opportunities and skills—than kids who have never heard the word *no*.

WHAT KIND OF PARENT ARE YOU?

The four parent types: authoritative, authoritarian,
permissive, and uninvolved.

Larry had high expectations for his son. He didn't want Liam to wreck the stereo, but, more important, he wanted Liam—at two years old—to learn how to inhibit himself from touching something off-limits. In other words, Larry wasn't prepared to plunk Liam in a playpen to keep him from touching the music equipment. Nor did Larry stick the stereo on a high shelf, out of his son's reach. He wanted to know that he could trust Liam around the stereo. Larry wanted to make sure that, even without anyone around to enforce them, Liam would eventually stick to the rules.

To achieve his goals, Larry was firm about the boundaries, and enforced them consistently at the outset—until Liam enforced the boundaries himself. Larry spent a lot of time with Liam, teaching him how to handle himself—and the music equipment—appropriately. And Larry was also quick to reward his son for keeping within the boundaries: "Hey, Liam, great job! Thank you for not touching Daddy's stereo! Thank you for being gentle!"

In other words, Larry showed high degrees of both *control* and *warmth*. It's that combination of these two qualities, in particular, that describes what developmental psychologists call an *authoritative parent*.

Back in the 1960s, psychologist Dr. Diana Baumrind pioneered current research into parenting styles. Now at the University of California–Berkeley's Institute of Human Development, Dr. Baumrind observed four different types of behavior that were key to describing a parent's style: *parental control, maturity demands, parent–child communications*, and *nurturance*.

Authoritative parents, Baumrind and others found, showed high degrees of all the above behaviors. For example, Larry showed a high degree of parental control:

- He was willing and able to influence Liam's behavior around the stereo. He didn't simply let Liam do whatever he wanted, and he actively taught Liam how to behave.
- Larry also placed high demands on Liam for maturity: He insisted that Liam could and would learn how to handle sophisticated stereo equipment in age-appropriate ways.

Four Parenting Behaviors

1. **Parental control:** The degree to which parents are willing and able to overtly influence their children's behavior. 2. **Maturity demands:** The degree to which parents are willing to pressure their children to act in ever more sophisticated and mature ways.	Control
3. **Parent–child communication:** The degree to which parents use reasoned discussions as a way of communicating with their children, how regular and clear those discussions are, and how often parents seek children's opinions and expressions of their feelings. 4. **Nurturance:** The degree to which parents are able to express love, compassion, pride, and pleasure to their kids through either their words or actions.	Warmth

At the same time, Larry was high on the warmth scale:

- He communicated reasonably with his son (when his son was being reasonable!). Larry clearly told Liam the reasons for his demands: "The stereo will break if you're not gentle, and then we can't hear music." Larry was consistent and clear in his demands; he didn't let Liam touch the stereo one day, but not the next. And Larry talked to Liam about Liam's feelings and desires: "I know you want to play with the stereo—it's really fun, isn't it? But we have to be very careful. Let me show you how to open and close the CD player. Gentle, gentle."
- Larry also nurtured Liam. He made it clear to Liam that he valued spending time with and wanted to play and share his interests with his son. He hugged and kissed Liam lots, got close to him, played with him, and praised him: "You're doing a great job at being gentle with the stereo! I'm really proud of you, Liam. Thanks!"

Baumrind also identified two other types of parents: the *authoritarian* parent and the *permissive* parent. If authoritative parents showed high degrees of both warmth and control, these other two parenting types were at either extreme:

- On the one hand, authoritarian parents show *high levels of control*, but display *low levels of warmth* toward their kids—they're the no-nonsense, "You'll do what I say, end of discussion" kinds of moms and dads. Yes, these types of parents have high demands for their kids' behavior and maturity levels, but they tend to rely on the threat of punishment to enforce those demands. "You eat all your peas or you won't get dessert!" Or, "If you're not in bed in five minutes, I'm going to get the wooden spoon!"
- On the other hand, permissive parents show *high levels of warmth* but *low levels of control* around their kids. We've all seen the parent who smiles helplessly and stands by as her

child refuses to share or ransacks the neighbor's living room. She may try to reason with her child—"Honey, wouldn't you like to share?" or "Come on, sweetheart, you shouldn't draw on the walls in other people's houses"—but she doesn't back up her reasons with action. "Oh well," she says, "I guess he'll learn how to share and behave better as he gets older."

As they relate to levels of warmth and control, the three parenting styles can be summed up by the following chart:

Parenting Styles as a Function of Warmth and Control

	Low Warmth	High Warmth
Low Control		Permissive
High Control	Authoritarian	Authoritative

But there's a blank space on the above chart. What kind of parent is low on both the warmth and control scales? Developmental psychologists Eleanor Maccoby[1] and John Martin developed a portrait of a fourth parenting style: the *uninvolved parent.*

This parent just doesn't spare the kids much time or attention. In its extreme form, uninvolved parenting borders on outright neglect. In less extreme forms, uninvolved parents are simply detached. They've got other things on their minds. They don't try to control their kids, and they make few demands for maturity or appropriate behavior. They don't have many conversations with the kids, nor do they demonstrate much nurturance or warmth. If their children *do* demand something, the uninvolved parent is often likely to give it to them, just to avoid confrontation. Uninvolved parents often want the kids to "Go off and play on your own, so I can have some peace and quiet."

---

[1] Martin, J. A., and E. E. Maccoby. "Socialization in the Context of the Family: Parent Child Interactions." In P. Mussen (series editor), *Handbook of Child Psychology*, Volume 4 (New York: Wiley & Sons, 1983): pp. 1–101.

Parenting Styles as a Function of Warmth and Control

	Low Warmth	High Warmth
Low Control	Uninvolved	Permissive
High Control	Authoritarian	Authoritative

If you haven't figured it out already, we're big advocates of an authoritative style of parenting—high expectations, high levels of control, and high levels of warmth and communication. As study after study shows, kids who grow up in homes with this parenting style have the best outcomes.

- Children raised by authoritarian parents *are* able to behave well—*if* a parent or adult is nearby. The problem, however, is that these kids are quick to abandon their good behavior when they can get away with it. Because they're used to a heavy-handed parent who constantly disciplines, they've never had to learn to discipline *themselves*. Unlike our friend Liam, they've never "internalized" self-control.
- What's worse, studies show that kids raised by authoritarian parents seem to lack spontaneity, affection, curiosity, and originality.[2] If that's not bad enough, they seem to be more unhappy and withdrawn, and boys in particular are more aggressive than kids raised in other parenting environments.
- Kids from more nurturing permissive families don't do much better. In fact, they do worse. At least the kids from authoritarian homes can behave when an adult is watching. Kids from permissive families are inclined to misbehave no matter who's looking. They've internalized the rules even less than kids raised by authoritarian parents.
- Studies have shown that kids from permissive families are also less socially responsible than kids from stricter homes. To add insult to injury, these kids are at risk for poorer self-reliance

[2] From Martin and Maccoby, p. 40.

and impulse control. They may be less liked by their peers (be-cause they're pains in the butt and other kids know it). They're more likely to whine and argue, and they're less independent than their peers. And they're more likely to do poorly in school.

The Good Stress of Challenge

Why do kids from authoritarian and permissive families falter? Interestingly, these two parenting styles have something in common: As Stanford University psychologist William Damon points out, both styles shield kids from the good stress of *challenge*.[3] Authoritarian parents do so by limiting kids' opportunities for exploration—unlike Larry, they'd simply stick Liam in a playpen or put the stereo system out of reach rather than actually teach him how to use it. Permissive parents, on the other hand, shield kids from stress by not confronting their poor behavior or demanding that they act in increasingly mature, appropriate ways. As a result, Damon notes, these kids "have similar difficulties in developing self-reliance, assertiveness, an autonomous sense of social responsibility, and tolerance for life's ups and downs."[4]

- If kids from permissive and authoritarian families can do poorly, then their peers raised by uninvolved parents can do even worse. These children are at greater risk for becoming more demanding or coercive, aggressive toward peers and adults, and less cooperative with adults. Many of these kids have a much harder time with controlling their impulses and delaying gratification: They want what they want, when they want it. And if they don't get it, look out![5]

[3] William Damon, *The Moral Child* (New York: Free Press, 1988): pp. 58–59.
[4] Ibid.
[5] In Martin and Maccoby, see Loeb et al. (1980); Gordon, Nowicki, and Wickern (1981); Hatfield, Ferguson, and Alpert (1967); Block (1971); Pulkkinen (1982).

Kids with authoritative parents are the big winners in the parenting style game. Researchers discovered that kids raised with an authoritative style are more independent and more socially responsible. They get along better with their peers and do better in school. They're generally happier, take more initiative, are more curious about the world, and are more likely to explore new activities. They also showed significantly less impulsiveness (that is, they're not the kids grabbing that one marshmallow!).[6]

Throughout the rest of this book, we'll take you through the ten steps of Drawing the Line with your kids and teaching them—like Larry did with Liam—the skills of appropriate behavior. We'll show you how to help your kids navigate the good stress of challenge. We'll help you confront even the most stubborn kids and intransigent behavior issues in order to move your kids to a whole new level of maturity. And you'll do that by using the kinds of techniques that authoritative parents use: You'll combine high levels of control with high levels of warmth.

In the process, we hope that your entire household will become a happier, less stressed, more peaceful, more fun, more productive place. But that's only one of our goals. In the long run, our larger goal is to help you raise successful adults. We want you to be the parents of the kids who can wait fifteen minutes for a marshmallow—and, in the process, we know that you'll be the parents of kids who will grow up to do wonderful things.

So What Do You Want for Your Kids?

Get out a pen and paper, because it's time to take the first step toward better behavior.

STEP 1: Identify your child's target behavior(s).

Let's have a look at a real-life example: four-year-old Aedan, his brother, Dylan, who's seven, and their parents, Melanie and Dennis.

[6] Baumrind, 1989.

With two kids, two jobs, a dog, and the usual round of daily activi-ties—school, hockey, judo lessons, volunteer work, grocery shop-ping, getting dinner on the table and the car serviced—life often feels hectic.

"Sometimes the days just go by and it feels like we're barely get-ting through," says Melanie. "I feel like we live in utter chaos, and that the boys' behavior makes it hard to get anything done."

When they think about it a bit more, though, Melanie and Den-nis can identify exactly what's going on in their household that makes it hard to get through the day.

First of all, their sons fight a lot. Aedan, in particular, likes to get things going. He's determined to show his older brother that he can do anything Dylan does—and, as a result, often antagonizes Dylan by getting into his space and his face. With two boys going at it much of the day, it's hard to get stuff done. Melanie and Dennis are constantly intervening in the boys' fights, and then they find them-selves delayed and late because they've lost so much time in their intervention.

Melanie and Dennis, then, have identified their first target behavior: Aedan and Dylan's fighting.

Because Aedan's in school only half days, he spends his after-noons with his mom, who works part-time outside the home (and full-time in it!). Often that means that Melanie takes her son with her on errands. And those errands get chaotic because she con-stantly has to wrangle her four-year-old. In the mall or the grocery store, Aedan bolts, running from one shiny thing to the next. He'll even bolt in the parking lot, where Melanie fears for his safety. Because she finds it so difficult to keep Aedan nearby, Melanie's constantly stressed when she's out with him, and her errands seem to take much longer than they need to.

Melanie and Dennis's next target behavior for Aedan, then, is his bolting in public.

Finally, both parents are getting frustrated with the level of ten-sion in their household. Much of that tension has to do, they realize, with Aedan's attitude. While Dylan's generally an easygoing kid,

Aedan's got a stubborn streak that manifests in defiance. Lately, it's been difficult to get him to speak politely—to say "please" and "thank you," and to ask nicely for things rather than demand them in an aggressive tone. His behavior is grating: It gets tiresome to listen to a four-year-old who constantly says "No!" Melanie and Dennis find themselves in a constant battle of wills with their son, and don't know how to proceed.

Aedan's final target behavior, then, is his rudeness and demanding, aggressive tone of voice.

Now it's your turn. Below, and on pages 231–234, you will find a Drawing the Line worksheet that you'll use as you identify your own kids' specific target behaviors. Drill down: What are your issues with your child? Does she refuse to eat at mealtimes? Does he scream and whine instead of using nice words? Does she dawdle all morning, making you late for work and her late for school? Maybe you can't get either of your kids to bed without the house turning into a war zone. Be specific: "I can't get out the door on time in the morning" is more useful than "Billy doesn't listen to me."

Drawing the Line: _____

Priority	Target Behavior	Positive Alternative	When/ Where Does It Occur?	Draw the Line	Drawing the Line: Reward?	Drawing the Line: Penalty?
1						
2						
3						
4						
5						
6						

When you've figured out what your top issues are with your kid, write them down under the heading Target Behavior. Complete a separate sheet for each of your children, if necessary. Here's what Aedan's Drawing the Line worksheet looks like, so far:

Drawing the Line: **Aedan**

Priority	Target Behavior	Positive Alternative	When/ Where Does It Occur?	Draw the Line	Drawing the Line: Reward?	Drawing the Line: Penalty?
1	Running away from me in grocery store.					
2	Fighting with brother.					
3	Rude, demanding tone.					

STEP 2: Identify positive alternatives.

Identifying problem behaviors is only half the battle. Yes, you want to eliminate those target behaviors, but nature abhors a vacuum. Next, you have to figure out what you want to *replace* those negative target behaviors. So for every item on your list, write down a positive alternative.

Positive alternatives tend to be fairly obvious. If your child refuses to eat anything but a couple of choice foods at dinner, a positive alternative would be to have her try at least a taste of everything on her plate, without whining. For a kid who screams and whines as a primary mode of communication, the positive alternative would be to use nice words and an "inside voice" to get what he wants. A morning dawdler needs to be able to get up, dress herself, and eat in time for the school bus or car pool. As for bedtime issues, parents would like children to go to bed (and then stay in bed) with a minimum of fuss.

Here's what Aedan's parents came up with for positive alternatives to his target behaviors:

Drawing the Line: **Aedan**

Priority	Target Behavior	Positive Alternative	When/Where Does It Occur?	Draw the Line	Drawing the Line: Reward?	Drawing the Line: Penalty?
1	Running away from me in grocery store.	Staying close by, being patient until I'm done.				
2	Fighting with brother.	Playing peacefully; sharing.				
3	Rude, demanding tone.		Saying "please," asking and talking nicely.			

"I Want My Kids to Grow Up Like My Cousin Paula"

You want a lot of things for—and from—your kids: for them to go to bed at a reasonable hour without the Third World War breaking out; to be able to cook one meal that everyone eats; to know that your son and daughter can play together for an hour without clobbering each other; to get your stubborn three-year-old out of diapers and using the potty; to be able to take your four-year-old into the grocery store without him pulling everything off the shelves, getting lost, or throwing a tantrum because you won't buy him the sugar-coated cereal he's seen on TV; to have a quiet, romantic evening at home with your partner while the kids are asleep; for the living room to stay tidy for five seconds; to have your daughter say, "Okay, Mom," when you ask her to set the table . . . and so on.

Whew.

It's so easy to get so caught up in the slew of all these daily desires that we lose sight of the future. At the same time, we know that all the above short-term headaches and heartaches—today's "micro" desires—are intimately linked to kids' long-term, "macro" success. So as you think about all the things you want for and from your kids today, also take some time to take the longer view. What do you want for your children when they're adults?

Those qualities might include professional success, having good relationships, empathy, consistency, creativity, generosity, good health, confidence, happiness, economic security, thoughtfulness, a strong sense of priorities, innovation, fairness, independence, intelligence and an ability to question, spirituality, leadership . . . the list goes on.

But that list is kind of abstract. It may help, instead, to pick a role model—maybe your grandfather, or your cousin Paula—whom you admire. Make a list, on paper or in your head, of the qualities that person possesses, the qualities you'd like your kids to emulate when they grow up. Why do you like him? What about her lifestyle, accomplishments, or character do you admire? How does he conduct his relationships, his career? Is she smart, creative, happy?

As you go through the day-to-day routines of life with your kids, keep that image of your granddad or cousin Paula in mind. And keep reminding yourself, as you insist on appropriate behavior from your kids, that there's a reason beyond the immediate for your insistence: You want them to grow up to be a role model to someone else.

Pick Your Battles

STEP 3: Prioritize: Which target behavior do you want to focus on first?

Next, you need to figure out where to begin. You can't do everything all at once, so which of the target behaviors that you've identified in the above steps do you want to work on first?

As you identify your target behaviors and positive alternatives, though, it's crucial to pick your battles carefully and to start small. You won't do yourself or your kids any favors by trying to do too much all at once. If you try to change every last thing about your kids, all at once, you're going to be exhausted and frustrated. And so will they. Worse, they'll feel picked on, resentful, and ashamed of themselves.

That means you have to prioritize: Decide which behavior(s) you want to tackle first. For some of you, the answer is obvious. Your kids do one or two things that just make you nuts. You may be at the breaking point—"If I have to sit through one more dinner like that/ clean up one more 'accident'/suffer one more sleepless night/referee one more battle between the kids, I'm going to lose it!"

You might pick the behavior that makes you craziest, the thing that seems easiest to deal with, or the behavior that, if eliminated, would improve your quality of life the most. It's generally a good idea to focus on harmful or dangerous behavior sooner rather than later. If your child is doing something that could hurt him (like playing with matches, or riding his bike into the street) or someone else (hitting her baby sister), you'll likely want to focus on that behavior early on.

If you've already got a clear idea which problem behaviors you want to target, that's great. Write them down (under the heading Target Behavior) on the blank worksheet on page 18. If you're not sure where to start, or aren't sure what's most pressing, it may help to ask yourself the following questions.

Which of My Kids' Behaviors Makes Me Craziest?

If you could magically eliminate just one behavior problem, which would it be? What one behavior—whining, throwing tantrums, fussy eating, refusing to sleep, fighting with siblings, toileting issues— detracts most from your happiness, peace of mind, or quality of life?

What Times of Day Are Most Difficult for My Family?

Break the day down into chunks. If you know that certain times of day are most difficult, try to figure out what's going on during those times, and see if you can isolate the behaviors that make it difficult.

For example, maybe your morning routine—getting everyone up, dressed, fed, and out the door to school, work, or day care—is a nightmare. Do you find yourself yelling at your kids and/or at your spouse? Are tears (the kids' or your own) part of the daily routine? Are you constantly late? Do you dread the alarm clock because it means another crazy morning? If so, then maybe you want to Draw the Line around a morning behavior—getting up, getting dressed, tantrums over breakfast, dawdling.

Do some similar sleuthing around midday, after school, dinner, bedtime, and—for those of you with up-all-night kids—the middle of the night.

What Situations Are Most Difficult for My Kids or My Family?

Sometimes problem behaviors surface in particular settings or situations, regardless of the time of day. Maybe your kids are hellions in the car. Maybe you dread going to the grocery store or the hardware store because the kids seem to explode in those settings. Maybe they act up whenever you try to have a phone conversation or chat with a friend over coffee. Or maybe the kids don't seem to be able to play with peers without picking fights.

If you know that certain situations are a recipe for trouble, you've got some clues around places to Draw the Line. You could set up trial runs in the car, at the grocery store, during "experimental" phone conversations or coffee dates with understanding friends—or their kids.

What Behavior Seems Easiest to Solve? Where Could I Most Easily Draw the Line?

We all need to feel successful. If you're feeling a bit cautious about tackling one of the bigger behaviors, try starting with something small, like getting kids to hang up their coats in the back hall every day. If you can Draw the Line and stick to your guns on something small, your kids will see that you mean business, and you'll feel like you've accomplished something. The high you get from creating even a small change can help you tackle the next problem behavior. And remember, change begets change: Tackling the smaller behaviors now will make it easier to tackle the bigger behaviors later on. As Sheldon says:

> Many parents are almost in a state of paralysis. They don't know what to do first, and that's because they see their problems as too big. If that's the case, start small. Take one little battle, like hanging up that coat in the hallway or sitting through dinner for fifteen minutes, but be willing to fight all day long to win it. Every marathon—every huge enterprise—starts with one step. Start with that one step. You'll be amazed—the next step will get easier and easier, and the one after that easier still.

With Aedan, Melanie and Dennis realized that the boys' fighting was the one issue that caused them the most grief. If they could get Aedan and Dylan to play nicely together and no longer had to referee the boys' constant fights, they felt that the general level of tension and chaos in their household would plummet. Once everyday life was more peaceful, they felt they'd have the head-space to tackle other issues. Melanie and Dennis ranked the boys' fighting as their top priority for change.

Melanie decided that the next most stressful thing for her was Aedan's bolting in public. She wanted to enjoy her time with her son and be able to get her errands done with less stress. She ranked this target behavior as her second priority.

Finally, Melanie and Dennis decided that Aedan's rudeness was their third priority. It was annoying, yes, but it didn't add as much stress or tension to their lives as the other two target behaviors. Once the fighting and the bolting were in check, they felt they'd have the time and energy to focus more on Aedan's attitude.

Here's what Aedan's worksheet looked like now:

Drawing the Line: **Aedan**

Priority	Target Behavior	Positive Alternative	When/ Where Does It Occur?	Draw the Line	Drawing the Line: Reward?	Drawing the Line: Penalty?
1	Fighting with brother.	Playing peacefully; sharing.				
2	Running away from me in grocery store.	Staying close by, being patient until I'm done.				
3	Rude, demanding tone.	Saying "please," asking and talking nicely.				

PUTTING IT ALL TOGETHER

You've created a list of target behaviors, positive alternatives. Armed with this information, you can make some pretty educated guesses about how and where you might be able to Draw the Line with your kids. We'll show you how in the next chapter.

— 2 —

Drawing the Line

*When the old ways just don't work—creating a
"new world order" for appropriate behavior.*

Four-year-old Jesse and his two-year-old brother, Ian, are two high-energy kids who constantly demand their parents' attention—and they'll use whatever behavior it takes to get it, including yelling and screaming, whining, throwing tantrums, and refusing to listen. They won't give their mom, Michelle, a minute to herself.

"I need some time for me," says Michelle. "That's what I don't have. If I try to go to the bathroom they'll open the door and come right in. If I'm trying to do my hair, they're right there: 'Mommy, I want this, I want that.' If I'm on the computer, they want to be on the computer. So I'll give in, and let them play on the computer and I'll come downstairs and start watching TV. And then they want the TV. At night, they won't stay in their rooms: They want to sleep in our bed. They always want my time."

"Sometimes when I come home it's bedlam in here, mayhem," says Kent, Michelle's husband. "I walk in and I can just tell. I'll look at the two boys and the first thing out of their mouths is something defiant or rude. I feel sorry for the day she must have had."

"There are days when I'll just sit on the couch, and I'm depressed because I don't know what to do anymore," Michelle continues.

"I've yelled. I've spanked them. I've sent them to their rooms. And nothing works. So I just sit on the couch and try to tune them out. I don't know what I'm doing wrong."

Kent and Michelle are desperate for a change. And they're not alone.

In our work with families, we've heard hundreds of parents say versions of the same thing. Again and again, they tell us, "I've lived with this"—and "this" is the fighting, the whining, the rudeness, the tantrums, the bedtime battles, the defiance, the fussy eating, whatever difficult behavior robs both parents and kids of peace—"for too long now. Something's got to give. This is not how I'm going to be a parent anymore. I need a new way of dealing with my kids, because the old ways just don't work."

Well, if the old ways don't work anymore, then prepare yourself for a new world order. You don't have to battle constantly with your kids. You don't have to resign yourself to a life of difficult, defiant, or inappropriate behavior from your children. It really is possible to live in a world where your kids play nicely, share, say "please," try new foods, get to sleep easily (in their own beds, at a reasonable hour), and give you a bit of time to yourself in the process. It really is possible to live in a world where you can have fun with and enjoy your children the bulk of the time.

We've taught hundreds of parents exactly how to create that new world. And in this chapter, we'll show you how you can begin to create it, too, through our trademark parenting strategy called Drawing the Line.

DRAWING THE LINE

When Michael Weiss met Jesse and Ian for the first time, he set up the following scenario. After introducing himself to the two little boys, he took them into the living room, where they got out some favorite toys: a train set and Robot Transformers. Then Michael told the kids, "Okay—your mom and dad and I are going to have a big, grown-up talk in the kitchen. So we need you guys to be really great kids and play by yourselves for a little while here in the living room. We'll keep coming back in here to check on you. And if you need us, you let us know."

Grown-ups talk in one room, kids play in another. In fact, Jesse and Ian were only about fifteen feet away from Kent and Michelle, on one side of an unofficial boundary marked by where the living room carpet ended and the kitchen tiles began.

Sounds innocent enough, doesn't it? Well, here's what happened:

Not content to stay in the living room, the kids started testing the boundary within seconds. First, Jesse crossed that carpet–tile border by charging into the kitchen with all the defiance his four-year-old self could muster. Quietly and efficiently, Michael imposed an extra-short time-out: He hauled Jesse out of the kitchen by taking hold of his upper arm and mechanically marching him back to the living room. "We need you to stay in the living room."

Almost immediately, Jesse was back in the kitchen, this time a little closer to the boundary. Michael quietly and quickly imposed another extra-short time-out, hauling Jesse out again, absolutely deadpan. "In the living room. We need you to stay in the living room."

And ten seconds later, Jesse charged in again, closer still to the boundary. This time, Michael hauled him out of the kitchen and up to his room for yet another ultra-short time-out: five seconds alone, with the door closed. Opening Jesse's bedroom door, he asked the little boy, "Why are you here?" and then answered for him, "You're here because we need you to stay in the living room. Do you want to come downstairs and play in the living room? You can come down whenever you're ready."

Kent and Michelle were stunned. "My time-outs are always so much longer," Michelle told Michael. "I make Jesse sit on the stairs for four minutes—one minute for every year of age. He hates it, though. It doesn't work."

"That's because four or five minutes is way too long," said Michael. "By the time it's up, the kid's forgotten why he was in time-out in the first place. For the most part, time-out is a really quick event: Five, ten, or fifteen seconds is usually all it takes to be effective."

And so it went. The scene repeated a few more times, but it quickly lost steam: Jesse took a few steps into the kitchen. Five-second time-out. Jesse put one foot over the line. Five-second time-out. Jesse tried to reach into the kitchen and turn off the light. Ten-second time-out. Jesse held on to the door frame and leaned into the kitchen with his entire body. Ten-second time-out.

But something else interesting also began to happen. The times in between Jesse's attempts to cross the line got longer and longer. At first, he didn't give his parents and Michael more than a couple of seconds in the kitchen before making a foray into the forbidden room. Then he waited half a minute. Then a minute, ninety seconds, a couple of minutes—long enough for Michael to go into the living room and tell him and Ian what a great job they were doing by playing well and staying out of the kitchen.

Finally, Jesse came right up to the very edge of the line, his toes just on his side of the boundary. He stood there, expectant. Was this going to be another time-out? What would this Michael guy do next?

"Hey, Jesse!" said Michael. "Look at you! You're doing exactly what I asked you to do by staying in the living room! Thanks!"

Over the course of about thirty minutes, a four-year-old boy (and his two-year-old brother, who'd been watching the scene closely and mimicking much of Jesse's behavior) figured out two important things: what the rules were, and, more important, that Michael would be credible and predictable in enforcing them.

Jesse also learned—very quickly—what would get him attention: playing quietly in the next room with his brother, and staying on his side of the boundary. In essence, he began to learn how to respect parental boundaries. And literally, he toed the line.

Jesse learned something else, too: that his usual strategies for getting attention—whining, arguing, getting in his parents' faces, defiance, yelling—weren't particularly useful in the situation. All they netted him was a bunch of time-outs, alone in his room. He was no longer getting a rise out of Michelle and Kent: They weren't yelling at him or threatening punishment. In fact, his defiance didn't seem to matter to them—he just ended up in his room with no one to bother.

In short, in about thirty minutes, Michael established—and a four-year-old boy figured out—a new world order.

WHY DRAW THE LINE?

If you haven't figured it out by now, Drawing the Line is simply a way to quickly set up an artificial situation that's virtually guaranteed to push your kids' buttons. Look at Jesse and Ian. Since these kids had a hard time giving their parents any space, Michael engineered a situation in which the kids had to play on their own and give Michelle and Kent some breathing room. The result? Instant conflict, as Jesse and Ian repeatedly tried to get their parents' attention using their usual, time-tested strategies.

Set up conflict with my kids? you may be thinking. *Why on earth would I want to do that? Isn't the whole point to have less conflict with my kids?*

Yes, it is. And here's the thing: By setting up artificial situations designed to push your kids' buttons, you set the stage for them to learn appropriate behavior. Depending on your kids and the situation, you may just have a fair bit of conflict at the outset. But that short-term pain leads to longer-term gain, as you and your children learn how to navigate these once stressful situations. In short, setting up controlled periods of conflict at the outset will net you much less conflict over the longer term.

What's more, when you Draw the Line, you set up conflict when you're ready, on your terms—and when you've armed yourself with the tools and strategies you need to teach your child how to behave appropriately in day-to-day situations. Instead of waiting, for example, for your two-year-old to throw a tantrum in the middle of a crowded grocery store ten minutes before dinner, Drawing the Line allows you to engineer her tantrum when you've got the time, energy, and tools to deal with it—for example, in the middle of a weekday morning, when the store isn't crowded and you don't need to buy a single thing.

And trust us: If you can create conflict, you can create a solution to that conflict.

You Can Draw the Line Anywhere

When Michael Drew the Line with Jesse and Ian, he literally drew a line—he showed the kids the highly visible boundary between the living room carpet and the kitchen tiles and, in effect, told them not to cross it.

We like this example because it's just so clear: *Here's the line, plain as day,* we're saying to the kids. *Cross it, and it's time out. Stay on your side, and the world's your oyster.*

Now, as we said earlier, Jesse and Ian had a hard time letting their parents—especially Michelle—have time to themselves. Wherever Michelle went, Jesse and Ian felt compelled to follow. So by setting up a situation in which the two boys weren't able to be near their mother for a brief period, Michael created a recipe for conflict.

But Drawing the Line doesn't necessarily have to be about drawing a physical boundary between two rooms. You can Draw the Line in almost any situation that's challenging for you and your kids. For example:

- For a toddler who bolts in the grocery store and other "fun" places, Drawing the Line might involve short, planned trips to the store to teach him how to stay close by. If he bolts, he's crossed the line—time out. If he stays close by, he's rewarded. (See chapter 3 for a description of how Melanie Drew the Line with her son Aedan in the grocery store.)
- If bedtime is a nightmare, then parents might choose to Draw the Line by insisting that kids stay in bed. If they get out of

bed, they've crossed the line—time out. If they stay in bed, they're rewarded. (See chapter 5 to learn how Arlene, a single mom of two wakeful little girls, Drew the Line with her kids around bedtime.)

- Your daughter eats only grilled cheese and peanut butter sandwiches—and it's making you nuts. You might Draw the Line at dinnertime, instituting a "taste one bite of everything" rule before she gets her sandwich. (This is what Anna and Cameron did with their fussy daughter, Madeline, at dinnertime. See chapter 5 to find out how.)

- Your son uses rude, demanding language and refuses to say "please." You can Draw the Line by offering him things he likes—ice cream or a favorite game—but only if he asks nicely. If he's rude, it's time out, and he doesn't get the treats. (Melanie used this strategy with Aedan. Read on to the end of this chapter to find out how.)

At the end of this chapter, we'll help you figure out when and where you can Draw the Line around your kids' target difficult behaviors. And in the next chapters, we'll show you how to pick effective rewards and penalties, and how, when, and where to talk to your kids when you Draw the Line. With these tools and strategies in place, you'll be able to Draw the Line with your kids—and begin to create a new world order where appropriate, pleasant, and fun behavior is the norm, not the exception.

Drawing the Line with ASD: Asher's Story

As we just saw, Michelle and Kent had a specific goal: They wanted Jesse and Ian to learn how to be able to play independently some of the time, instead of constantly demanding attention and stimulation. For them, Drawing the Line meant insisting that their two boys spend some structured time each day playing on their own.

Other parents might Draw the Line in the service of very different goals. Take Asher, for example. He's a four-and-a-half-year-old kid who's been diagnosed with autism spectrum disorder (ASD). Like many kids with an ASD diagnosis, Asher really likes to organize his environment. He especially likes to arrange things—such as his toy cars—into lines, and he can get extremely upset if those lined-up toys are rearranged.

Unlike Jesse and Ian, Asher doesn't have any problems playing on his own. What he needs to work on, however, is social interaction—Asher needs to learn to see his parents and other people as sources of comfort, information, and fun. So his parents, Nima and Andrew, Draw the Line by picking times each day to disrupt Asher's quiet play and arranging. During these times, Nima Draws the Line by picking up and holding on to Asher's next car so that he must interact with her in order to continue his play. Or Andrew sits down in the path of Asher's arrangement so that Asher must interact with him to get him to move. In essence, Asher's parents are telling him, *In the new world order, sometimes the best way to get what you want is to interact with us and with other people.*

Of course, Asher isn't happy about the new world order. At first, he gets mighty upset. But Nima and Andrew just keep insisting, every day, that Asher interact with them to get what he wants. Over time, however, and with consistent practice, Asher begins to calm down. He learns that he can use words and phrases—like "Please move, Mom," or "Daddy, I want my blue car, please"—and eye contact to get what he wants. In other words, he's finding appropriate and creative ways to break down the barriers Nima and Andrew have thrown up in the way of his favorite activities.

Asher also learns that his parents are kind of fun to play and interact with—and, by extension, so are other people. In fact, he begins to look forward to their "interruptions": He comes to see them as a game, as a puzzle for him to solve. In the longer run, he's learning that, sometimes, the best way to get what he wants is by interacting with other people: an important lesson for any child, and especially important for a child dealing with an ASD diagnosis.

FIGURING OUT THE NEW WORLD ORDER

Let's take a closer look at Jesse and Ian. We haven't banished them to torture in Siberia for weeks. They're warm, well fed, well loved, wanted kids. They're surrounded by toys, playing in a safe, familiar setting, with both parents within sight and earshot. All we're asking is that they let Mom and Dad and a guest talk quietly in the kitchen for half an hour or so, without undue interruption.

Is that so hard? On the surface, it shouldn't be. There's nothing inherently difficult, even for a four-year-old, about playing with toys and staying out of the kitchen.

Then why is Jesse putting up such a fight? Well, because this isn't really about the kitchen. This is about control and desire. In other words, it's about Jesse figuring out how to negotiate and control the new world order—as laid down by Michael (and eventually, Michelle and Kent)—in order to get what he holds most dear.

And what does Jesse hold most dear? On the surface, of course, it looks like what he wants most of all is to come into the kitchen. He certainly keeps running in there, even though he keeps getting hauled out. But, of course, there's nothing inherently fantastic about the kitchen; he doesn't want to be there because the room in and of itself satisfies some deep longing in him.

In fact, Jesse wants *attention*. And his experience up until Michael's visit—the old world order—has taught him that the best way to get attention from his parents and other adults is to demand it, by getting right in their faces and, if necessary, acting up: whining, arguing, shouting, yelling, fighting, or disregarding their requests and their boundaries. That's the behavior that's got Michelle yelling, sending him to his room, spanking him, and finally sitting on the couch and tuning him out completely. (And of course, the more Michelle tunes out her sons, the more they're compelled to act up to get her attention. And on goes the vicious cycle.) According to Jesse's logic, any attention—even being yelled at, scolded, or swatted on the bum—is better than none. (As we'll see in chapter 3, even negative forms of parental attention can be extremely rewarding to kids.)

FUTURE LEADER—OR FUTURE TYRANT?

So Jesse wants attention. And why shouldn't he? We all do. That's a good thing. Over the course of his four years, Jesse has become very skilled at taking control of most situations to get what he wants. That's good, too. Really. We want our kids to be able to figure out how to get what they need in this world, and to be confident in their abilities to go out and get it. That's how leaders are created.

The problem, however, is Jesse's set of strategies. He's priming himself to be a future tyrant, not a future leader. Under the old world order, he's figured out that his most direct route to attention is inappropriate behavior. And so he behaves inappropriately as much as he can, essentially bullying Michelle into reacting. Which she does—by shouting, yelling, spanking, fighting and arguing with him, and sending him to his room so she can take a breather. (In fact, Michelle's reaction to her son's behavior can look an awful lot like that behavior.)

Jesse—and, lately, Ian—is giving his mom such a run for her money that she's too tired to pay attention to her kids when they do give her the occasional moment of peace or cooperation. (And really, because those moments are so rare, when Michelle *does* notice her sons' quiet, appropriate behavior, she's scared to comment on it or interrupt: Why ruin a good thing? Does that sound familiar?)

Rewriting History

"Establishing a new world order in half an hour? That'll never work with my kid."

You're right. It won't. It wouldn't work with any kid. No one, including us, can change a child's entire life in thirty minutes or less. Kids are complex beings, and change takes time.

What's more, what Michael can do with Jesse and Ian in half an hour will likely take Michelle and Kent a lot longer. That's not simply because Michael is the "expert," but more about the fact that he doesn't have any history with Jesse. He can Draw the Line without getting emotional—unlike a frustrated parent who's dealt with her kid's defiant behavior for far too long. At the same time, because Jesse doesn't know Michael all that well, he doesn't know how to push Michael's buttons to get a rise out of him. In other words, when Michael establishes a new world order for Jesse, that's one thing. When Michelle and Kent try to change things, however, they're rewriting a lifetime's worth of history between them and their sons—and they're bound to meet with a lot more resistance. Parents and kids will need time to adjust to the new world order.

What anyone *can* do in thirty minutes is establish a few simple guidelines—
Mom needs to spend some time by herself in the kitchen, and kids need to
play by themselves in the playroom for a little while—and show kids that
they're serious about enforcing those guidelines. In that half an hour, we can
help kids begin to figure out how to get what they want without resorting to
inappropriate behavior. (We're also teaching them that you don't always get
what you want, or that you don't necessarily get it right away. That's life.)

No, your child isn't suddenly going to become a compliant little angel
with thirty minutes of magic. But that half an hour is enough time to make a
start. So be patient. And be persistent. We promise: If you're able to devote
thirty minutes most days to Drawing the Line with your kids, the other
twenty-three and a half hours will start to get easier.

When Michael arrives and Draws the Line, he turns the old world
order on its head. As Jesse quickly discovers, his usual attention-
getting strategies simply don't apply anymore. In the new world
order, all of a sudden, Jesse doesn't get the attention he craves when
he acts up and ignores parental boundaries—he no longer gets a rise
out of Michelle and Kent, who just quietly and mechanically plop
him in his room, alone. (Yes, they're still responding to his behavior,
but in a much more predictable, quiet, boring fashion—not the
high-energy histrionics Jesse has come to cherish.) In the new world
order, Jesse gets attention when he respects the boundaries, when he
plays quietly with Ian in the other room. So very quickly, he begins
to develop a new set of strategies, ones that will net him precious
attention under the new regime.

KIDS IN CONTROL

Under the old world order, it was pretty clear that Jesse controlled
the situation. Acting up got him attention, and so he secured that
attention by acting up. In essence, he controlled his parents' response to him by establishing a vicious cycle of negative attention.

What's crucial to note, though, is that *Jesse is also in control of the new world order*. He's still in charge of when and whether he gets attention—it's just that the rules have changed. Under the old world order, playing quietly didn't net him attention and acting up did, so he acted up. Under the new world order, the reverse is now true, and so Jesse begins to learn to play quietly with his brother and act up less.

Not convinced? Think of it this way: If our real goal was to control kids' behavior for them, we could do it easily. If Michael wanted to force Jesse to stay out of the kitchen, he could have put up a gate, closed and locked the kitchen door, stuck Jesse in his bedroom behind a locked door, or sent him to play outside in the backyard. (He could have stuck two-year-old Ian in a crib or playpen for half an hour.) Or Michael could have tried to distract—or redirect—Jesse and Ian by popping the boys' favorite DVD in the player and hoping that the lure of the movie would outweigh the lure of parental attention in the kitchen.

And in fact, parents use precisely these strategies all the time in the service of controlling their kids. But while they're effective in the short term (no kids in the kitchen), they don't really teach kids much about how to behave appropriately when the external barriers come down (kids back in the kitchen). The more difficult—but ultimately more rewarding—task is to teach kids to control themselves, to respect the barriers even when no one's around to enforce them. That's what authoritative parents do.

Drawing the Line by Parent Type

In chapter 1, we learned about the four types of parents: authoritarian, permissive, uninvolved, and authoritative. Here, in a nutshell, is how each type of parent tends to react when their kids challenge the rules:

- **Authoritarian** parents are likely to enforce the boundaries by using physical force and barriers: They'll put up gates, close and lock doors, send kids outside or to their rooms "until you can behave." At extremes, authoritarian parents will use physical violence—or its threat—to control their children. "You try coming in here one more time and you'll get a spanking!" "I smacked you because you came in here when I told you not to. Now you'll learn."

- **Permissive** parents don't tend to set up many boundaries or to enforce them with any great consistency. They're more likely to use redirection as a means of controlling their children: "Here's your Barney video. Why don't you watch this instead of coming in here?" "Don't cry because you can't come in—look, here's some ice cream. It's okay." Or the boundaries simply break down under the weight of kid pressure: "Fine, you can come into the kitchen—but just this once, and don't tell your dad!"

- **Uninvolved** parents don't tend to set or enforce boundaries. "You're in the kitchen? Fine, whatever. Just don't bother me right now."

- **Authoritative** parents set and enforce reasonable boundaries, but their ultimate goal isn't to intimidate or bribe kids into toeing the line. Rather, they want their kids to develop both the skills to respect boundaries even when they're not compelled to and the wisdom to know when to cross the line.

From Banana Peels to Real Self-Esteem

Instead of controlling Jesse with locks and gates and distractions, Michael sets up the situation so that Jesse is in control. The little boy can just keep on coming into the kitchen. And he does, for a while. Each time he crosses the line, however, Michael keeps enforcing the boundaries with time-outs. His goal isn't to prevent Jesse from coming in (even though that's what it looks like). Rather, he wants to teach Jesse how and when to come in, and that *he's in charge of the situation.* Jesse needs to know that his behavior determines the outcome: *Cross the line, and you're outta here! No attention for you, big boy! Toe the line, give your mom and dad a short break, respect the boundaries, and you get freedom and parental attention that's fun as opposed to unpleasant.*

Think back to the Marshmallow Test we described in chapter 1.

As we stressed there, kids who learn self-control at an early age—kids who can inhibit their impulses and delay gratification in order to secure a larger reward—have a distinct advantage over their peers who can't control themselves. When Michael Draws the Line with Jesse, his ultimate goal is to help Jesse learn the skill of self-control.

But that's only part of the picture. Ironically, once Jesse has that self-control, once he can inhibit himself from breaking the rules, he also gains the even more sophisticated—and crucial—skill of *judgment*. In other words, once Jesse learns how to follow the rules, he can also learn when it's appropriate to break them.

When we Draw the Line, we're not looking for kids to conform blindly to a set of rigid, arbitrary rules. We're looking to teach children how to behave appropriately. Instead of creating an obedient little robot who blindly follows his parents' orders, we're working on creating a discerning little boy who can think for himself. So—and this is crucial—when Jesse wanted to know if he could come into the kitchen to throw away a banana peel, Michael let him, no problem. It would have been unreasonable—in fact, it would have been downright stupid—to enforce the "no kids in the kitchen" rule in that instance.

Let's take a closer look at that banana peel situation:

Jesse was fairly sure that he wasn't allowed to come into the kitchen. But he was also fairly sure that the banana peel belonged in the compost bucket, and that his parents would have wanted him to put it there. So he was faced with a dilemma: Of the two conflicting rules, which one applied? Would this Michael guy put him in a time-out if he came into the kitchen to throw away the peel? What would happen if he tested the "no kids in the kitchen" rule on these new grounds? And so he came to the kitchen door, stayed on his side of the line, and asked if he could come in to get rid of his banana peel.

And Michael and Michelle and Kent said yes. "Yes, yes, yes! Of course you can come in and throw out that peel! What a great guy you're being, Jesse!"

In that moment, Jesse aged developmentally about two and a half years: from an eighteen-month-old baby to a four-year-old boy. Over the course of, again, about thirty minutes, he cleared a bunch of developmental milestones in terms of testing the boundaries: from running into the kitchen and yelling like a banshee to a much more logical and sophisticated—not to mention polite!—form of questioning. In other words, he's developing judgment and discernment—and the ability to think for himself.

Jesse knew the "no kids in the kitchen" rule, but he also knew when it shouldn't be enforced, to everyone's benefit. And you don't get people making brilliant innovations without knowing the rules—and testing them when they're not useful or fair. In other words, Jesse is figuring out not only what the rules are, but also how and when to respect them, when he can get around them, and when it's appropriate to break them.

All this from a banana peel.

Rule Making and Rule Breaking

Life is full of rules: Stay out of the kitchen. Don't tattle. Respect your elders. Stay in your bed. $E = mc^2$. As parents and caregivers—as human beings—we all have different values, and the rules we create reflect those values.

We believe that one of the most important things parents can do is to give their children the skills they need to figure out when they should and shouldn't follow the rules—now and in the future. Mostly, we want our kids to respect the rules. Sometimes, we want kids to break the rules. Always, we want them to be able to use reason and good judgment to figure out the difference. For example:

- **Stay out of the kitchen:** What if I have to throw away a banana peel?
- **Respect your elders:** What if a strange adult tells me to get in his car? What if an adult says something racist?
- **Don't tattle:** What if my friend tells me that her babysitter is hitting her or touching her in ways that make her feel uncomfortable? What if the fifth-grade bully is beating a second-grader to a pulp in the schoolyard?

- **Stay in your bed:** What if the house is on fire? What if I just threw up—or think I might? What if I have to pee?
- **E = mc²:** What if I've thought of a new theory that seems to contradict or enhance Einstein's?

When you Draw the Line with your kids, you're not creating little robots who blindly follow orders. Instead, you're helping them learn how to tell the difference between potentially useful and potentially harmful rules, between legitimate and illegitimate authority. You're teaching them to think for themselves and make considered, wise decisions—and that's a crucial life skill.

THE NEXT STEP: DRAWING THE LINE WITH YOUR KIDS

We've seen how Michael Drew the Line with Jesse and Ian. Now what about you?

In chapter 1, you figured out your kids' target behaviors: those frustrating things in your children's behavioral repertoire that you want to change or eliminate. You also figured out the positive alternatives to those target behaviors. And you prioritized: You decided which target behavior to work on first.

Now it's time to get out your worksheet for your kids and take the next steps.

Let's go back to four-year-old Aedan, from chapter 1. His parents, Melanie and Dennis, have targeted three behaviors: fighting with his brother, Dylan; bolting in the grocery store; and rude language. They've figured out their positive alternatives: playing peacefully with Dylan, sticking close by Melanie when they're out in public, and using polite language and a pleasant tone. And they've prioritized those behaviors. Here's what Aedan's worksheet looks like so far:

Drawing the Line: **Aedan**

Priority	Target Behavior	Positive Alternative	When/ Where Does It Occur?	Draw the Line	Drawing the Line: Reward?	Drawing the Line: Penalty?
1	Fighting with brother.	Playing peacefully; sharing.				
2	Running away from me in grocery store.	Staying close by, being patient until I'm done.				
3	Rude, demanding tone.	Saying "please," asking and talking nicely.				

What next?

STEP 4: Figure out when, where, and under what circumstances the behavior occurs.

When it comes to Drawing the Line, information is power. When you know when, where, and why your kids are liable to act up, you can use this information to engineer conflict. In other words, you can set up your kids so that those target behaviors will emerge. And then you can Draw the Line.

Melanie and Dennis did some thinking to figure out when, where, and under what circumstances Aedan's target behaviors occurred. First, fighting: Sometimes it feels as though Aedan and Dylan fight pretty much whenever they're in the same room. But Melanie knows that the worst time of the day for fighting tends to be right after school, after the boys have been apart for a while. Usually, the scene for fights is the living room, where the toys are. Specifically, they tend to fight when they're playing video games.

Figuring out the whens and wheres of Aedan's second target behavior, bolting in public, is pretty easy: It happens when he and

Melanie go out shopping together, at the mall or grocery store. Aedan's so excited and distracted by all the shiny things in the world that he runs off to explore.

As for the rude language and that aggressive, demanding tone that make up Aedan's third target behavior, well, that seems to happen a lot. Lately, it feels as if whenever Melanie or Dennis asks Aedan to do something, they're going to face defiance. And when Aedan wants something from his parents, he doesn't ask nicely or say "please"—he just demands it. When they Draw the Line with their son, Melanie and Dennis may need to focus on a couple of really compelling instances of this target behavior. We'll explain how shortly.

After Melanie and Dennis have taken this step, here's what Aedan's worksheet looks like:

Drawing the Line: **Aedan**

Priority	Target Behavior	Positive Alternative	When/ Where Does It Occur?	Draw the Line	Drawing the Line: Reward?	Drawing the Line: Penalty?
1	Fighting with brother.	Playing peacefully; sharing.	After school, with video games.			
2	Running away from me in grocery store.	Staying close by, being patient until I'm done.	At the store.			
3	Rude, demanding tone.	Saying "please," asking and talking nicely.	Almost always! (And particularly when he wants something he really likes.)			
4						
5						
6						

Now it's your turn. Take the time to identify when, where, and under what circumstances the target behaviors most often occur. Fill in the information for each behavior on your kids' worksheets on page 18.

ENGINEERING CONFLICT

STEP 5: | Engineer conflict: How will you Draw the Line?

When you know when, where, and under what specific circumstances your kids' target behaviors occur, you will be able to make some pretty educated guesses about where you might be able to Draw the Line.

Let's see how Melanie and Dennis figured out how to set up some conflict with Aedan in order to trigger those target behaviors. Since Aedan and Dylan most commonly fight after school over the video games, figuring out when, where, and how to Draw the Line is easy here: Dennis and Melanie simply have to set up their two boys with the PlayStation after school, and then intervene with rewards for good behavior and penalties if and when the boys—especially Aedan—cross the line by fighting. (You'll learn more about penalties and rewards in chapter 3.)

Similarly, if Aedan bolts in the grocery store, then the obvious place to Draw the Line with him is at the grocery store. Again, Melanie will engineer the situation to set up potential conflict. If Aedan crosses the line and bolts, he'll be penalized. When he sticks close by Melanie, then he's rewarded. And note: When Melanie goes to the grocery store with Aedan, she should go when she's got plenty of time to deal with him. If she needs to take two hours to practice with him, she can. If she needs to leave immediately without buying a thing, she can do that too. She's creating conflict—but she's creating it on her terms, when she has the time, energy, and tools to deal with it most productively.

Drawing the Line: **Aedan**

Priority	Target Behavior	Positive Alternative	When/ Where Does It Occur?	Draw the Line	Drawing the Line: Reward?	Drawing the Line: Penalty?
1	Fighting with brother.	Playing peacefully; sharing.	After school, with video games.	Set kids up to play together after school; if they fight, they've crossed the line.		
2	Running away from me in grocery store.	Staying close by, being patient until I'm done.	At the store.	Go to the grocery store with Aedan (when we've got time to practice); if he bolts, he's crossed the line.		
3	Rude, demanding tone.	Saying "please," asking and talking nicely.	Almost always! (And particularly when he wants something he really likes.)			
4						
5						
6						

Sometimes, however, a situation may not be so clear-cut. For example, kids might be whiny, aggressive, rude, or defiant at any time or in a variety of situations. In these cases, it's often a great idea to set up an activity that your child really enjoys, like painting, or playing with Play-Doh, or making cookies. In this case, the reward is implicit in the activity: If kids behave appropriately, then they get to have fun with the activity. If they don't, their penalty is a time-out away

Drawing the Line: **Aedan**

Priority	Target Behavior	Positive Alternative	When/ Where Does It Occur?	Draw the Line	Drawing the Line: Reward?	Drawing the Line: Penalty?
1	Fighting with brother.	Playing peacefully; sharing.	After school, with video games.	Set kids up to play together after school; if they fight, they've crossed the line.		
2	Running away from me in grocery store.	Staying close by, being patient until I'm done.	At the store.	Go to the grocery store with Aedan (when we've got time to practice); if he bolts, he's crossed the line.		
3	Rude, demanding tone.	Saying "please," asking and talking nicely.	Almost always! (And particularly when he wants something he really likes.)	Set up a situation (painting) in which Aedan has to ask nicely to get something he really wants; if he's rude, he's crossed the line.		
4						
5						
6						

from the activity. To deal with Aedan's rude language, Melanie and Dennis set up a painting table. If Aedan wants to paint—and he does—he has to ask nicely. If he's rude, he's crossed the line, and Melanie and Dennis simply ignore him and don't let him paint.

Now it's your turn. Try to think of how you can engineer a situation that's bound to push your kids' buttons. Often it's as simple as figuring out when target behaviors occur: If bedtime or mealtime is problematic at your house, then you'll Draw the Line at those times by deciding on a certain minimum standard of behavior (eat two bites of each food; stay in your own bed). Sometimes the setting or situation is key: If your child has a hard time containing himself at the mall, that's where you'll Draw the Line. If she throws tantrums instead of sharing, you can Draw the Line by inviting over a couple of trusted friends and their kids to practice sharing. And so on.

Stuck for ideas? It may help to read the case studies in chapter 5 for ideas around bedtime, mealtimes, good behavior in public, toilet training, and sibling battles. In the next chapter, the section Thirty-one Thousand Flavors of Drawing the Line also provides some suggestions. Finally, this book includes lots of examples of parents Drawing the Line with their kids.

From Drawing the Line to R.I.P.: Relating in Peace

When you Draw the Line, you use a set of tools—rewarding, ignoring, and penalizing, or *R.I.P.*—that guide your children through the new world order. These three tools make Drawing the Line effective. In chapter 3, we'll help you understand these three tools and how they can help you keep your kids on track.

—3—

Relating in Peace, or R.I.P.

Rewards, ignoring, and penalties: your children's global positioning system.

Imagine that your child is walking, alone, on an unfamiliar path through the woods. It's nighttime, and it's dark. Sometimes the path is straight and clear, but it also winds and twists, dips and rises. The path has plenty of obstacles: tree roots and rocks that threaten to trip up your child, thorns and low-hanging branches that can scratch skin and tear clothes, muddy patches in which to lose shoes, the occasional stream or waterfall to drink from—or fall into. By the way, you've heard there are bears in these woods, too . . . and steep cliffs . . . and poisonous berries . . .

Now imagine the same scenario, except that this time you're walking behind your child—and you've got a powerful flashlight. At each new twist and turn in the path, each boulder or tree root, each low-hanging branch, thorn, stream, berry, waterfall, or each rustle of leaves that might signal wildlife, you briefly flick on your flashlight, illuminating the way ahead. With your constant guidance, your child is able to navigate the path and arrive safely at his or her destination.

Put yourself in your kid's shoes: If you were walking through the woods on your own in the dark, wouldn't you want the lights on as much as possible? We would. We'd want to be able to see as much as we could as we negotiated the bumpy terrain.

Rewarding, ignoring, and penalizing (R.I.P.) are like your flashlight in the woods. These three tools give your children the information they need to gracefully negotiate the often bumpy terrain of life. And they're the tools that will allow you and your kids to Relate in Peace.

When we Draw the Line with kids, we're creating a new world order. And we help kids negotiate that unfamiliar new world by using rewards, ignoring, and penalties. Especially at the beginning, we use these three tools almost constantly, creating a continuous source of feedback and information—a constant source of light in the dark—for kids as they learn to make sense of the place. After a while, with lots of feedback and practice, kids will become adept at negotiating the path without so much help, anticipating twists and turns and avoiding or clearing obstacles. After a while, you don't have to flick on the flashlight at every juncture. And eventually, you can hand it over and say, "I trust you to navigate the path on your own; I'll be here for you if you need me, but I know you have the skills to get to your destination safely."

Rewards, Ignoring, and Penalties Are Information—That's It!

Any discussion of rewarding kids, ignoring them, or penalizing (or punishing) them is by nature a loaded discussion. Most of us have grown up with some pretty entrenched ideas of what these three things—and especially reward and penalty—mean.

Maybe, when you were growing up, *reward* meant a great toy at Christmas or Hanukkah or on your birthday—as long as you were "good." Maybe it meant dessert if you ate all your brussels sprouts. Maybe you think of reward as the new toy or outfit you got for bringing home all A's or winning the spelling bee. Maybe that trip you're planning to Disneyland with your family counts as a reward in your head. Maybe reward was (or is) associated with religion and good deeds: If you're good enough, one day you'll go to heaven. Or maybe you think of rewarding kids as "spoiling" or "indulging" them.

When we say *penalty*, on the other hand, some parents hear "punishment." And *punishment*, like *reward*, can be a very loaded term. What did punishment mean to you when you were a child? For some of us, it meant being yelled at, going to bed without dinner, having our mouths washed out with soap, being grounded, or having privileges or allowance taken away. For others, it meant being hit: from a swat on the behind to vicious beatings. For still others, it conjures up threats of hellfire and damnation. Many people think of punishment as a form of revenge or retribution: getting back at kids for their "bad" behavior. There's no doubt that the idea of punishment is a charged one, conjuring up images of parents using force against defenseless children.

If *reward* and *penalty* (or *punishment*) are loaded terms for you, we'd like you to do your best to put aside the associations they conjure up for a little while and consider the following:

Rewards and penalties are information.

Repeat that one a few times to yourself. Think of that flashlight illuminating the path and guiding your child to his or her destination. In the same way, rewards and penalties keep kids on the path. Rewards let children know that they're going in the right direction—and to keep going. Penalties say, "Okay, a little to the right . . . now a little to the left . . . a little more to the left . . . great!"

Repeat it to yourself again. *Rewards and penalties are information.* That's all.

You might want to think of rewards and penalties as a game of "hot and cold": As kids stay within the boundaries, we give them positive feedback: "Great job! Stay on track!" When they cross the line, we give them negative feedback: "You're warm, getting warmer, cooling down, getting colder, colder, icy, heating up, warmer, warm . . . ooh, you're getting hot, hot, hotter, a bit cooler, cooler, warmer . . . Wow! You're on fire!"

With this in mind, start getting used to scanning your kids' behavior—all the time, not only when they're interacting with you or acting up—and asking yourself the following question: *Should I reward, ignore, or penalize this behavior?*

In the rest of this chapter, we'll explain what we mean by rewarding, ignoring, and penalizing behavior. Armed with this knowledge, you'll be able to take the next step in creating your new world order: identifying effective rewards and penalties for your kids—and what you can ignore, at least, for now.

REWARD

Take a look at the following two scenarios.

Scenario 1: Playroom Battles

Phoebe is three and a half years old, all long blond curls and big blue eyes—but don't let her china-doll appearance fool you, because this kid's a slugger. Phoebe's brother, Daniel, is a year younger than her, and he's no slouch in the tough-guy department, either. And boy, can these kids fight. When Phoebe and Daniel go at it—and they go at it much of the day—the playroom turns into a war zone.

The fighting—hitting, shoving, scratching, biting, screeching, and crying—worries Lisa, Phoebe and Daniel's mother, to no end. She can't stand the thought of her kids hurting each other. So when the kids try to murder each other in the playroom, Lisa wades right into the fray. "Stop that!" she'll tell one, then the other. "No hitting! No, no!" "Why can't you play nicely?" "Oh, baby, are you hurt?" "Give that back to her!" "He had it first!" "Here, let me kiss it better." "Leave him alone!" "Stop bugging her!" "You're being very bad right now!"

Every day, it's the same thing: Despite Lisa's interventions, the kids just seem to be drawn to picking on each other. Lisa's really hoping they'll grow out of this phase soon.

Scenario 2: Toilet Training

At age two and a half, Mitchell just doesn't seem to want to be toilet trained. It's driving his mom, Linda, a bit around the bend, especially when Mitchell has what feel like on-purpose "accidents" all over the house. So Linda and her husband, Barry, set up a new toilet-training regime with Mitchell. As one part of this regime, Mitchell gets gummy bears—and lots of praise, hugs, and kisses— whenever he successfully uses the toilet. (But he never gets the gummy bears anytime else.) Over the course of a few weeks, Mitchell begins to use the potty regularly, graduating from diapers and accidents to "big-boy" underwear and a new sense of accomplishment and freedom.

Okay, pop quiz: In the above two scenarios, which parents—Lisa, or Linda and Barry—rewarded their kids for their behavior?

If you chose Linda and Barry, you're right.

But if you chose Lisa, you're also right. In fact, in the above scenarios, *both* sets of parents rewarded their kids.

How do we know that both sets of parents rewarded their kids? Because in both instances, the behaviors the parents targeted increased. The more Lisa paid attention to Phoebe and Daniel's fighting, the more the kids fought. And the more Linda and Barry paid attention to Mitchell's success on the toilet, the more successful he was at toilet training.

It seems fairly obvious that when Linda and Barry give Mitchell gummy bears, they're rewarding his efforts at toilet training. What may be less obvious is that when Lisa gets in the middle of Phoebe and Daniel's duels and gives the kids all her attention, she is in fact rewarding—or reinforcing—the fighting. But in fact, she is.

Adding Fuel to a Fire

Rewarding is like adding fuel to a fire: It causes the fire to burn brighter and hotter. Whenever you give something to your kids—be it praise or harsh words, gummy bears or threats—in response to their behavior and, as a result, that behavior increases, you've just rewarded your kids. Simply put, rewards feed or reinforce behavior, just as logs fuel a campfire.

If rewarding behavior is like adding fuel to a fire, however, it doesn't particularly matter whether the fire will be used to cook dinner or to burn down the house. In other words, it's entirely possible to reward inappropriate, mean, aggressive, nasty, and annoying behavior. Parents—like Lisa—do it all the time.

The classic example of a parent rewarding inappropriate behavior is the kid (maybe your kid, maybe someone else's) whining in the grocery checkout line because she wants a chocolate bar. "Mommy, I want candy. Mommy, I want candy. Mommy, I want candy. Mommy, I want candy! Mommy! I want candy!" Finally, the kid's frazzled mother can't handle it anymore and buys her the blasted chocolate to stop the whining—and the nasty looks that the other customers are shooting her way. That mom has just rewarded—and therefore reinforced—her daughter's whining. To absolutely no one's surprise, the next time she's at the checkout counter, the child whines even more. Rewarding the kid's whining with chocolate has increased her whining.

Perhaps perversely, it's also worth noting that rewards aren't limited to good or pleasant things, like gummy bears and chocolate, or trips to Disney World. As we saw with Lisa and her kids, scolding and yelling can be very potent rewards for kids. Think about four-year-old Jesse from chapter 2—for him, even being swatted on the rear is rewarding. How do we know? Because when his mom spanks him, his aggressive, defiant, disruptive behavior increases. That's why we so often hear parents say, "The more I yell, the more I spank, the more I tell them no, the more I give them time-outs, the more they act up!" They act up more because the yelling, spanking, and five-minute time-outs alone on the steps all reinforce—and therefore increase—the inappropriate behavior. Parental attention, even if it's unpleasant, is hugely motivating for children. (That's why, as you'll read in the next section, an essential part of Drawing the Line involves the *I*-word: ignoring some instances of inappropriate behavior.)

On the other hand, just because something might seem to be pleasant, that doesn't mean it's a reward—at least not in the classic sense. If you give your son ice cream every time he finishes his dinner, and he never really seems to be that interested in finishing his dinner, then the ice cream isn't a reward. (And if you gave him a big bag of garbage for finishing his dinner, and as a result he becomes a mini vacuum cleaner at the dinner table, eating everything on his plate, then, well, the bag of garbage is a reward. That's just how it works.)

Your Attention: The Most Potent Reward

So we've discussed the fact that rewards are one form of information, or feedback, for kids. And we've talked about the fact that technically, rewards are anything that increases, or reinforces, behavior—much the same way as fuel feeds a fire.

But what, specifically, are rewards? What kinds of things can and should parents use to reinforce children's behavior?

When we talk about rewards, often parents' first inclination is to think about stuff, especially big stuff: expensive toys, wonderful meals and desserts, hours of television, clothes, trips to interesting places, money. And while it's true that all these things are potential rewards, it's also important not to confuse doing nice things for your kids with rewarding them.

Are Hugs and Kisses Rewards?

It's absolutely true that hugs and kisses can reinforce—or reward—behavior. And it's perfectly acceptable to hug and kiss your kids when they're behaving appropriately.

But we want parents to hug, kiss, and otherwise show warmth and affection for their kids all the time, not just as a reward. In other words, warmth and affection aren't negotiable. They don't depend on your kids' behavior, and they shouldn't be limited only to the times when your kids are behaving well.

Think about taking your kids to Disneyland, or on any big, fun trip or outing. There's no doubt that taking your kids somewhere fun is doing something nice for them. But is it a reward? Not likely—not unless the trip increases some (hopefully good) behavior that you've targeted for your child. So if a trip to Disneyland miraculously toilet trains your stubborn three-year-old, then it's a reward. Otherwise, it's just doing a nice thing for your kid.

We're not saying that parents shouldn't do nice things for their kids. In fact, we encourage parents to do nice things for their kids all the time. But when it comes to rewarding children in the service of reinforcing behavior, we encourage parents to move away from the idea of big, showy, expensive rewards and think small, especially in the context of Drawing the Line. Often your attention—in the form of eye contact, a smile, a few words, a brief touch, or simply getting nearer to your child—is the most potent, and effective, reward around.

Act, Don't Yak!

In their desperate desire to make inappropriate and ugly behaviors go away, parents can inadvertently reinforce the very behaviors they want to get rid of. How do they do this most often? By talking.

Talking is one of the most rewarding or reinforcing things a parent can do. Having a long conversation with kids who are behaving inappropriately simply adds fuel to the fire. So act, don't yak! One important step in stopping the inappropriate behavior is to stop the talk.

Don't get us wrong. We're big believers in having conversations with kids—but not in the heat of the moment. In fact, scolding is almost never an effective strategy with young kids. Think about it: When you scold little kids, often you're simply telling them what they're doing. And they already know what they're doing. It's like telling them the weather in Europe. They don't care.

Talk to your kids, but talk to them when they're calm—and when you're calm. They're more likely to listen and respond to you then. When they're mid-tantrum, though, act—don't yak! (In chapter 4, we'll guide you through the basics of how, when, and where to talk to your kids when you're Drawing the Line.)

When you're Drawing the Line, especially at first, you give out small rewards for small units of behavior. Think back to Jesse in the previous chapter. Whenever he stayed in the living room for more than thirty seconds, Michael made sure to let him know that he was doing a good job. The reward was small and swift—and it came in response to a small unit of behavior.

Remember that flashlight illuminating your child's path: It's much easier to praise your child every few minutes for staying on track than it is to haul the whole family off to Disneyland every time your kid does something well. So think small, and think about yourself—your smiles, your praise, your attention, your proximity—as the most potent reward around.

What Moves the Earth for Your Child?

Take a bit of time to think about potential rewards for your child. Remember, you (your attention, your proximity, your words, your eye contact) are often your child's most motivating reward. Here are some ideas for quick rewards that parents can use when Drawing the Line.

Smaller, In-the-Moment Rewards (for small units of behavior: thirty seconds to ten minutes)

- Smiling at your child.
- Looking at your child, or at the toy he or she is playing with.
- Your comforting physical presence: sitting or standing near your child, getting closer.
- Touching your child: ruffling hair, stroking a back, tickling, snuggling, or cuddling.
- Genuine, specific praise: "You're doing a great job stacking up those blocks!" "I appreciate how nicely you're waiting for me in this lineup."
- High-fiving your kids.
- A sticker or a gold star.
- A small treat, like an M&M or a gumdrop (see more on food, page 61).

Medium-Size Rewards (for larger chunks of appropriate behavior)

- Being silly with your kids.
- Dancing with your kids.
- Reading a book to your child.
- Singing or listening to music with your kids.
- Setting up painting, Play-Doh, or arts and crafts for your child.
- Fifteen to thirty minutes of TV, or watching a favorite video or DVD.
- Baking cookies with your child.
- Letting your child help you with a grown-up task, such as gardening, feeding a pet, cooking, baking, sewing, or home repairs.
- Playing catch in the park.
- Going for a walk.

Rewarding Is One of the Hardest Things for Parents to Do

Parents hear all the time that "punishing your kids is one of the hardest things you'll have to do." Nobody, however, tends to say anything about rewarding being harder.

Would it surprise you if we said that rewarding kids may be one of the hardest things for parents to learn to do? In fact, for many parents, learning how, when, and how often to reward their kids is the hardest part of Relating in Peace. On the surface, it doesn't make sense: Why should it be harder to reward your kids than to penalize them?

Well, it can be harder for a whole bunch of reasons.

It's Easier to Spot Bad Behavior than It Is to Notice the Good Stuff

It's often much easier to spot inappropriate behavior than it is to notice when the kids are being angels. Which is more noticeable: a kid throwing a temper tantrum in the middle of the grocery store or a kid playing quietly in the next room? The child staying in his bed or the one who refuses to? The whiny, clingy toddler or the cheerful two-year-old engrossed in her blocks? The kid who says "Yes, Daddy," or the kid who shouts "No!"?

When kids are being downright good, they can slip under our radar. And if it's hard to notice consistently good behavior—say, a child who stays in bed or plays quietly in the next room while you fix dinner—imagine how much harder it is to notice small moments of good or even relatively good behavior, sandwiched in between bouts of worse behavior?

"Who Has Time—or Energy?"

Let's go back to Jesse. For a while there, he had Michael and his parents working pretty hard. Every ten, twenty, thirty, sixty seconds at first, Jesse crossed the line. And every time he crossed the line, Michael penalized him—time-out.

Eventually, though, Jesse also spent brief bits of time playing with his brother in the living room. And when he did, Michael seized upon those opportunities to tell Jesse he was doing a great job of staying in the living room. If Michael worked hard at penalizing Jesse's inappropriate behavior, he worked even harder to find even small bits of appropriate behavior to reward or reinforce.

Yeah, it's true that Jesse didn't stay in the living room all that much, or all that long. And yeah, he was being kind of a pain most of the time, at least for the first little while. And yeah, it's really tempting to rest in between bouts of line crossing rather than stand up, walk into the other room, and tell a four-year-old how much you like the way he's playing. But penalty is pretty much useless without reward, so Michael made sure he found some good behavior—however small—to reward in the midst of those time-outs.

Sometimes you can miss the boat with reward: By the time you're on your feet telling your kid he's being good, he's already gotten into the next mischievous thing. But with vigilance, you'll probably find plenty of opportunities to reward.

"But She's Playing Quietly—I Don't Want to Interrupt Her!"

We hear this one a lot: Why get in the way of a good thing?

In fact, noticing and rewarding your child for playing quietly is likely to prolong his quiet play in the longer term. Think of Jesse in the living room. His goal is to get attention, so if he sits quietly for a while and no one pays any attention to him, he may up the ante in order to make sure that his parents see him.

If they acknowledge his good behavior—even with a quick smile, wave, or "Hey, you're doing a great job of playing with your brother"—Jesse gets the attention he needs, and his quiet play is reinforced.

In essence, by not paying attention to kids' good behavior, we're telling them, *Your good behavior has no effect on me.* (In fact, that's the equivalent of ignoring, which we'll talk about more on page 64.)

Rewards don't have to be huge interruptions. They can be a quick smile, touch, hug, or even a look. Just enough so that your child knows you're paying attention.

But, you may be thinking, *when I do go in and pay attention, my child starts to act up. I'm better off just leaving him be.*

Trust us—you're not! Yes, we know that kids will often act up when you first start paying attention to their good behavior. Think of this as a bad habit. With time and repetition, however, you can break this habit, helping your kids get used to the idea of enjoying and peacefully welcoming your "interruptions"—and the attention they bring.

"Why Should I Reward My Kid for Something He Should Be Doing Anyway?"

One of the hardest parts of behavior management is to reward children for doing what you'd expect them to do anyway. "Why should I reward my kid for sleeping at night, eating his vegetables, or playing nicely? Isn't he supposed to do that?"

Yes, he's supposed to do that. Unfortunately, without positive reinforcement or reward, he often won't know he's supposed to do that—just as, without penalty, he won't know what he shouldn't do. Again, remember that rewards and penalties are just information, or feedback. These constant yeses and nos, nos and yeses, distributed in real time, let kids know both how they're doing and what they should be doing. (Think back to the flashlight: Yeah, your kid's supposed to stay on the path, but he needs to be able to see it in order to stay on it.)

Rewards and penalties are both necessary forms of feedback. Without both of them, it becomes incredibly difficult to see substantial developmental change. So even if it feels like it should be obvious to your kid, let her know you appreciate it when she does what she's "supposed to do." Eventually, she'll do it on her own.

"It's Really Hard to Praise Her When She's Been Getting on My Nerves All Day"

We hear you. Let's face it: Sometimes your kids can get on your very last nerve. Let's say your four-year-old daughter has been whiny and rude all morning, ignoring most of your requests to pick up her toys, turn off the TV, get ready for ballet class. You're pretty annoyed—and frankly, not really in the mood to praise her for the small bits of cooperation she's demonstrated throughout the morning.

It's not nice to admit, but sometimes we hold grudges against our kids. After all, if our spouses, partners, or friends treated us with the same disrespect, we'd probably be mad for a couple of days. But our kids are our kids and our job is to teach them how to behave appropriately—which means rewarding appropriate behavior even in the midst of the crap. Hard as it sometimes is, we've got to put aside grudges, switch gears, and let kids know when they're doing okay. (And in the next chapter, we'll discuss how timing, talking, and proximity will help prevent parental grudges against kids.)

Tip: Reward Close to the Line

When you're Drawing the Line with your kids, notice when your child is getting close to the line, and reward her *before* she crosses it. For example, if you've asked her to stay in the living room while you talk in the kitchen, if she comes right up to the kitchen door, praise her *before* she has a chance to cross the line: "Hey, sweetheart! You know what you're doing? You're doing exactly what I asked you to do by staying in the living room! What a great job you're doing—I appreciate it." Or if you know that your son typically can sit at the dinner table for fifteen minutes before whining, praise him at fourteen minutes: "What a fantastic job you're doing of staying in your chair at dinner! Thanks— I really like having dinner with everyone as a family." Similarly, if the kids have been playing well together for a while but you sense a fight brewing, step in with the praise and rewards. Get down on the floor and join in their play for a little bit, and tell them: "Wow—you guys are playing together so well! Thanks for doing such a great job!"

When you reward close to the line, you help your children stay within the boundaries—and often, you extend their appropriate behavior. By praising a child at the kitchen door, fourteen minutes into dinner, or just before a fight is about to erupt, you can often avert the coming storm and get your kids accustomed to ever increasing standards of behavior.

Bring on the M&M's! When Food Is an Appropriate Reward

We're going to say something here that a lot of parents will find controversial: We think food is a great reward. By food, we mean whatever turns your child's crank, including cookies, candy, chocolate, colas, and cake. Sugar, sugar, and more sugar—as far as we're concerned, bring it on!

Okay, we admit it: We're being provocative here. But we want to address an often sore point for parents and caregivers, and that is the use of food (especially junk food, and, for that matter, TV, video games, and anything else "bad" for your kids) as rewards.

Why junk food? Well, simple. Most kids really like it. It moves the world for them. And that means that it's a good tool—in certain situations—for reinforcing appropriate behavior.

Let's take a look, again, at Aedan, our four-year-old grocery store bolter. While his mom, Melanie, shops, Aedan's liable to dart off, attracted by whatever catches his eye. Aedan's bolting is frustrating and scary for Melanie: It makes shopping twice as long, and she worries she'll lose him in the crowd. She wants him to learn to stay close by her without having to stick him in the cart.

Now, when Melanie and Aedan go grocery shopping, the very first thing they do is go to the bulk food section, where Aedan chooses a potential treat—he'll get that at the end of the trip if he doesn't bolt. That's his big reward.

But half an hour is a long time to wait for any four-year-old, so Melanie also keeps chocolate coins in her pocket. At regular intervals of good behavior—as small as every two or three minutes or less, at first—she hands Aedan a tiny bit of a chocolate coin and tells him, "You're doing a really great job staying close by me! Thanks!" (When Aedan looks like he's about to wander off, Melanie very quickly reins him in, telling him, "Stay by me, please—great job!") At the end of the successful shopping trip, Melanie and Aedan return to the bulk food section to pick up a small bag of gummy bears or whatever Aedan's picked out.

Why does Melanie use candy? Well, as she puts it, "If I said to Aedan, 'I'll buy you a pound of grapes and dole out grapes on our way through the store,' he'd just laugh at me. You've got to use something that's going to get their attention." If, on the other hand, Aedan were some kind of grape fiend but didn't like chocolate all that much, then grapes would be an entirely motivating choice of reward. You've got to use what works with your kid.

Now, food probably shouldn't be your first choice as a reward. Remember, in most cases the best reward for your kids is your attention. In certain circumstances, though, food is a very useful choice.

What are those circumstances?

- First, when you're out in public and need a portable reward. Being out in public can be a challenge for kids—so much stimulation, so many interesting things, or a lot of waiting around for Mom or Dad to finish grown-up errands, such as grocery shopping or banking. Being out in public is also potentially more dangerous: Kids can get lost, wander off, risk getting hit by a car. And let's face it: Being out in public with misbehaving kids isn't just potentially unsafe—it's potentially embarrassing for parents. In highly charged, highly distracting public places, your attention may not be reward enough for a child who wants to climb all over the machinery in a hardware store. In public—in any volatile, higher-risk situation, like in the car—food may be your own, and your kids', saving grace.

- Second, when you're helping your kids through a particularly difficult or significant transition or developmental milestone, such as toilet training. For a child who's having a lot of diffi·culty with toilet training, lots of praise—and a really special treat like gummy bears or M&M's—every time he uses the toilet successfully can speed up progress and ease the transition.

- Third, to compete with other, enjoyable activities. Say your daughter is watching television and you want her to pick up her toys and get ready for bed. Well, moving from TV to cleanup isn't the most enjoyable transition for her—in fact, she can start to throw tantrums in this situation. If she really likes chocolate kisses, you might say to her, "Do you want a chocolate kiss? Great—that's what you get as soon as the TV's off and the toys are all picked up."

A Few Guidelines for Using Junk Food as a Reward

- Think small! A junk food reward doesn't have to be a whole chocolate bar. It can be as small as one M&M (or even one-quarter of an M&M), one mini marshmallow cut in half, or a chocolate chip. Those Halloween-size treats, cut in quarters or eighths, are a good place to start.

- Don't use junk food as a replacement for nutritious, "real" food. If your kid is eating so many junk "rewards" that she doesn't have room for dinner, you're probably going overboard. (Again, think small.)

- If you use junk food as a reward in certain situations, then use it only as a reward. If Aedan gets chocolate as a reward for staying near Melanie in the grocery store, then he never, ever gets chocolate any other place. If your toddler gets gummy bears for using the toilet, then she never, ever gets gummy bears at any other time. If a kid can get his or her junk fix at any time, then it ceases to be a motivating reward.

- Don't rely on junk forever. It's a temporary, transient kind of reward. As kids begin to internalize and get comfortable with the new world order, phase out the junk. Eventually, your praise, the pleasure in a job well done, and the occasional treat will be reward enough.

- Give junk *after* good behavior, not before. It's a reward to reinforce good behavior, not a bribe that you hope will compel it.

The bottom line? Small amounts of so-called junk food can be a very effective—albeit temporary—reward for your kids. Use it sparingly and strategically—as one part of your overall strategy in dealing with kids' difficult behavior. And don't worry: Studies show that, used wisely, a few bits of chocolate or a couple of pretzel pieces or gummy bears doesn't add up to food-addicted, anorexic, or obese children.

Still, if you're not comfortable using food as a reward, don't! Ultimately, it's your choice.

IGNORE

If rewarding is like adding fuel to a fire, then ignoring kids' behavior is like letting a fire burn itself out. You're not feeding the fire (reward), and you're not actively putting it out (penalty), you're just letting it run its course—while keeping a watchful eye on it to ensure that a stray spark doesn't catch on some dry tinder and get out of hand.

When you ignore a child's behavior, you're essentially telling her that that behavior doesn't count. It has no impact, no force, no sway in the world. It makes no difference at all.

Let's look at some situations in which parents or caregivers ignore their kids' behavior, from least to most dramatic.

Situation 1: Whining at the Table

Madeline is three and a half, with bright red hair and equally dramatic opinions about food. If she doesn't like what's for dinner, she gets pretty vocal. When Madeline starts up—"I don't waaant it, I don't liiike it"—her parents, Cameron and Anna, have learned to ignore the whining behavior.

"I know you don't like it," Cameron will say smoothly as he passes the chicken, "but we're not talking about that right now."

And he and Anna and the rest of the family continue on with dinner. Madeline's pouting simply doesn't matter. It doesn't net her any attention, nor do Cameron and Anna penalize it. Rather, they're just not interested.

Situation 2: Staying on Track

Five-year-old Sam can really push his parents' buttons. He's one of those kids who always seems to be up to something, whether it's riding his bike out of bounds and into traffic, picking fights with his brother or other kids, or actively defying his parents' wishes.

Yeah, Sam has a lot of issues. But when Dr. Michael Weiss Draws the Line with Sam, he focuses on just one thing at a time, like getting Sam to stay on the driveway with his bike. Michael rewards Sam's appropriate cycling with praise and high fives, and penalizes him with a brief time-out (holding his bike for ten seconds) when he rides into the street.

But when Sam starts to act out in other ways—like muttering swearwords under his breath—Michael ignores that behavior. His expression doesn't change, his manner doesn't change, and he gives Sam no reaction. He just carries on talking to Sam as if the four-letter words never happened. He's not Drawing the Line about swearing, he's Drawing the Line about the bike.

Sam's swearing has the potential to distract Michael from the task at hand—which is to show Sam how to ride his bike responsibly. But Michael's not biting. When Sam mutters the *F*-word, Michael's deaf to it. "You ready to try riding your bike again?" he asks. "Great! Let's go."

Situation 3: Screaming to Be Heard

Two-year-old Violet has entered a screaming phase. If she wants something, she screams. If she doesn't want something, she screams. If her parents, Nima and Andrew, ask her to do something, she screams.

For a while, Nima and Andrew ignored the screaming by saying, "Use your words, Violet," and then calmly continuing on as though the screaming wasn't happening. They simply weren't interested in the screams, and the screams had no impact. At the same time, Nima and Andrew rewarded Violet with specific praise when she did use words to communicate.

After a while, however, Nima and Andrew decided that Violet's screaming was too distressing to ignore anymore. So they upped the ante and Drew the Line. Now when their daughter lets go with a good shriek, Nima and Andrew still tell Violet to use her words. But then they calmly turn their backs and walk away (time out). At this point, passive ignoring has turned into active ignoring—a subtle form of penalty. Violet's behavior does have an impact, but it's not one that she likes. Over the course of a few weeks, Nima and Andrew begin to notice that Violet screams a lot less.

Ignore the Behavior, Not the Child

In each of the above situations, you'll notice that Michael and the kids' parents ignored the kids' *behavior*, not the kids. Cameron and Anna acknowledged Madeline, but ignored her whining. Michael ignored Sam's swearing, but didn't ignore Sam or the fact that Sam wanted to ride his bike. And Violet's parents ignored the screaming, not their daughter.

Learning to ignore the behavior rather than the child is the hardest part of understanding the *I* in *R.I.P.* Keep in mind that ignoring—at least for our purposes—is not the silent treatment. It's not pretending that your child doesn't exist. And it's not tuning out your kids. Ignoring is simply sending kids the message that a specific behavior has no impact, no power. It's the opposite of paying attention.

So when do you choose to ignore a child's behavior?

Well, the thing about parenting is that you have to choose your battles. So if your child is doing something that's irritating but relatively benign (like Madeline whining at the dinner table), and you've got your hands full with managing the two other kids, getting dinner on the table, and catching up with your loved ones at the end of the day, you may just choose to ignore her whining.

Similarly, if you're actively focusing on changing certain behaviors—such as ensuring that Sam learns how to ride his bike appropriately on the street—you may just have to ignore others, like the swearing. You can't focus on everything, nor should you; you'd drive yourself, and your kid, insane.

If You Can't Ignore It, Don't!

"Mom? Mom? Mom? Mom? Mom? Mom? Mom? Mom? Mom? Mom?..."

"*What!?*"

We've all done it: We think we can ignore something annoying our kid is doing, but after twenty times, we can't ignore it any longer, and then we explode.

Here's a tip. If you're not sure you'll be able to ignore something, don't sweat it. You can acknowledge a child's behavior without reinforcing it. Or you can penalize the behavior.

For example, say your child's trying to get your attention, and you're busy doing something else. Don't ignore his repeated requests. Instead, take a quick break from your activity to acknowledge your kid—immediately. You can say something like, "I hear you calling me, but I'm busy right now. I'll come see you in five minutes." Or, "I can't talk to you right now, Sean, because I'm talking on the phone. I'll talk to you in a few minutes."

When you respond after your child repeats your name twenty times, you're simply reinforcing the repetition. Essentially, you're saying: *Keep calling my name. If you do it long enough, eventually I'll respond.* (Bad lesson to learn!) If you can't ignore it, better to nip the situation in the bud by responding immediately and letting him know you're unavailable.

If you're going to ignore a behavior, you have to learn how to truly ignore it. Even subtle body postures or fleeting eye contact—not to mention explosions—indicates that you're still paying attention. Kids, even toddlers, pick up on subtle messages that their behavior has an effect on you, and that's reinforcing. So don't respond to demands. Either use a time-out or just walk away.

And sometimes you'll find—like Nima and Andrew—that you can't ignore a behavior anymore. When Violet's screaming continued, Nima and Andrew felt they had to take a more active approach to teaching their daughter how to communicate effectively. And so they began to penalize the inappropriate behavior by turning their backs and walking away in response to Violet's screams.

You Can Only Ignore Ignorable Behavior

Nima and Andrew's changing response to Violet brings us to a key point: You can only ignore ignorable behavior. Think once more about the fire slowly burning itself out in the pit. Well, it's still fire, and potentially dangerous. You're still going to keep one eye on it to make sure that a spark doesn't catch somewhere and escalate into something unmanageable or dangerous.

Say your son decides to throw a temper tantrum in the middle of a restaurant, or goes after his sister with a pair of scissors. As far as we're concerned, those are examples of unignorable behaviors. When parents ignore or tune out unignorable behavior, they're sending a strong message to their children—not to mention the general public or the sister who has to endure the kid's awful behavior—that they don't really care.

So what to ignore? It's all relative. Pick your battles, and stay focused on your goals.

Penalize

If rewarding is like adding fuel to a fire, and ignoring is a slow burnout, then penalizing is like throwing water on the flames. When you penalize a certain behavior, that behavior decreases.

What Is Penalty? And What Is Effective Penalty?

When two-year-old Remy gets out in public—say, to a shopping mall—he can get a little out of hand. He'll try to run off in pursuit of all the shiny, exciting things he sees. If he can't get what he wants, he'll pull the old "stop and drop," falling to the floor and beginning to scream, essentially bringing the outing to a halt.

Remy's parents, Nolan and Camille, handle Remy's behavior in two different ways. Nolan simply picks up his son, holding him tightly so that he can't escape or pull the flop-and-scream maneuver. Nolan's a big guy, and he can easily contain Remy for the duration of a shopping trip if he needs to.

Camille, on the other hand, is less comfortable with the hands-on approach. Yet she can't seem to stop Remy from running off or throwing tantrums. Her solution? She's stopped going out with Remy, unless she absolutely has to. And then the outings are quick and stressed.

"Penalty" or "Punishment"?

Why do we use the word *penalty* instead of *punishment*?

Well, an obvious reason is that *punishment* conjures up a lot of potentially nasty associations that we'd like to get away from. *Penalize* is a more neutral word, one less likely to evoke thoughts of revenge, retribution, or being mean to kids.

But the real reason we use the word *penalty* is that it paints a more accurate picture of what's going on. Imagine a penalty box at a hockey rink: When a player gets out of line, the referee pulls him (or her!) out of the game and into the penalty box for a set amount of time. That time is time away from the opportunity to play. When the time's up, the player's back out on the ice. No grudges, no retribution, nothing nasty—just time out.

In the same way, as you'll see over and over again in the examples we use in this book, penalty isn't about retribution, nastiness, or holding grudges. It's time out from the opportunity for reward.

Both Nolan and Camille are penalizing Remy. How do we know they're penalizing their son? Because in both cases, the target behavior has decreased: Remy isn't running around a shopping mall. In the short term, both Nolan's strategy of containment and Camille's of avoidance do work.

In the longer term, however, these strategies aren't particularly effective. Essentially, Camille and Nolan control Remy's behavior with external barriers—through sheer physical force, or by keeping him, in effect, a prisoner in his own home. In other words, Nolan and Camille take control away from Remy. And while taking control nets them some momentary peace, it does nothing to achieve their larger goal of teaching him how to behave appropriately outside of the home. Because these penalties contain Remy without teaching him *how* to behave out in public, they don't prevent him from running off or dropping to the floor every time he doesn't get what he wants.

Effective penalties don't simply stop behavior in the short term by removing a child's control. Instead, *effective penalties eventually give control back to children.* In combination with effective rewards, effective penalties decrease the likelihood of a target behavior recurring—even when the external barriers do come down. Camille and Nolan's goal is to find a way to teach Remy how to control himself—to behave appropriately in exciting public places, without the threat of containment or avoidance.

As Sheldon says, "You can lock up toys. You can put locks on doors and cupboards and refrigerators and things like that, but the only lock that can't ever be picked is the lock in the child's mind."

Extra-Short Time-Outs—from the Opportunity for Reward

Almost always, the most effective form of penalty is a time-out. We're not talking, however, about the popular—but completely misguided—notion of "five minutes of time out on the stairs" or "one minute of time out for every year of life" (where a four-year-old sits in his time-out chair for four minutes).

When we say time out, we're often talking about a matter of seconds. If penalty is an opportunity to help teach kids how to behave appropriately, then we want as many of those opportunities as possible. One five-minute time-out provides only one opportunity to teach (and it's generally too long a time to be effective for most kids). Five one-minute time-outs, on the other hand, provide five times the opportunity—and ten thirty-second time-outs provide ten times the opportunity. (And twenty fifteen-second time-outs ... well, you get the picture.) In the case of time-outs, think swift, think brief, and think often. (In chapter 4, we'll talk more about timing.)

A Million Repetitions: Pick Those Battles and Be Prepared to Win

If reward and penalty are information, then Drawing the Line is a way of conveying that information. When you Draw the Line with your kids, you're letting them know that there's a new world order, where inappropriate behavior has no currency and appropriate behavior does.

In One Father's Words . . .

I've stopped yelling for the most part. It just doesn't work. It doesn't achieve any end. I don't like to have to penalize my children, to put them into time out, but that's the most effective way to do it.

So if the kids aren't getting along, and they start winding up, I'll say, "Listen, stop. Stop now." If they don't stop, the instigator, he's the guy that gets put into time out. He goes up to his bedroom.

Well, the penalty isn't a day or a month or an hour. It's just "stop." Knock it off, it's finished now. Stop. Go up to your room. Be done with it and come down when it's over. And it's over right away. You know, just the act of going upstairs and coming back downstairs again takes the heat off the argument. And then it's time to move on to the next phase of play or work or whatever you're doing. So it's very effective. And there's a calmer feeling in the home.

Sometimes it can take a while for kids to get that message. When you Draw the Line, they may wonder if you're for real this time. And so they test the boundaries—sometimes repeatedly. Think about Jesse, from chapter 2, who kept running into the kitchen to see what would happen. When kids test the new boundaries, parents have to be prepared to keep mechanically enforcing the rules for as long as it takes to convince the kids that they won't get away with misbehaving. And if that takes ten, twenty, a hundred trips to time out, and another ten, twenty, or hundred small rewards, so be it.

In other words, pick your battles—and be prepared to win them.

Let's take a look at Ashleigh. She's three and a half years old, and she—like her little sister, Amanda—can throw one whale of a tantrum. When Ashleigh gets going, watch out! She'll scream, cry, throw herself down on the floor, and kick. She used all these strategies when Michael Drew the Line with her and Amanda. As a last-ditch effort to wring some attention from her shell-shocked parents, Ron and Susan, Ashleigh started to retch. "I'm gonna puke!" she called to them: "Mommy! Daddy! I'm gonna puke!"

Ashleigh and Amanda—and this is a wild, wild understatement—did not take kindly to having Michael Draw the Line with them. In this case, time out was a five- to ten-second stay in a high chair with a locking tray table. Mid-scream (or mid-retch), Michael simply picked up Ashleigh (or Amanda) and put her in the chair. Then he walked away. After a few seconds, when the little girl quieted even a bit, Michael returned.

"Why are you sitting here?" he asked. "You're sitting here because we need you to stay in the living room and play quietly. Do you want to get out of the chair? Okay, let's go play in the living room."

After repeated forays into the kitchen and trips to the time-out chair, even these two world-class tantrum throwers lost steam. Eventually, after a good hour or so of drama, the two little girls were giggling away with Michael on the living room couch.

After her initial histrionics wound down, Ashleigh decided to further explore the new world order. She wanted to figure out the boundaries, and how credible Michael would be in enforcing them. Her exploratory vehicle? A marble. Ashleigh lay on "her" side of the boundary between the kitchen and the playroom and dropped her marble onto the kitchen floor.

Now, the marble on the kitchen floor was noisy, and annoying. And yes, it was potentially unsafe; if someone stepped on it, they could end up flat on their back. Decent reasons, both, to insist to Ashleigh that she play with it elsewhere. But Ashleigh was also using the marble to attract attention back from Michael and her parents. In essence, she was using the marble to say, *I may not be in the kitchen, but I can still insist on being the center of attention.*

And what did Michael want to do? He wanted to teach Ashleigh how to take control of the new world order without resorting to tantrums and projectile vomiting. In other words, he wanted to teach her how to get what she wanted—attention—using appropriate behavior.

And so Michael began a second round of time-outs. Each time Ashleigh dropped the marble on the floor, Michael simply picked it up and put it in his pocket. Time out. (Yes, something as simple as taking away a marble is a form of time out—it's time away from the opportunity for play and reward.)

"I want my marble," Ashleigh would say.

"You want your marble?" he'd ask. "Okay, you can have it. But where does it stay? It stays on the rug. On the rug. Thattagirl."

And he'd hand her back the marble. And then, pretty soon, she'd drop it on the kitchen floor again. And the scene would repeat.

Marble on the floor. Time out.

"Okay, that's not where the marble goes. And now I'm keeping it. Do you want the marble? Where does it stay? It stays on the rug. Here you go."

And repeat. Marble on the floor. Time out.

"If you keep the marble inside the living room on the rug you can have it. Okay, you want it? Thattagirl. Thank you. Thank you, thank you, thank you, thank you, thank you! Here you go."

And repeat. Marble on the floor. Time out—this time in the high chair for five seconds.

"Why are you sitting in the chair? You're here because I asked you to keep the marbles in the living room. Do you want the marble? Here you go. But you have to keep it on the rug."

And repeat. Marble on the floor. Time out.

"Do you want the marble? I have it. Why did I take it away? Why did I take it away? Because it came in the kitchen. Okay? So now I'm going to keep it for a while because that's too many times."

"No!"

"Yeah, for a little while, because that was too many times. If you want the marble back, you show me you can play nicely with your sister, okay? Okay, I'm going to go talk to your mom and dad for a little while, Ashleigh. You know where that marble has to stay. Thattagirl, thattagirl. Thattagirl. Now, how good are you? Ashleigh! Thank you!"

And so on.

Sound tedious? No kidding. It's tedious to write, and it's even more tedious to do—especially after listening to two little girls scream in stereo for upward of an hour. It's sorely tempting to just take the damn marble from Ashleigh, or to give in and let her play with it in the kitchen. In fact, Ron and Susan—not to mention

Ashleigh—couldn't quite believe that Michael kept giving the marble back.

"There's a point at which I would just take it away," he told them, "but Ashleigh has to test my limits six million times before I'm going to actually pull the plug on her. I'll keep giving the marble back to her, but it belongs in the living room. Every time I hear this thing in the kitchen, it's mine. And you know, I'm tired. I don't want to do this, either. But I'll do it one more time. And I'll do it one more time after that. And if I have to stay here with you guys for the next three weeks, I'll do it one more time. I need to show Ashleigh that I have one more time than she's got. She's got to get that message."

And the message is simple: This is the new world order. Tantrums have no currency here, but appropriate behavior does. So if you want to throw tantrums, fine—but they're not going to get you anything but time out. If you want to drop the marble over the line, fine—but I'll take it away. If you want to toe the line, play with the marble in the living room, well, the world's your oyster. It's up to you: You're in charge.

In Drawing the Line with Ashleigh, Michael is trying to teach her how to play with the marble, not prevent her from playing inappropriately. That's why he just keeps giving the marble back to her—and taking it away when she crosses the line. He's not getting mad or worked up. He's just saying, *Welcome to the new world order. This is how it's going to be.* And those five- or ten-second time-outs provided him with umpteen opportunities to teach Ashleigh about the new world order.

Those multiple learning experiences are also teaching Ashleigh how to get the grown-ups' attention in ways that are more mature and appropriate than screaming and retching. So when she asks nicely to come into the kitchen, Michael lets her—as long as she doesn't roll the marble on the floor. And she doesn't. Like Jesse, Ashleigh aged several developmental years over the course of a couple of hours.

The Next Step: What Moves the World for Your Kids?

In order to Draw the Line, you'll need to think about rewards and penalties for your own children. Pull out your worksheet from chapter 1, because it's time to take the next steps.

| STEP 6: | Identify effective rewards and penalties for your kids.

Let's take a look, once again, at our friend Aedan. His parents have targeted three behaviors: fighting with his brother (usually over the PlayStation after school), bolting in the grocery store, and rude language.

Melanie and Dennis have identified three places where they can Draw the Line with Aedan on these behaviors. To deal with the fighting, they set up Aedan and his older brother with their PlayStation after school—and they're prepared to deal with the boys' conflict if it arises. To deal with Aedan bolting in the grocery store, Melanie takes him to the store. And to deal with Aedan's rude language, Dennis and Melanie set up an activity he really likes, such as painting: They can be fairly sure that they'll face some conflict when Aedan has to say "please" in order to paint.

Melanie and Dennis's next step is to plan appropriate, effective rewards and penalties for each situation. Here's what they come up with.

1. Fighting

If the boys start to fight over the video games, they've crossed the line. The penalty is that the game is turned off—at the first sign of conflict—for five or ten seconds. Again, this is a time-out from the opportunity for fun and reward. Melanie and Dennis will use this penalty a few times. If the boys keep fighting, they'll move to a second, more disruptive, penalty: The instigator (usually Aedan) will go to his room for a different form of brief time-out.

Here's what Aedan's time-out will look like: Melanie or Dennis will mechanically take Aedan upstairs (by firmly holding on to his upper arm or carrying him if need be), put him in his room, close the door, and count to five.

"Putting him in his own room for two or three seconds gives you a breather as a parent," says Dennis. "It's a chance to calm down and to come to your senses instead of getting angry. And then—because you got that two- or three- or five-second break—you can talk to him instead of screaming."

After those five or so seconds in his room, whether Aedan's quiet or not at that point, Melanie or Dennis will then open the door. "Why did I put you in your room?" they'll ask. And then they'll answer for Aedan if he doesn't answer for himself: "I put you in your room because you're fighting with Dylan. You guys have to play nicely together. Do you want to play nice? Then come on downstairs whenever you're ready. Want to come downstairs?" At that point, Aedan's free to come downstairs and continue playing. Or he can stay in his room and sulk—it's up to him. If he chooses to sulk, however, he's on his own: Melanie and Dennis aren't going to stick around to watch (and reinforce) his pouting.

What about rewards? If the kids play well together, Melanie and Dennis will reward them by telling them so, using specific praise ("I really like how well you guys are playing together without fighting!"), and Dennis will get down on the floor and play with them. Their parents' attention and praise, plus Dennis's physical closeness, are hugely reinforcing to the two boys. As well, keep in mind that the PlayStation is a reward unto itself—it's a fun toy to play with. Melanie and Dennis turn on the game when the boys' behavior improves.

2. Grocery store bolting

When Aedan stays near Melanie at the store, she rewards him in several different ways.

First, at the beginning of a trip, Melanie and Aedan visit the bulk food section of the supermarket, where Aedan gets to pick out a special treat. But they don't buy that treat right away—at the end of a successful trip, if Aedan stays close by Melanie and comes back to her when she asks, they'll return to the bulk section and pick up Aedan's treat. Melanie uses that larger treat as an incentive throughout the trip. "I'll say to him, as he's about to wander off, 'Remember your special chocolate or those gummy bears that you wanted? You have to stay close by me to get those.' And he'll say, 'Oh, yeah. Okay.'"

Second, throughout the shopping trip, Melanie rewards Aedan with specific praise: "You're doing a great job staying with me. Thanks!"

Finally, as she praises her son, Melanie hands Aedan small bits of chocolate at regular intervals of good behavior. She keeps a couple of chocolate coins in her pocket and breaks off small pieces of them. (For more on using food as a reward, see page 61.)

If Aedan bolts, on the other hand, he's crossed the line. When that happens, Melanie penalizes him by stopping the grocery cart, pulling him back by taking his upper arm, and telling him, "Stay with me, please." That simple act of pulling Aedan close to her is a form of time-out: Melanie has stopped her son from moving away from her.

If Aedan continues to bolt, Melanie will let him know that he risks losing his larger, end-of-trip treat. Finally, if Aedan's behavior gets to be too stressful for Melanie, they can simply leave the store—with no candy—so they can both take a break.

3. Rudeness

To tackle the rude language, Melanie and Dennis come up with the idea of painting. Since Aedan loves to paint, it's a highly rewarding or reinforcing activity. The catch is, he has to ask nicely in order to be able to paint. Here, the rewards and penalties are implicit in the activity. If Aedan refuses to ask nicely, he's crossed the line, and the penalty is that he doesn't get to paint. The minute he asks nicely, however, he's rewarded by being allowed to paint.

Every so often, Melanie and Dennis will ask Aedan if he'd like to paint: "Are you ready to paint? Yeah? Okay, then all you have to do is ask nicely. Nope? Don't want to? Well, that's okay. Just let us know when you're ready." They can repeat the question as many times as they'd like, until either Aedan asks nicely or painting time is over.

If Aedan sits quietly at the kitchen table, sulking and refusing to say "please," that's fine. Melanie and Dennis can ignore the sulking. If he ups the ante with a tantrum, yelling, or some other form of inappropriate behavior, Melanie and Dennis can take him off to his room for a time-out there. The message they're sending Aedan is simple: Rudeness gets you nowhere in this house anymore. But say "please" and ask nicely, and the world's your oyster.

"Now," says Melanie, "if either boy talks back or gets rude, I say, 'If you want to act like that, you can go into your room. It's okay to talk that way in your room by yourself, but if you want to stay out here with us we're going to have fun and laugh.'"

So what about you? Get out your worksheet and start to think about penalties and rewards that might work when you Draw the Line with your kids.

Remember, your praise, attention, and proximity (that is, getting close to your kids—right down on the floor with them!) are often the most potent reward.

On the other hand, a brief time-out—stopping your child, for a few moments, from doing something he or she wants—is usually the most effective penalty. Remember: Time out isn't a place, it's an event. It's time out from the opportunity for reward. What's more, time out is a very short event—maybe a few seconds in duration. That's just enough time to interrupt your child's inappropriate behavior and provide a chance to learn. Often, the longer the time-out, the less effective it is. Compare ten thirty-second time-outs to one five-minute time-out—the shorter time-outs provide ten times the opportunity to learn!

Drawing the Line: **Aedan**

Priority	Target Behavior	Positive Alternative	When/ Where Does It Occur?	Draw the Line	Drawing the Line: Reward?	Drawing the Line: Penalty?
1	Fighting with brother.	Playing peacefully; sharing.	After school, with video games.	Set kids up to play together after school; if they fight, they've crossed the line.	• Praise/attention. • PlayStation. • Dad can play with them.	• Time out from Play-Station (turn it off for 5 seconds; restart game). • Time out to bedrooms.
2	Running away from me in grocery store.	Staying close by, being patient until I'm done.	At the store.	Go to the grocery store with Aedan (when we've got time to practice); if he bolts, he's crossed the line.	• Little bits of chocolate for short periods of sticking with me. • Praise. • Promise of bigger treat at end of trip.	• Pull Aedan back when he starts to wander. Say, "Stick by me, please." • Stop moving briefly (he wants to *go!*). • Leave store with no candy.
3	Rude, demanding tone.	Saying "please," asking and talking nicely.	Almost always!	Set up a situation (painting) in which Aedan has to ask nicely to get something he really wants.	• Praise. • He gets to do do the activity (Play-Doh) if he asks nicely.	• Time out from being able to play with Play-Doh.
4						
5						
6						

Look for rewards and penalties that make sense in the context of what you're doing. For example, when Aedan and Dylan play at the PlayStation, one obvious reinforcement is the game itself, while one obvious penalty is simply turning it off.

Stuck for ideas? See if any of the suggestions in the box below help out. And have a look at chapter 5 for detailed examples of how real parents Drew the Line with their kids around bedtime, toilet training, mealtime, car trips, and sibling battles.

Thirty-one (Thousand) Flavors of Drawing the Line: Penalty and Reward

Stuck for creative, appropriate ideas for Drawing the Line? Here are some suggestions for rewards and penalties:

- Your daughter won't get dressed. Remove her favorite article of clothing or jewelry, such as a bracelet, watch, or headband (penalty). Give it back when she starts dressing (reward).
- Stop the car—*safely!*—(penalty) when the kids start fighting in the backseat. Start moving once they calm down (reward). (Parents: If you use this time-out, remember that safety is your number-one priority. Choose a quiet street where there's not a lot of traffic, and always make sure that you can pull over safely, without risking your own health or that of your kids or other drivers. If you don't see a safe opportunity to pull over, *keep driving.*)
- Your five-year-old son is playing with his food or eating with his hands. Remove the plate (penalty). Offer it back after a few moments (reward) so he can resume eating—like a big boy, not a baby.
- The kids start to argue about which TV program to watch. Use the remote control to turn off the TV (penalty). When the kids stop fighting and negotiate calmly, turn on the TV again (reward).
- Your daughter is engrossed in a book, the television, or the PlayStation and ignores your requests to please set the table. Take away the book or turn off the TV (penalty). Give back the entertainment after she's set the table (reward). (Hint: Here, it would make sense to time your requests logically. Ask your daughter to set the table at the end of the chapter, the TV show, or the game.)

- Your toddler son is biting, shoving, and hitting. Take away his favorite toy or stuffed animal when he's aggressive and put it in solitary confinement, such as a locked or high-up cupboard (penalty). Give it back (reward) when the aggression subsides.
- When your child acts up, take away a coupon that represents a future reward—say, for ice cream after dinner (penalty). Give it back when and if your child begins to behave appropriately (reward).
- Stop pushing a swing (penalty) when your daughter demands rudely to be pushed "higher!" Start pushing again when she asks nicely (reward).
- Walk away from a child when he speaks rudely or disrespectfully (penalty). Get closer (reward) when he speaks politely.
- Your ten-month-old infant likes to strip the leaves off your potted plants. When she makes a beeline for the plant, say, "No." Pick her up and move her back three or four feet (penalty). When she crawls away, tell her, "That's right! Good girl!" (reward).
- Turn away when your son whines (penalty). Tell him, "That's whining. I don't talk to you when you whine. Use a nice voice and we can talk." Pay attention when he speaks in a nice voice (reward).
- Stop the stroller (penalty) when your daughter leans out of it. Start pushing (reward) when she sits up.
- When your son begins to whine or cry at the dinner table because he doesn't want to eat, turn his high chair away from the table for a few seconds (penalty). Turn it back (reward) when the whining subsides.
- Close the bubbles for five seconds (penalty) when your daughter begins to pour the liquid instead of blow. Open the lid (reward) so she can try again.
- Teachers: Delay releasing the kids for recess (and signal the delay by turning off the lights) when the kids are too loud (group time-out). Let them go when they quiet down (reward).
- Your daughter starts to throw a tantrum. Walk away (penalty). Get closer as she calms (reward). If she persists, or becomes more aggressive, take her to a time-out in her room (five seconds with the door closed) or in a high chair with a locking tray. Take her out of time out when she quiets.
- When your kids are playing computer games, turn off the computer screen (penalty) in response to their fighting or rude behavior. Turn it on again (reward) when they're ready to cooperate and be polite.
- Take away Play-Doh for a few seconds (penalty) when your daughter starts to eat it. Give it back (reward) so she can play appropriately.

- Place yourself briefly out of reach—such as in the car, in your room, or in the bathroom—in response to clinginess, whining, tantrums, or rudeness (penalty). Get closer (reward) when the inappropriate behavior subsides.
- Your daughter wanders off or tries to touch everything in the store. Leave the store and sit on a bench (penalty). Let her know you can go back in (reward) when she's ready to stick by you and not touch.
- If your son won't walk with you through the mall (he insists on running off in every direction), hold his hand, stop walking, make no eye contact, and count to three to yourself (penalty). Then turn to him and say, "Stay with me so that I don't have to hold your hand." Resume your journey (reward).
- Sit your son on the back steps (for a few seconds!) when he goes out of bounds in the backyard (penalty). Let him know he can get up anytime he's ready to stay within the boundaries (reward).
- If your toddler is the type to get up and run from the stairs when in a time-out, put her in her high chair with the tray locked for a few seconds.
- Use startling your child as a penalty. If your two-year-old bites you, suddenly and firmly take hold of his chin, turn his face toward yours, and say, "No biting!" The shock of your reaction is a penalty. Praise his more appropriate behavior (reward).

CHARGING THOSE BATTERIES

So reward, ignoring, and penalty are your powerful flashlight, helping you guide your child along the twisting path of life.

Well, here's the thing about even the most powerful flashlights: The batteries work only so long before they run out of juice. In other words, even with the powerful tools of R.I.P., parents are still working on borrowed time. The years from birth until age six are the crucial years for kids to acquire the skills they need to successfully navigate that path.

Remember, the goal of rewarding, ignoring, and penalizing kids is to give them control. It's to teach kids how to navigate the path of life independently and appropriately, following the rules when they're fair and just, and challenging them when they aren't. With R.I.P., parents help kids learn and internalize a moral code that can guide them even when the parental flashlight batteries finally give out. In other words, with R.I.P., parents are giving kids their own perpetual source of illumination in the woods.

In the next chapter, we'll talk about timing, less talking, and proximity—and why they're the key ingredients in your plan's success.

— 4 —

Becoming Credible: Timing, Less Talking, and Proximity

How, when, and where to talk to your kids—
and when not to talk at all.

Lori is planning dinner for her family. She's in the kitchen while her five-year-old son, Kevin, is downstairs, playing video games. She'd like him to bring up a bag of spaghetti from the pantry in the basement, so she goes to the top of the stairs and calls down to him to help her.

"Kevin, would you like to bring Mommy some spaghetti, please?"

Silence.

"Kevin! Did you hear me? Can you bring me some spaghetti from the pantry?"

Silence.

"Kevin!

Still no answer. (Tell us that this has never happened in your home!) Lori's starting to get just a little bit angry.

"Kevin, how old are you?"

Silence.

"Is something wrong with your ears? Kevin!"

No response from the basement.

"Kevin, I'm going to count to three and then you'll be in big trouble . . . one . . . two . . . three . . . Kevin!"

Silence.

And so on. With each repetition, Lori gets more agitated—you can hear it in her voice. Here she is, making a perfectly reasonable request, and her son is ignoring her.

After a few more repetitions of her son's name at increasingly higher pitches, Lori gives up and stomps down the stairs to the pantry.

"Never mind Kevin, I'll get it myself—like I normally do."

The situation isn't new. If Kevin doesn't want to do something, he simply ignores his parents.

"When it's suppertime and he's downstairs and we're upstairs, we flick the downstairs light on and off to tell him to turn off the TV and come upstairs to eat," says Lori's husband, Wayne. "We could tell him that five and six and seven times, and he won't come up. You'll have to go downstairs and turn the TV off and take him by the hand and bring him upstairs. If you tell him to do something, he will not listen to you—"

"Unless it's something he wants," adds Lori.

"Yes," says Wayne. "If you tell him to come upstairs and get ice cream, he'll be right up."

"He'll pretend that he doesn't hear us," says Lori. "It got so bad that we had his hearing checked by a specialist. But there's nothing wrong with his hearing. It's perfect."

While his parents are getting more and more frustrated, Kevin's feeling pretty good: He gets to keep playing video games while avoiding tasks he doesn't want to do and activities that don't interest him. In the longer run, however, he's learning that the best way to get the things he wants is to ignore and disrespect his parents and other adults. Over time, he's going to internalize an image of himself as a "bad kid," a kid who doesn't listen. And meanwhile, Lori and Wayne are feeling pretty bad about resenting their son.

That bad feeling lasts well beyond the spaghetti incident. Kevin's parents get so frustrated with his nonresponsive behavior that they end up fighting. "By the end of the night we'll be at each other, because of the situation a few hours ago," says Lori. "Kevin's been in

bed for hours, and we still have so much frustration that we're arguing. It's like a stew pot and we're still going through it."

There may be nothing wrong with Kevin's hearing—but there's a
lot wrong with the dynamics of the situation. In a nutshell, it's too
long, too loud, too far, too angry, and too much! Timing, talking,
and proximity—and, as a result, scale—are all off in Kevin's interactions with his parents, just as they are in countless other incidents
between parents and their kids.

Timing, Less Talking, and Proximity: Your "Early Retirement" Parenting Plan

We're all familiar with those advertisements for retirement savings.
You know, the ones where they compare the person who started saving in her early twenties with the forty-year-old who just got around
to contributing to his retirement account last year? The message is
startling: The twenty-year-old who starts saving early on can put
much less cash into her retirement fund—*and stop saving before the
forty-year-old even starts*—and still end up with much more money in
the end. (This news is either heartening or depressing, depending
on whether you're an early savings bird or a later financial bloomer.)
In other words, a little bit of extra effort earlier on yields tremen-
dous results, and greatly reduces efforts down the road.

The same holds true when dealing with kids' problematic behaviors. A little extra effort at the very beginning of an episode can
greatly reduce parental effort—and stress!—down the road. When
kids act up just a little—like the first time Kevin ignores Lori—
parents often choose to ignore it, and the situation drags on, and
escalates. When a situation drags on, however, parents get increasingly angry and frustrated. Voices and blood pressure rise, and before
we know it things get blown out of all proportion. A simple request
for a bag of spaghetti can turn into an all-out battle, with kids in
tears, parents furious, and bad feelings permeating the whole house.
And all over a bag of spaghetti. In other words, the *scale* is way off.

Had Lori upped the scale of her response, just a little, at the out-set of the spaghetti incident, it's likely there wouldn't have been an incident at all. So let's rewrite the scene. Imagine what would have happened had Lori nipped the situation in the bud by reacting immediately to her son's disrespectful behavior. The *moment* she realized she was being ignored, Lori could have stopped talking, gone downstairs, turned off the TV, gotten close to Kevin, and calmly but firmly repeated her request, close-up. If need be, she could have taken him by the hand and walked him through the task of getting the pasta from the pantry and bringing it upstairs.

In the short run, of course, this approach seems counterintuitive: Lori would actually be doing the job she asked Kevin to do. But by taking this approach, she's also showing him that she means what she says. Practiced consistently, that's a lesson that will stick in the long run. In time, there's a great chance that Kevin will learn how to cooperate with his parents and respect their reasonable requests. And in the meantime, Lori's saving herself a lot of aggravation by not getting worked up: She keeps her cool with Kevin, and—as a bonus—doesn't end up fighting with her husband all evening.

When we talk about scale, we're talking about three crucial, interrelated elements that will make or break parents' efforts to deal with disrespectful, nonresponsive, or noncompliant behaviors—often before these behaviors even occur. If parents can master the basics of timing, less talking, and proximity, then they're well on their way to creating an atmosphere in which it's easy for kids to cooperate. By acting quickly, closing the distance between parent and child, and keeping talk to a minimum in the heat of the moment, parents can help keep situations manageable and in per-spective—and in the process, teach kids how to act appropriately.

That, in a nutshell, is our next step.

STEP 7: Make yourself credible: Stop talking, get close, and start acting to nip inappropriate behavior in the bud.

In this chapter, we'll explore each of these crucial elements in turn, so that you can integrate them into your plan.

"How Long Has This Been Going On?": Timing

As parents, we've got a lot on our plates: the usual round of work, housekeeping, child care, and finding time for our partners or spouses—not to mention ourselves. It's easy to get distracted. Not surprisingly, we're often slow to react to our children's behavior, both the good stuff and the annoying stuff.

Take Kevin and Lori. She stands at the top of the stairs for a good few minutes, calling to her son. And in this situation, those minutes might as well be hours. If we were timing this scenario with a stopwatch, the clock would have started *the moment after* Lori made her first request. At that point, Lori needs to wait just long enough to know whether or not Kevin's responding. If she hears his footsteps to the pantry, or an "Okay, Mom," the clock stops. She's done. If, on the other hand, Lori hears only silence—or the sound of the Nintendo—that's her clue that Kevin is ignoring her. And at the *first* sign of his inappropriate behavior, it's time to act.

Now, part of the problem is that Lori thinks she *is* acting when she stands at the top of the stairs and repeats herself. She calls, she cajoles, she threatens, she uses sarcasm. And she uses up a fair amount of energy. Every time she repeats herself—"Kevin, bring up some spaghetti! Kevin, bring up some spaghetti!"—Lori lets the situation drag on even longer. The longer she lets Kevin ignore her, the angrier and more frustrated she gets. So the situation escalates, just as a snowball rolling down a hill grows into a huge snow boulder. Lori's voice gets higher and louder, her blood pressure rises, her body tenses, and Kevin becomes more entrenched on the couch: If he wasn't going to listen to his mother the first time, he's hardly going to go upstairs when she sounds *really* mad. By the time Lori finally gets the spaghetti herself, she's furious.

What's more, the more Lori repeats herself, the more time passes. And the more time passes, the farther she and Kevin get from the original incident. By the time she finally acts, her actions have lost immediacy—and, by extension, clarity: Is she furious because Kevin didn't listen to her the first time? Because he didn't listen to her the ten times she asked next? Because he never listens to her? Because she can't seem to figure out how to solve this problem? It's no longer clear—to us, or to her. And if Lori were to penalize Kevin at this point, he probably wouldn't know exactly why, either. As a result, the consequences wouldn't teach him much. By reacting immediately, it's clear to both parent and child what behavior is at stake and how the parent expects the child to behave.

Instead of standing at the top of the stairs getting angrier with each passing minute, Lori needs to stop talking—immediately!—and back up her requests with actions. If Kevin doesn't respond the first time, that's long enough. As we noted above, Lori needs to deal with her son's inappropriate behavior by going downstairs, turning off the television, and calmly insisting that Kevin cooperate with her by getting the spaghetti.

By responding immediately, Lori sends a strong message to Kevin that she means what she says. Over time, that message will sink in—and Kevin will begin to listen to his parents' reasonable requests because he knows that, if he doesn't, those requests will be backed up by their immediate actions.

How do you know if the situation is dragging on too long? Here are three simple clues:

- **Do you sound like a broken record?** "Kevin, bring me up some spaghetti! Kevin, bring me up some spaghetti! Kevin, bring me up some spaghetti!" If you notice that you're repeating yourself, there's a good chance your timing is off.
- **Are you repeating requests or negative statements, like "Stop that"?** If yes, it means that your child is either ignoring you or acting in an unacceptable way. Rather than repeating yourself and nagging, hear these statements as signals to yourself to stop talking, get up, and act!
- **Are you getting upset?** Do you feel angry or frustrated? Is your voice rising? Are you yelling? Are your fists clenched, or is your jaw tight? Does it feel like your blood pressure's rising? All

these physical and emotional signs are powerful signals that you've let a situation escalate for too long. Act quicker, to nip unwanted behavior—and your own rising blood pressure—in the bud.

Of course, no one is expecting you to be able to respond immediately to every single instance of inappropriate behavior—especially when you're dealing with other children or several activities at the same time. Reality simply dictates that we can't always react as immediately as we'd like to. Don't be too hard on yourself—just respond as quickly as you can, as often as you can. And keep in mind that the faster you're able to respond within the moment, the more time, energy, and aggravation you'll save later.

Timing and Reward

We've talked a lot about responding quickly to inappropriate behavior. But how should you time your responses when kids are behaving well?

In general, we'd love it if parents noticed kids' appropriate behavior just as much as they noticed the inappropriate stuff—and responded quickly to it. In reality—as we discussed in the last chapter—we know it can be more difficult to pick up on good behavior, simply because it doesn't register on our radar screens the way the in-your-face annoying stuff does.

When you're actively Drawing the Line with your kids, however, it's crucial to recognize and quickly reinforce their appropriate behavior. Whether you're potty training, teaching table manners, negotiating tantrums, or trying to make bedtime a peaceful time, you need to reward kids—usually with specific praise and attention—often, and immediately following any display of the desired behavior. So the moment your child uses the toilet successfully, says "please," quiets down from her screaming fit (even just a little), or stays in bed for five minutes, reward him or her: "Way to go! I'm so proud of you for making a pee-pee in the toilet!" Or, "You're doing a great job staying in bed. I'll be back in five minutes to check on you. Sweet dreams."

To reinforce Kevin's appropriate behavior, Lori could praise him after he's gotten the spaghetti from the pantry and brought it upstairs—even if she's just walked him through the entire exercise: "That's great, Kevin. I really do appreciate your help. Now you can go back to watching TV." In time, with consistent penalty and reward, Kevin will learn to do the job on his own. And the positive reinforcement of praise—however forced it sounds at the beginning—is an important tool in helping him learn.

In the beginning, err on the side of rewarding too much rather than too little. As new behaviors and accomplishments become a bit easier for your kid, then you can start to vary the availability of the rewards. For example, at first you might praise your daughter every time she follows your direction to put away a toy. As she becomes more reliable and adept at putting away her toys, start to reward her every two or three times she shows the behavior. Eventually, save the reward for after she finishes cleaning up all of the toys. You can also give unexpected bonus rewards if she does a really good job: "Wow! This playroom looks fantastic! What about we read a story to celebrate?" In other words, start with very frequent and regular rewards, and gradually reward less frequently and less predictably—a process called "thinning" or "fading" (more on this in chapter 6). When kids don't expect to be rewarded, rewards are even more valuable, and underscore special behavior.

Swift, Yes, but Also Short

Hopefully, it's clear by now that parents need to react quickly, especially when confronted with kids' problematic behaviors. Whether doling out penalties or rewards, however, parents should keep in mind another aspect of timing: Keep the rewards and penalties brief. Often five or ten seconds of time out is all it takes to get a kid on track again, while a reward can be as simple and fleeting as eye contact or a smile. (For more on brief rewards and penalties, see chapter 3.)

Old adages such as "one minute of time out for every year of life" are, frankly, wrong. Long time-outs or rewards shift the focus from the activity at hand to too-lengthy negative or positive consequences. Instead of worrying about how long positive and negative consequences should be, focus instead on how *frequent and brief* the consequences are. You can divide up five minutes of penalty time a bunch of different ways:

- One time-out that lasts for five minutes.
- Five time-outs that last one minute each.
- Ten time-outs that last thirty seconds each.
- Thirty time-outs that last ten seconds each.

They all add up to the same amount of time. But trust us: All things being equal, the final scenario is by far the most effective. Why? Because it provides the most opportunities to learn. Virtually all learning theories link repetition rate with speed of learning. The more frequently you penalize a child for inappropriate behavior, the faster she'll learn to avoid it and to behave appropriately. The more frequently you reward appropriate behavior, the faster she'll gravitate toward it.

"Thirty trips to time out? You must be joking. Who has that kind of time or energy?" Well, we can tell you this: We have far more energy for thirty ten-second trips to time out than we do for forcing a stubborn four-year-old to sit in a chair for five minutes at a time, several times a day. And we certainly have more energy for thirty tiny trips to time out than we do for putting up with days, weeks, or months of battles with children. Sometimes, consistently penalizing or rewarding your kids can be tiring—in the short run. That's why we often suggest that parents pick a specific time to Draw the Line: to deal with certain problematic behaviors when they have the time and energy. We'll often tell the parents we work with, "You've got to have one more repetition of penalty in you than your child has of difficult behavior. You've got to show him that you're willing to go all day on this issue."

But we'll tell you a secret: It's a rare child or situation that gets to thirty repetitions of a time-out. (For what it's worth, our record is twelve. Twelve.) Most kids will give up on inappropriate behavior long before you get that far. It boils down to your own persistence and determination in demonstrating to kids that you really mean what you say. Keep the consequences really short, and deliver them relentlessly—over and over again. Your child will grow really tired of the same old drill.

Really Use Your Words: Talking *Less* Is *More* Effective

Let's return, again, to Kevin and Lori and the bag of spaghetti. Here's a perfect example of the classic broken-record scenario. Lori stands at the top of the stairs and talks. In fact, she talks in all kinds of ways: She asks nicely, she cajoles, she repeats herself, she yells, she uses sarcasm, she threatens—but she doesn't actually *do* anything. Once more, Lori needs to act instead of talk, and act quickly, by going to where her son is and physically insisting that he listen to her.

"We are a society of the biggest mouth talkers on the face of the earth," says Michael. "We gab, gab, gab, talk, talk, talk. And talk is the cheapest thing on the planet."

Now, don't get us wrong. We have elaborate discussions with really young kids, but we also know when to keep discussions short and to the point, and when to keep quiet altogether.

So how do you talk to your kids—in the heat of the moment, and after? What should you say, and how should you say it? In what order? How loud? What ratio of positive to negative to neutral statements should come out of your mouth? What about tone of voice and facial expressions? And where should you be when you talk?

Clearly, there are a lot of dimensions to talking. And to make things more complicated, those dimensions will change with the situation. But read on—we'll help you figure out when, where, and how to talk to your kids.

In the Heat of the Moment

We love talking to kids. They say the smartest, cutest, craziest, funniest things—and we're constantly amazed by how acutely they observe the world and how much they understand. We can talk to kids—our own, and other people's—for hours.

That is, if they are not acting up.

In the heat of the moment—when a child is behaving inappropriately—we often say nothing. If we do talk, we keep conversations with kids short and to the point ("Use your words" and "No biting" are good examples). And most important, we back up those words with action. For example, instead of repeatedly calling to her son, Lori needs to go to him and physically guide him through the act of getting the spaghetti from the pantry. To do this, she might first go to him and turn off the TV (that's the penalty). Then she can get down to his eye level, and take him gently but firmly by the arm. Only then would she say: "Why did I turn off the TV? Because I need you to help me by getting the spaghetti. In this house, we help each other. Do you want to play video games? You can play once you've helped me. Let's get that spaghetti."

Let's break that sequence down again, using a different example. Three-year-old Jana's parents, Todd and Clara, really value dinnertime as family time, and want to eat that meal with their three kids around the dining room table. They're having trouble convincing Jana to stay at the table. They've decided to Draw the Line around sitting at the table. They want her to stay at the table for a minimum of twenty minutes. If Jana leaves, she's crossed the line, and the penalty is simple and straightforward: One of her parents escorts her back to the table. When she and her siblings sit at the table and eat with their parents, Todd and Clara take pains to remark on what nice manners they have, on the good job they're doing, and on how much they like spending time with their kids. They also use the incentive of dessert to motivate their kids to stick around just a little longer. (For a more detailed account of Drawing the Line around dinnertime, see chapter 5.)

Consequence and Reason: Creating Moral Kids

Drawing the Line. Rewarding, ignoring, penalizing. Timing, less talking, and proximity.

Sometimes we can get so caught up in the details of managing our kids' behavior that we forget the larger goal in all of this. What is it that we're trying to do with all these techniques?

Of course, we'd be lying if we said that we weren't trying to find ways to increase our kids' cooperative behavior and bring more peace, quiet, and pleasure into our parent–child relationships.

But we don't want our kids to listen to us because they've become subdued little robots. Nor do we want children to "obey" only because they know they'll be punished if they don't and/or rewarded if they do. And we don't want them to behave simply because it will make our lives easier— although it will. Instead, through all these exercises, we want kids to de- velop and internalize a moral code of conduct. In other words, we want kids to learn to share, consider the feelings of others, help out when asked, be polite, treat others fairly, take care of their bodies, strive to do well in school and beyond, and more—all examples of so-called pro-social behavior— not because they fear they'll get caught if they don't or because they want rewards, but because they've come to internalize a system of values (gen- erally, your values) and know *for themselves* what's appropriate and what's not. And then we want them to be able to act on the knowledge, even when we're not around to make them act.

This whole process of internalizing a moral code is known as "induction": We want to "induce" certain moral standards in our kids. Induction has been researched at length by developmental psychologists William Damon, Linda Eisenberg, and Paul Mussen, among others. Along the way, they've discovered some critical concepts about how best to talk to kids to help them develop and internalize these pro-social behaviors. In a nutshell, say Eisenberg and Mussen,* the process of induction requires two things:

- Holding children accountable for their actions (through rewards and penalties).
- Offering meaningful explanations for those consequences.

By reasoning, say Eisenberg and Mussen, parents and caregivers can model pro-social behavior—consideration and concern for others—and a

* Eisenberg, Linda, and Paul H. Mussen. *The Roots of Prosocial Behavior in Children* (New York: Cambridge University Press, 1995).

logical, orderly approach toward social interactions. At the same time, parents teach their children about acceptable standards of behavior and other people's feelings, and communicate that kids are responsible for their behavior.*

Let's look at a classic example: the preschool thief. Two-year-old Sarah snatches a toy dump truck from her classmate, Zane, who bursts into tears. Obviously, the snatching and grabbing so typical of toddlers is something we'd like to discourage. Instead, over time we'd like Sarah, Zane, and all their peers to internalize the values of respect for other people's property, sharing, asking nicely, and all the other pro-social behaviors that tend to make life more pleasant for us all.

In a perfect world, a vigilant teacher takes the dump truck from Sarah and hands it back to Zane. That's Step 1: the penalty, or consequences. Then the teacher says to Sarah, "Why did I give the truck back to Zane? Because he was playing with it first. You made him sad when you took it away without asking. I bet you would be sad if he took a toy away from you. Can you say, 'Sorry, Zane'?" That's Step 2: the reasoning behind the consequences.

Obviously—as anyone who's had any exposure to two-year-olds will tell you—it's going to take dozens of repetitions of the lesson for Sarah and her peers to fully internalize the moral code of conduct around sharing. Over time, though, the message should sink in—as a result of the combination of both meaningful consequences and meaningful explanations for those consequences.

In other words, it's not enough merely to penalize a kid for her transgressions: If you consistently impose the penalty on its own, not backed up by any reasoning, you might end up with a kid who obeys—that is, when you're around. In the absence of an authority figure, however, she's quite likely to revert to the snatching and grabbing, because she hasn't internalized the moral code of sharing and considering other people's feelings. (This is the kind of approach often taken by authoritarian parents, as discussed in chapter 1.)

The reverse is also true. Reasoning on its own, not backed up by meaningful consequences, doesn't do much to induce behavior. We often see this approach with overly permissive parents, who will say something to the effect of, "Oh, Sarah, it's not nice to take toys away from other people. See, now Zane's crying. He's sad because you took his truck away. Do you want to give it back?" But what if Sarah says, "No," and walks off with her booty?

* Ibid., p. 82.

Unless a caregiver follows up with meaningful consequences—that is, requiring Sarah to give the truck back—the lesson has pretty much zero value.

Consequence (both positive and negative) and reason—in a nutshell, these are the two ingredients that create moral kids.

When Jana wanders away from the table, however, Todd and Clara stop talking and act. First, one or the other gets up and physically escorts Jana back to her seat (penalty). Only then, after the penalty, do they say anything—and the comments are short and to the point: "Why did I have to help you back to your chair?" After a moment, if Jana doesn't answer, her mom or dad will answer for her: "Because we haven't finished dinner yet. You need to wait until we're done."

In the heat of the moment (and, admittedly, these moments aren't particularly charged), Todd and Clara don't get into long explanations of why they think it's important for the family to eat dinner together. Only after the moment has passed, and after the penalty has been imposed—and their kids are calm enough to hear them—do they talk with Jana and her siblings about the reasons behind their rules. "Dinnertime is when we're together as a family. We want to talk to each other and hear what we did today."

When is the wrong time to try to have a reasonable discussion with your kids? When they're being unreasonable: ignoring you, walking away, crying, whining, screaming complaining, or otherwise acting inappropriately. You can only reason with a reasonable person.

Yes, No, Maybe So: Positive, Negative, and Neutral Statements—How Much of Each?

Here's a sometimes painful exercise: For one day, monitor what you say to your kids. How many positive, neutral, or negative statements do you make?

- **Positive statements** are, well, positive: "Yes, you can," "Good job," "I'm proud of the fact that you did that on your own," "You were so polite with your grandmother. Thank you."
- **Neutral statements** tend to convey information: "Dinner is in five minutes," "Let's go to the bathroom before we leave the house."
- **Negative statements** are all those times you say no in its various forms: "Don't," "Stop," "Not right now," "You can't . . . ," "You're not allowed," "That's inappropriate," "You're wrong." Negative statements can also be questions ("How many times do I have to ask you?") or sarcastic remarks ("Never mind, Kevin, I'll get it myself—like I always do"), or seemingly neutral statements when they're shouted angrily ("Dinner is in five minutes!").

You may be surprised—or not—to find out that the majority of your statements are negative in tone. In fact, the majority of things you say to your kids should be positive or neutral in character.

Negative statements make you feel bad—who wants to be known as a nag? But they also weigh on children. If kids hear negative statements in relation to themselves, and they hear the statements repeatedly, over time they'll come to believe the message behind the words: that they are not good kids. As we said earlier, for example, the more often Kevin hears messages to the effect that he's not a cooperative child, the easier it will be for him to believe those messages.

Now, we're not suggesting that you become a syrupy giver of false praise. And we're not telling you never to say no to your kids. We say no all the time. What we are saying is that if you hear yourself saying something negative, it should mean that your child is engaging in a behavior that you want to discourage. Rather than repeating negative statements ad nauseam, hear these statements as a signal to yourself to stop talking, get up, and act!

If words are coming out of your mouth, try to make sure it's because you're chatting with your kids, conveying information to them, giving clear directions or explanations, offering a perspective, or just telling them how great they are. If negative statements are coming out of your mouth, they should be short and to the point—and not repeated. Negative statements should signal to your kids that you are about to take action.

Why Scolding Doesn't Work

Scolding is almost never an effective strategy with young children. As Sheldon says, "It's like telling them the weather in Europe. They don't care." Scolding is simply another way of paying attention to the kids when they're doing something they shouldn't do. Mostly, when parents scold, they're just telling their kids what they're doing wrong—and the kids already know what they're doing, so the information isn't particularly useful. If you find yourself scolding your kids, that's a sign that you're talking too much. Get up and *act*!

Tone of Voice

One note: When you're negative, act negative.

Too often we see adults giving mixed messages to kids. We've seen parents smile brightly as they say sweetly to their offspring, "Oh, sweetheart, it's not nice to bite. Can you say 'sorry'?"

Many of the words are right, but the tone isn't. In fact, it utterly contradicts the words. Coupled with a lack of action, the words are ultimately meaningless to a biting three-year-old.

A more appropriate response? Again, think short, curt, to the point: "No biting!" Add to that a stern look or frown, and deliver the message at the child's eye level. (If necessary, take his or her chin in hand—gently but firmly—to make sure that you can make eye contact.) That quick, curt approach startles a child, and is itself a penalty. Once the penalties have been delivered, you can offer reasons and corrective measures: "Biting hurts Mommy. It makes her want to cry. You wouldn't like if someone bit you, would you? Now say you're sorry, please."

Are You Repeating Yourself?

Both parents and teachers fall into the trap of repeating rules, expectations, and consequences. We've already discussed the fact that repeating yourself is a sign that your timing is way off, and that each repetition takes you farther away from the original incident—by the time you finally act, the lack of immediacy renders the consequences less effective. As well, with each repetition, you're likely getting angrier and more frustrated.

But there's another problem with the broken-record routine: You lose credibility with each repetition. If you really meant what you said, you wouldn't stand there repeating yourself—you'd do something. When Kevin ignores Lori, it's because he knows from past experience that he can ignore her and get away with it. Her requests aren't credible to him, because he knows there won't be any real consequences if he doesn't listen to her. In short, her constant repetition,

---

123 . . . Magic? Why Counting to Three May Not Be Your Best Strategy

Some parents like to give their children three "warnings" before sending their offspring to time out. You know: The kid will do something inappropriate, and Mom or Dad says, "That's one." The kid repeats the behavior, and Mom or Dad says, "That's two." And the kid repeats the behavior yet again, and Mom or Dad says, "That's three— you're out."

We're not big fans of counting to three. Most of the time, it doesn't work. And it doesn't work because it's not clear and it's not immediate. When a kid acts up and parents count to three, they're essentially telling that kid that he can get away with misbehaving twice before the rules kick in—so he may as well just keep on doing what he's doing until Mom or Dad gets to three. *That's only a one or a two,* a child thinks. *It doesn't matter until Mom gets to three.* As a result, kids get mixed messages: *Sometimes I can get away with hitting, and sometimes I can't.*

Our advice: The first time your kids act up, bust 'em! Take them to time out immediately. That way, your demands for appropriate behavior are consistent and crystal clear.

---

not backed by any action or consequence, teaches Kevin that his mom isn't credible.

Don't get caught in this trap. Don't accidentally turn into a broken record. Decide at the outset how many times you are going to repeat yourself—we suggest no more than once after the initial request—and then act.

Most people repeat themselves because they are busy doing something else—or they're just plain tired! But if you find yourself saying, "I wish my kids would listen to me," then stop repeating yourself and take action. One way to nip your child's behavior in the bud is to nip your own repetitions in the bud.

Request or Requirement? Watch Your Grammar

"Kevin, would you like to bring Mommy some spaghetti, please?"

"Is it time for bed now?"

"Do you want to pick up your toys?"

"Would you please eat just one bite of chicken?"

For various reasons, many of us have a difficult time asking for things directly. We have an even harder time stating clear requirements. Whether it's because we want to be friendly or low-key, or because we're afraid of sounding pushy or rude, we tend to soften our directions and requirements and make them sound more like requests. We do this by turning what should be statements into yes-or-no questions, and prettying up those questions with "would you like," "do you mind," "do you want," and the like.

The problems with this kind of verbal approach are at least three-fold:

- First, it takes away clarity. Are you asking or demanding? Are you giving your child a choice or not? If you're not clear, you can't expect your child to automatically understand what you want and comply with your wishes.
- Second, it puts you in an awkward position and takes away your credibility. If you ask, "Do you want to pick up your toys?"

and your child—quite legitimately—answers, "No," then you look foolish and now have to repeat yourself. "I mean, it's time to pick up your toys." *Well, why didn't you say so?* thinks your kid.

- Third, it sets you up for conflict. By asking a yes-or-no question, you're giving your child the opportunity to say no to you—about something that may be nonnegotiable. By disguising your requirement as a request, you've now opened yourself up to a battle that you could have avoided.

Requirements—bringing Mommy some spaghetti, going to bed, picking up toys, tasting one bite of a new food—are nonnegotiable. Requests, on the other hand, are things your children have some choice about: talking to Grandma on the phone, wearing the red sweater, having another helping of peas, deciding which bedtime story they'd like to hear.

Decide what's a requirement and what's a request. Often we'd like our children to do things, but we recognize that ultimately it's up to the kids. When you say to your two-year-old, "Would you like to talk to Grandma on the phone?" you likely know that there's the good chance he'll say no, and you're probably not prepared to force him to talk on the phone—even if you (and his grandma!) would really like him to. This type of situation is, by definition, a request. You aren't going to back it up with a meaningful consequence, and you're not going to get into a head-butting match with your child. In the end, he'll do what he pleases.

If it's a requirement, don't ask your kids if they'd like to do it. Instead, tell them to do it. Use statements, not questions or requests—and back up those statements with actions, either a reward when your kids listen ("Thank you! I appreciate your help!") or a penalty (for example, turn off the television until they complete the required task) if they don't.

Just because it's a demand, it doesn't have to sound nasty. There's nothing rude or wrong about saying:

"Kevin, please bring Mommy some spaghetti."

"It's time for bed now. Let's go."

"Pick up your toys, please."

"Try one bite of chicken, and then you can have dessert."

Get a Little Closer: Proximity

Let's return, again, to Lori and Kevin and that bag of spaghetti.

Lori needs to think about where she's standing in relation to her son. She's at the top of the stairs, while Kevin's in the basement, absorbed in Nintendo. By standing at the top of the stairs, Lori's essentially making a long-distance request. And that's a problem, one we refer to as "long-distance behavior management."

Parents can successfully offer attention, rewards, and praise from a distance. If you want to, you can shout, "Hey, Billy! You're being a really great kid," from another room or from the kitchen window to the backyard. You can blow kisses across the playground. You can write funny notes and put them in kids' lunch boxes. All these activities can reinforce appropriate behavior—from a distance—while making your children feel loved and as though you're paying attention.

But when it comes to trying to minimize difficult behavior—too much noise, kids making messes, siblings trying to kill each other, or garden-variety not listening—parents need to get up close. Why? For several reasons:

- First, long-distance behavior management—which usually involves calling or yelling from another room—sends kids the message that their behavior isn't important (or offensive) enough to get you to come closer. As long as you send that message, the kids will likely continue to beat up on each other, scream, or ignore you. And why shouldn't they, if it's not that important to you?
- Second, long-distance behavior management by definition often involves yelling, as you struggle to make yourself heard

above the noise and across the house. Even if you're not yelling out of anger, you're still yelling. And when you yell, as we discussed, the situation escalates: Your blood pressure goes up, the noise increases, the kids get spooked—and you're well on your way to getting angry.

- Third, getting up close sends a strong message that you mean what you say. While a kid can ignore you yelling from another room, it's virtually impossible to ignore a parent who is making eye-to-eye contact from six inches away. By getting close, you make your message more credible.

Don't fall into the trap of being an ignored broken record, yelling from the other room. If your kid is doing something you don't want her to do, close the gap between the two of you: Stop what you're doing, go over to her, and redirect her behavior. When Kevin ignores Lori, she needs to discourage his rude behavior by getting close to him. As Michael points out, "If you don't hear Kevin's footsteps within three or four seconds, you know he ain't listening. Now you have one of two options. You can either get progressively angrier, and keep calling and keep calling, or you can stop talking, go downstairs to where he is, and close the physical gap between you and him. Get in his face, speak in a low voice, and physically redirect him to action. I swear you'll save time and aggravation in the end."

When we say get close to your kids, we mean get really close, like a couple of inches. Get in their space. Get down to their level and make eye contact. If you need to, turn off the TV or the video games, or gently but firmly take a child's chin in your hand and insist that she look at you. Then, when you have her attention, you can give the reasons behind the consequences.

Similarly, if you'd like your child to do something, don't shout your request across the house. Again, get up, go to him, and ask him—in an "inside" voice politely—to help you out.

Let's look at another family, getting ready for dinner in another city. Marian would like her nine-year-old daughter, Chelsea, to set the table. Busy in the kitchen, Marian shouts across the house to Chelsea, who's upstairs in her bedroom: "Chelsea! Come and set the table!"

The simple effort of shouting causes Marian's blood pressure to rise.

Chelsea, at the receiving end, hears her mother's raised voice and hears one thing: trouble. She didn't want to set the table in the first place, but now she's also confused: Why is her mother yelling at her when she hasn't done anything? *I'm not going down there*, she thinks. *I'm just going to pretend I didn't hear.*

A few moments later, Marian notices that her daughter hasn't responded. Her solution? She yells louder. "Chelsea! I said, come and set the table!" Her blood pressure goes up a little bit more. *What's she doing?* Marian wonders of her daughter. *It's like she's deaf.*

Up in her bedroom, Chelsea's in a quandary. Her mom's yelling louder—she must be getting madder. And now Chelsea's kind of peeved at her mom. *Why is she so mad? I haven't done anything*, she thinks. *She yells at me all the time.* Chelsea considers going downstairs to set the table, but she really doesn't want to face her mom.

You can see where this is going—and the end isn't pretty. Marian, who was originally yelling to make sure her daughter could hear her, is now yelling because she's mad. Chelsea is feeling injured and put upon because her mom yelled at her for no good reason. In the end, Marian stomps upstairs to yell at her daughter up close for a change: "I can't understand why nobody in this house ever listens to me! Get downstairs right now, young lady, and set that table! And if you're not careful, you'll be grounded for a week."

Chelsea bursts into tears and yells back at her mother, "You're always yelling at me! It's so unfair! I hate you!"

The point is simple: Marian could have averted a fight by going up to her daughter's bedroom and politely asking her to set the table. It may take a bit more effort at the outset to get close and talk rather than stay put and yell, but we promise you this: It'll save you a lot of hassle in the long run.

Tip: Make a Pact Never to Yell Again

"One of our house rules is simple," says Andrea, a mom of a one-year-old: "We can't shout. If I need to communicate with my partner—to ask her a question, or tell her the phone's for her—I have to get up, go over to her, and talk to her. And she has to come to me. It doesn't matter if she's upstairs and I'm in the living room or the basement. Sometimes it seems like a pain, but it really adds to the peace in the house and cuts down on the frustration of not being heard the first time. Since we have two phone lines, sometimes we'll even phone each other rather than yell. Occasionally, we've e-mailed each other rather than yell."

If you could do precisely one thing, make precisely one change, to the way you talk not only to your kids but to everyone in your house, make it this: Never, ever, shout across the house again. If you need to talk to one of the kids or to your partner, get up, walk over to where they are (even if it's up or down a flight of stairs), and talk to them in a calm, quiet voice. Just try it for a week—see what a difference it will make.

Get Close to Reward

As we noted above, you *can* reinforce good behavior from far away. But just because you *can* doesn't necessarily mean that you should. Most of the time, make a point of getting close to your kids when they're behaving well.

As Ron, the father of two little girls, says, "If I see them playing nicely, even if it's just for a brief moment, I'll jump in there and at least point it out to them: 'You guys are playing great!' Don't be afraid of interrupting good behavior."

Sometimes your physical closeness is in itself a reward. In chapter 5, you'll read about how Arlene, a single mom, Drew the Line around bedtime. To reward her daughters, Morgan and Jacqueline, when they stayed in bed, Arlene got close to them: As long as the girls were quiet and in bed, Arlene kept the bedroom door open and checked on them constantly. Her proximity to her daughters was the reassuring presence they needed, at first, to stay in bed. If the girls got out of bed or acted up, Arlene closed their door, effectively penalizing them by cutting off her presence.

Your physical presence can be enormously rewarding to your kids. Routinely get close to the kids to tell them how great they are doing. Pay attention to the good behavior by coming into the room and saying hello, or joining in kids' activities and playing side by side, even just for a moment. Then leave them to carry on. Your physical closeness will make your kids feel acknowledged and comfortable, while your eventual departure will allow them to further develop independence and explore the world on their own.

Are You Credible?

As we've seen throughout the course of this chapter, timing, talking, and proximity are inextricably intertwined. The faster you respond, the less angry you're likely to get, and the quieter your voice can stay. By responding immediately, you're also less likely to repeat yourself—and won't get caught in the broken-record trap. The closer you are, again, the quieter you can be, and the harder it is for a child to ignore you, so the chances of repeating yourself go down enormously. And so on. Together, these three strategies keep the scale of almost any childhood transgression reasonable, and the parents keep their wits while guiding their kids toward appropriate behavior.

We guarantee that by responding quickly, keeping talk to a minimum, and getting close to your kids, you'll find it easier to be consistent in your demands for decent behavior. Parents who are consistent don't give an inch one day and a mile the next. They don't penalize kids for certain behaviors one day and let the same behaviors go another day. They don't make demands they're not prepared to enforce. They don't say one thing and do another. And when parents can be consistent, they gain credibility with their kids.

When children see their parents as credible, we mean that children view their parents as honest, reliable, believable, and predictable, as people who have integrity, whose words are consistent with their actions. Credible people say what they mean to say and they follow through the way they said they would. Every technique we use with families—every technique in this book—is rooted in credibility. We're utterly consistent and predictable with kids, and so kids know that we mean what we say and are serious in our requirements for cooperation. Why is this important? Because as goes your credibility as a parent, so goes your child's respect for you.

For the last time, let's look at Lori, Kevin, and the spaghetti. Kevin doesn't get the pasta for his mom because he knows that he doesn't really have to: Experience has taught him that if he ignores her for long enough, eventually she'll get it herself, and he gets to keep playing his video games, uninterrupted by household chores. He doesn't see Lori's requests as credible, because he knows that there won't be any consequences if he doesn't respect them. Therefore, he doesn't respect them. (And why should he? Obviously, if his mom really meant what she said, she would back up her words with actions.) Over time, Kevin has come to see Lori as not credible and therefore not worthy of respect.

Every time Kevin doesn't listen to his mother, he practices being disrespectful. The more he practices, the better he gets at it—and the more entrenched the disrespect becomes. Lori needs to learn how to make herself (and her requests) credible to Kevin. Kevin needs to see that his mother means what she says, and that she will follow through on her expectations that he'll cooperate with her requests. If these two things don't happen, Lori is setting herself up for a lifetime of disrespect from her son. Further, she's setting up Kevin for a lifetime of difficult interactions with the world.

As you Draw the Line with your kids, please remember timing, talking, and proximity: Get up, get close, stop talking, and *act*—at the first sign of inappropriate behavior. And how exactly do you act? In the next chapter, we'll show you five examples of how real families Drew the Line with their kids.

—5—

Practice Makes Parent

Putting your plan into action.

Car rides are a nightmare for Corinne. Whenever she tries to drive anywhere with Rhys (sixteen months), three-year-old Peter, and five-year-old Caleb, the minivan turns into a war zone. Caleb teases Peter. Peter hits Caleb. Caleb hits back, harder. Rhys fusses in his car seat. Peter begins to cry as he tries to kick Caleb, who's busy trying to undo his seat belt so that he can *really* whack his brother. Corinne yells at all of them. Caleb starts crying, too. Rhys begins to shriek.

By the time they arrive at their destination, all three boys have worked themselves into hysterics, and Corinne's nerves are shot. At the wheel, she feels helpless: She can't intervene, and she feels she's putting herself and her kids in danger because their behavior is so distracting, she can't pay proper attention to the road. She's taken to avoiding car trips unless they're absolutely necessary.

Of course, Corinne's avoidance strategy doesn't do her or the three boys any favors in the long term. It means she gets less done. It also means that the boys are deprived of potentially fun, enriching experiences because their mom won't take them out "until this phase passes." But the phase likely won't pass, because unless Rhys, Peter, and Caleb actually learn the skills of decent car-ride etiquette, it's unlikely that they'll ever behave appropriately on car trips. (And if they can't behave appropriately in the car, it's unlikely that they'll be able to behave appropriately in similarly challenging situations—such as on the school bus.)

Corinne needs to Draw the Line on good behavior in the car. To do that, she and the boys need to *practice* car trips. And that's our next step:

STEP 8: Draw the Line! Set up conflict: small windows of time where you can practice dealing with challenging situations with your kids.

Yes, that's right. Although it may seem counterintuitive, parents (and kids) need to practice new behaviors. Too often, we think that parenting is an intuitive skill, one that we shouldn't have to practice. As the examples throughout this book make clear, however, it takes planning, practice, and repetition to change behavior and learn new skills. Just as your golf game or your piano-playing abilities or your yoga routine won't improve without practice, neither will your parenting skills or your children's behavior.

Now's the time to set up regular periods where you and your kids can practice and get comfortable with the new world order. You may need fifteen minutes a day in the playroom, or twenty minutes in the car most days. You may Draw the Line each night at bedtime. You can Draw the Line on diapers or dinnertime. In fact, in almost any scenario with your kids, you can find a regular time and place to Draw the Line and practice the new world order.

But *exactly* how, when, and where do you Draw the Line? It's one thing to write down your goals, rewards, and penalties on a worksheet. It's another to actually put your plan in action. If you're looking at your worksheet and feel at a loss for how to proceed, worry not! In this chapter, we're going to show you how to put it all together by walking you through some of the most common, real-life, *Real Families* scenarios that families face: frustrating car rides, battling siblings, kids who won't eat, nightmarish bedtimes, and toddlers who can't seem to get out of diapers.

HECK ON WHEELS: PUTTING THE BRAKES ON FIGHTS IN THE CAR

Working with Michael, Corinne figures out some good rewards for her kids when they're behaving well (fun CDs with stories on them to play while they're driving, and tiny pieces of chocolate: M&M's cut into quarters). At regular intervals—say, every five minutes or so of good behavior (think small!)—she tells the boys what a great job they're doing and hands them each a tiny treat. The ultimate reward? Getting to their destination happy.

Corinne also figures out a penalty that will nip the teasing, whining, hitting, and crying in the bud: At the *first sign* of any inappropriate or dangerous behavior (remember: timing!), Corinne doesn't say a word (she's no longer yelling—she's acting). She presses STOP on the CD player and pulls over. Yup, she pulls over and *gets out of the car.* She gets close to her kids (proximity!) by opening the back door and leaning into the backseat, and tells her kids, calmly and briefly (talking!): "Why did I stop the car? I stopped it because you guys were teasing each other. That's dangerous. When you're ready to stop teasing and have fun, we can get going again. Are you ready? Then let's go." When the boys are quiet, Corinne gets back in the driver's seat, turns on the CD, and takes off again.

Corinne's worksheet for her sons looked something like this:

Drawing the Line: Caleb, Peter, and Rhys

Priority	Target Behavior	Positive Alternative	When/ Where Does It Occur?	Draw the Line	Drawing the Line: Reward?	Drawing the Line: Penalty?
1	Fighting, whining, hitting, screaming— generally awful behavior in the car.	Peaceful road trips where the kids keep their hands to themselves and get along instead of fight.	In the car, almost every time we go anywhere.	Insist on appropriate behavior: quiet, cooperative, peaceful, fun!	• Praise. • Small pieces of chocolate M&M's, given out for very small units of good behavior. • Fun CD to listen to.	Pull over and make kids wait until they've calmed down and stopped fighting.

Now, this strategy seems pretty involved. It could take up a lot of time, especially at the outset. (And no, it won't work on the interstate.) That's why Corinne needs to create certain times where she has nothing to do but practice, on roads that let her pull over easily. She and the boys are going for a drive not because they need to be somewhere on time, such as a birthday party or the doctor's, but because they all need to learn how to behave safely in the car, and have a good time to boot. If the trip goes poorly, Corinne has the freedom to turn around and go back home. (And when she and the boys absolutely do have to be somewhere in the car, she leaves herself plenty of time to get there with as many stops as she needs to make her point.)

And the truth is, the boys are quick learners. They like the attention their mom gives them for behaving well, and they like the treats and stories. They also hate stopping: Like anyone else, they want to get where they're going, quickly. When Corinne pulls over and gets out to talk to them, the strength of her reaction lets them know she's serious. And because Corinne reacts so quickly to the first sign of mutiny, no one has a chance to get worked up, and her nerves are no longer shot. The improvement is immediate, and dramatic. All in all, it takes only about three weeks of practice before car rides are smooth sailing for the family. Soon Corinne hardly ever has to stop, and she slowly phases out the M&M's while keeping up the praise and the fun CDs. Her investment of time and her willingness to practice have given her and the boys the freedom once more to be out in the world, having fun.

BROTHERLY (AND SISTERLY) LOVE:
DEALING WITH SIBLING BATTLES

"The kids are fighting again? Ah, leave them alone—they've got to learn how to figure it out for themselves."

When it comes to sibling battles, we consider those fighting words. As Sheldon says, letting young kids figure out how to get along "for themselves" is about as effective as sending them into heavy traffic on a bike to "figure out" the cars—and hoping that the drivers will give them good feedback. Young children haven't yet learned the skills of sharing, negotiation, fair play, and the like. (Think about your average two-year-old: Does she share voluntarily? We doubt it.) And unless parents or caregivers teach them these skills, it's a safe bet that the kids won't just pick them up out of thin air.

When parents leave kids alone to figure things out, what happens is a playroom version of "survival of the fittest." The dominant child, the one who's stronger or more willful in a relationship, learns that force wins and that he can get what he wants by bullying or manipulating his sibling. And since the weaker child can't win by force, he learns to win by other means, such as whining, crying, screaming, retreating, or calling on Mommy and Daddy. In the end, kids polarize: The stronger one gets stronger while the weaker one gets weaker and whinier. In cases where both kids have a dominant streak, parents often end up, literally, with blood on their hands, as kids battle constantly to maintain the position of top dog. No matter how things shake down, kids learn all the wrong strategies for solving problems.

Take Mickey and Aaron. At three and four years old, these brothers can't seem to play nice with each other. Whether it's LEGO, marbles, or their favorite toy cars, if Mickey is playing with something, his older brother wants it. If they're playing a game, Aaron wants to be in control. And if Mickey is off playing by himself, Aaron will barge in and insist on joining him—and taking over the show. Mickey, understandably, doesn't take kindly to his older brother's constant interventions: He'll scream and cry when Aaron grabs his toys. Or he'll try to hit his brother. More recently, however, he's taken to retreating, avoiding Aaron altogether by playing alone in his room and hiding from Aaron, who then gets upset when his playmate disappears.

The boys' parents, Lily and Jim, seem to spend a lot of time dealing with their sons' fights and tears. They'd really like their sons to be able to get along in the playroom. What these parents need to realize is that Aaron and Mickey are going to learn the skills of good play only by being taught.

The *skills* of good play? Yes, it's true. Kids' play is the foundation for all kinds of skills—such as sharing, negotiation, collaboration, and deferred gratification—that will carry over into adulthood. When parents and caregivers teach kids how to play, they help kids learn skills that will benefit them for a lifetime.

So if your kids fight a lot, don't just leave them to work it out for themselves. Teach them how to play together peacefully and how to work out their differences without resorting to fistfights and other problematic behaviors. In other words, *practice playtime*. Once they've got the skills, *then* you can let them learn to negotiate the world on their own.

Drawing the Line in the Playroom

When Michael came by to play with Aaron and Mickey, he set out to do two things. On the one hand, he wanted to Draw the Line around all the boys' troublesome play strategies, such as bullying, hitting, screaming, retreating, grabbing, and the like. And so part of his plan was simple: Whenever the boys resorted to any of those behaviors, he'd simply send them to a quick time-out—five or ten seconds away from the action.

But it's not enough to simply penalize inappropriate behavior with these warring little boys. Equally, if not more, important is to replace the inappropriate behavior with better alternatives. In other words, we need to show kids not only what they *can't* do, but also what they *can* and *should* do. To do that, parents need to set up times to model and teach appropriate play strategies to their kids, rewarding them for playing nicely with each other.

So how do you teach kids appropriate play strategies? Simple. By getting down on the floor with them and modeling appropriate play. For ten or fifteen minutes a day, most days, set up little practice lessons in "how to play" for the kids. Act as referee and peacekeeper—

as well as playmate!—to teach skills such as taking turns, trading, negotiating, sharing, and collaboration. Give the kids the opportunity to see just how to go about being pals. If Lily and Jim had a worksheet for Aaron and Mickey, it would look something like this:

Drawing the Line: Aaron and Mickey

Priority	Target Behavior	Positive Alternative	When/ Where Does It Occur?	Draw the Line	Drawing the Line: Reward?	Drawing the Line: Penalty?
1	Mickey and Aaron fight instead of play; Aaron interferes with Mickey's play or insists on dominating play. Mickey retreats, screams, cries, hits.	Having the boys learn to play well together and on their own.	In playroom, mostly, when-ever the boys are together (after naps, often). They often fight over toy cars.	Sit down with boys and the favorite toys (cars). Model lessons on appropriate behavior: taking turns, sharing, negotiating, trading, collab-orating.	Pay attention to the boys and praise their cooperative be-havior; get right down on the floor and play with them.	If either boy resorts to tactics such as grabbing, hit-ting, hoarding toys, bullying, whining, etc., he goes to a brief time-out.

So how do these little lessons in appropriate play actually work in real time?

Lesson 1: Divide and Conquer—Taking Turns

Well, with Aaron and Mickey, Michael first scouted around for a toy that both boys really, really wanted—something that they'd be likely to fight over. He was also looking for something—cars, marbles, blocks, dolls, or LEGO, for example—that could be divided between the kids. In this case, that something was toy cars.

Then he sat down on the floor with the brothers (remember, proximity!) with a big pile of toy cars in the middle. The first lesson was turn taking. As both boys lunged for the cars, Michael stopped them.

"Wait a second," he told the would-be drivers. "You know what we're going to do first? Let's keep all the cars right here for a second. We're going to divide them up. I want to pick and choose."

The kids looked at him blankly. Aaron tried to grab a car. Michael stopped his hand (time out!).

"Hang on there, buddy. Do you want to play with some cars? What we're going to do is we're going to take turns. You're going to pick a car, and then Mickey is going to pick a car. How's that?"

Mickey started to get up and wander away—his usual strategy of retreating from play with his big, bullying brother. Michael caught him before he was even on his feet (timing!) and sat him down again.

"Okay, Mickey, wait, wait, wait. Come here. Right here. I need you to sit down. Have a seat. Okay, right there, have a seat. Can you sit? Thattaboy."

With both boys in line, Michael seized on the opportunity to launch into the lesson on taking turns.

"Okay, it's Mickey's turn. Okay, Mickey, you pick a car. Pick one."

Mickey did—and then reached for another. Michael stopped his hand.

"Okay, that's it. Just one. Thattaboy. Okay, Aaron's turn. You pick a car, Aaron."

Again, Mickey tried to sneak in another car. Again, Michael nipped the thievery in the bud by catching his hand.

"No no, hold on. Now it's Aaron's turn. Wait for Aaron. You pick, Aaron. We're waiting for Aaron."

Aaron picked a car

"Thattaboy, Aaron!"

Now Aaron tried to grab a second car. Michael stopped his hand. "Just one. Just one car on your turn."

Then both boys had to wait a moment: "Okay, wait, wait, wait," Michael told them. "It's my turn, my turn. I want this one." Michael picked a car. "Okay, now it's Mickey's turn. Okay, Mickey, your turn. You pick. Just one."

And so it went, over and over, as Mickey, Aaron, and Michael sorted through the entire pile of cars, about thirty in all. Michael praised each boy as he took his turn or waited for his brother to take a turn. And when either kid tried to grab a car out of turn, Michael physically stopped him by catching his hand (time out!) and saying, "No. Wait your turn." Had either boy kicked up a fuss—for example, if one tried to hit the other or started to whine, scream, or cry— Michael would have mechanically escorted him to a more obvious time-out: five or ten seconds on the couch, in his room, or in a high chair with a lockable tray. "Why are you here?" he would ask the offender. "You're here because you need to share with your brother and use your words. Wanna come play? Okay, then you've got to share and not hit or cry."

"This may seem tedious," Michael told Jim and Lily, who watched the entire exchange. But over the course of the ten minutes or so of dividing up the cars, the boys had had thirty mini opportunities to practice turn taking. And that was the whole point of the exercise: to practice cooperating in a controlled setting.

"We want to set up these daily little rehearsal sessions in order to get the boys in the habit of using more sophisticated skills, like language, in their play," says Michael. "At the beginning both Aaron and Mickey don't trust each other: They're grabbing for toys and clinging for dear life to what they get because they're afraid of losing it. And that's why we need a parent right in the middle of the two, to act as a referee, actually demonstrate the act of sharing, and convince them that they'll both get their fair share.

"As we repeat the routine, the situation becomes less adversarial. They start to see that when they give they can also get, and that it can actually be fun to play with each other. Aaron learns that he can give up some control, and Mickey learns to trust that Aaron isn't going to completely dominate him."

Lesson 2: Fair Trade on the Auto Market

In the end, Aaron, Mickey, and Michael ended up with ten cars each. For a while, the boys were content to play with their own cars, and Michael made sure to reward them for their good behavior as they vroomed the cars around without fighting:

Fair Play: Timing, Talking, and Proximity

Remember, when you're teaching your kids the rules of fair play, timing, talking, and proximity make all the difference:

- **Timing:** At the first sign of any trouble—a hand reaching out to grab a toy or punch a sibling, a whine or scream—intervene! Physically reroute wandering hands, tell kids, "Use your words," and don't hesitate to take an offender off for a quick time-out to regroup. At the same time, be quick to praise cooperative behavior: "Thattaboy! I like the way you're playing so nicely with your sister!"
- **Talking:** The whole point of collaborative, cooperative play is to get kids to use words, not fists. When you're modeling appropriate behavior, feel free to talk lots as you teach kids the skills of turn taking, trading, and playing creatively together. But when kids act up, stop talking and act! Yelling, "You guys have to share!" ten times from across the room won't do you much good. Getting close to your kids and insisting on sharing will.
- **Proximity:** We can't say this enough: Get close to your kids! When you're modeling appropriate play, the best place to be is right down on the playroom floor, in the thick of the action with your kids. That way, if things get out of hand, you can intervene quickly. And your physical presence is immensely rewarding to your children: By getting close and paying attention, you reinforce their cooperative play.

"Hey, guys! I just want to tell you, the fact that you guys are sharing so nicely, I really appreciate it. You're really doing a good job of sharing. Do you know what sharing means? Do you know what sharing means, Aaron? It means that you're taking a turn and then Mickey is taking a turn. Great stuff!"

Eventually, however, the boys began to notice each other's cars. The seeds for a fight? Possibly. Or the opportunity for another lesson on fair play: trading and negotiating.

Kids like the act of the trade—just think about the old games of trading baseball cards or marbles. Kids need to learn that trading is a two-way street: Sometimes you give and sometimes you get, but you don't get without giving. Kids also need to learn that trading is a form of negotiation: You have to cut an acceptable deal with the other guy in order to get what you want. When kids understand these concepts, they've mastered two important social skills. And they learn that trading can be a lot of fun.

When Aaron decided that he wanted Michael's fire engine, he immediately resorted to his usual tactic of grabbing. Michael, however, intervened, nipping Aaron's thievery in the bud by stopping the little boy's hand. As he had with turn taking, Michael then modeled the art of the trade for the boys.

"No, Aaron, that's my car. What do you want? Use your words."

"I want it," answered Aaron.

"Well, if you want my car, you have to trade me for it," said Michael. "What do you have that I want? I'll tell you what . . . I like that motorcycle you've got. I'll give you my fire engine for your motorcycle."

"This," said Aaron, holding up a different car.

"No, I don't want that one," answered Michael. "I want the motorcycle. I'll give you my fire engine for the motorcycle. I like that motorcycle a lot."

"My motorcycle?" Aaron looked doubtful.

"Yeah, your motorcycle. You can keep it if you want. You don't have to trade it. But I'm not giving you my fire engine if you don't give me one of your cars. Is there another you want to trade? We can find another one."

Aaron looked at his cars. "Ice cream truck," he finally said.

"All right, cool," said Michael. "I like the ice cream truck."

"That's cool," said Aaron.

"All right, it's a deal. Trade. Okay."

After trading the fire engine for the ice cream truck, Michael brokered a deal between Mickey and Aaron: Aaron would exchange his "Thomas the Train" for "Gordon," another train engine.

"What do you need?" Michael asked Aaron. "Use your words. Do you need Thomas? Is that one of the ones that Mickey has?"

"Yeah," said Aaron, reaching for Thomas the Train. Michael stopped his hand.

"No, you can't just take it from him. You have to give him one of yours if you want one of his. Why don't you see if you can trade? Find one that Mickey wants and see if you can trade."

Aaron picked up Gordon and tossed the train at his brother. Again Michael intervened.

"No no no, that's just throwing it at him. That's not a trade. Pick it up and offer it to him. Say, 'Mickey, if I give you Gordon . . .'"

Aaron finished the sentence: ". . . can I have Thomas?"

Mickey held out his hand for Gordon the Train.

Michael intervened once more: "Now wait, Mickey, if you're going to take Gordon you have to give him Thomas. Mickey, can we do this trade? You're going to get Gordon, he gets Thomas? Is that okay?"

"Yes," said Mickey, handing Thomas the Train to Michael, who completed the deal by handing each boy his new train. "Okay, that-taboy! Great trading!"

Several times, Michael modeled trades between the two boys. He encouraged Mickey and Aaron to use their words, and intervened quickly with a time-out if one or the other resorted to grabbing, hitting, crying, or other illegal tactics. And he praised the kids each time they made a deal. Finally, he sat back and let the boys complete an entire deal without his intervention. Lily and Jim looked on, astonished, as their sons came to an agreement over a trade.

The Outcome: United We Stand—Playing Together

By this point, Aaron and Mickey had a basic understanding of both turn taking and trading. Equally important, both boys were having fun, and were comfortable because they knew that Michael wasn't going to let one have something over the other. They also knew that he wouldn't stand for any foul play, such as hitting or grabbing. With these rudimentary skills in place, and secure in the knowledge that neither would lose out, Aaron and Mickey could collaborate and play together.

Once again, Michael joined the boys down on the floor, this time in some less structured play: vrrrroooming the cars around the floor and over the kids' bodies, racing cars, and smashing them up. Again, he intervened at any hint of foul play. And he praised the boys mightily for their cooperation. As the kids' play became more established, Michael began to fade out his participation, moving to sit on the couch with Lily and Jim, or to grab a cup of coffee from the kitchen.

Fair Play: A Recap

So do your kids fight a lot? Well, they've got to learn to get along: Playing fair, sharing, and collaborating aren't simply nice things for children to do; they're developmental imperatives, absolutely crucial skills for kids to learn.

And kids do have to *learn* these skills: Everyone thinks that kids know how to play together, but they don't. So show them!

- First, identify when and where your kids are most likely to fight. That's the time you want to go in and play with them.
- Next, show kids how to share, how to take turns, and how to use words rather than fists or tears. Find toys that they both want, and set up situations in which they have to practice taking turns, negotiating, and sharing. Your kids are watching your every move, and they imitate you. When parents model how to play, kids watch and learn.
- Really control the situation at the outset, brokering deals and walking the kids through each step. If trouble does break out, don't hesitate to enforce the rules by redirecting the kids' actions, or with brief trips to time out. On the other hand, remember to tell your kids how well they're doing when they play nicely. Your praise and attention are positive reinforcement of their good play.

Give Me Some Space!

Yes, kids need to learn to play well together. And sometimes, kids need to learn when to play alone.

Sometimes, kids—especially older siblings—just need their own space. An older child might need to make a model, read a book, or work on his or her own stuff without a little brother or sister always interfering.

As much as they need to model peaceful play together, parents also need to respect their kids' needs to be apart some of the time. That means, on occasion, dividing kids up and saying to the younger sibling, "Look, your big brother needs some time to be on his own. Come with me. Let's do a puzzle together." In that way, you give each kid individual time and let them have the space they need in the family.

Over time—as you'll read in the next chapter—you can begin to fade out your participation. Once you've got your kids playing nicely, leave them on their own for just a few minutes, and then come back and check on them. Eventually, you'll find that you can leave for longer periods of time.

The skills of cooperative play start on the living room rug, but these same skills carry on into the school playground, the classroom, and, eventually, the boardroom and bedroom. Start now to teach your kids the crucial life skills of taking turns, sharing, and collaboration.

GETTING THE KIDS TO EAT—AND ENJOY—DINNER

"Hectic, frenzied, and up and down. We're constantly trying to get the kids to sit and eat and not get distracted or fight with each other."

That's how Anna describes dinnertime with her three kids: six-year-old Lauren, four-year-old Madeline, and Ryan, who's twenty months.

"And then Madeline's a bit of a finicky eater," says Anna's husband, Cameron. "If it's not chicken nuggets or a peanut butter or grilled cheese sandwich, you're in for trouble. She'll out-and-out decide that she's not going to eat any of it. She's not even going to try it. She'll just say, 'I don't like this,' and push it away. That's kind of irritating when you've just finished making dinner."

"You know," sighs Anna, "sometimes, I could just do without all the fuss."

Well, guess who's coming to dinner? Yup, Michael showed up one evening to chow down with Cameron, Anna, and the kids—and to give the harried parents and kids some pointers on how to come together as a family and enjoy dinner.

The Lost Art of the Family Dinner

Why should we care about family dinners? Why not just hand the kids sandwiches and let them eat in the playroom? Better yet, why not let them eat bowls of sugary cereal and milk in front of the television each night? (Yeah, yeah, we've all done it in a pinch . . .)

We could go on and on about the social value of families eating together. Especially in families where one or both parents work and kids are in school and enrolled in activities, dinnertime is one of the only times of the day that all members of a family can be together. It's a time to relax, reconnect, communicate, and have fun together. It's also a chance for children to learn social and developmental skills, such as good manners, taking turns, delayed gratification, sharing, and the art of conversation.

Kids and Food: Some Basic Truths

Kids eat because they're hungry and stop eating when they're full.

This is a basic, but profound fact. Kids don't eat because they're bored, or lonely, or frustrated. They don't look at the clock and say, "Hmm, it's noon— I guess I'll eat lunch now." Those are learned, adult (and often not-so-healthy) behaviors around food.

Left to their own devices, kids will usually choose to eat small quantities of food when their stomachs actually tell them they're hungry. And once they're full, they stop. That's a good thing. If more adults ate only when they were hungry and stopped when they were full, the entire dieting industry would likely go belly-up.

If you try to make a child eat when he's not hungry, you'll face a losing battle and, over the longer term, run the risk of instilling some poor eating habits in him. Instead, work with your child's rhythms by losing the empty calories (junk food, too many bottles of milk and juice) and offering a variety of healthy foods to your child when he wants them. Then let him eat when he's hungry.

Most little kids don't eat very much.

This isn't news to most parents, who despair of ever getting their children to eat a decent meal. But in fact, little kids don't need very many calories to get by: The average three-year-old probably needs an astonishing *eight table-spoons of food a day* to meet all her caloric needs. That's it.

With that in mind, consider that it's really easy for kids to fill up on eight tablespoons of chocolate cake, cookies, candy, or juice and milk, leaving little room for the healthy stuff and solid food. So if you're worried about how little your child eats, cut down or eliminate the junk, and leave room for healthy food.

Kids don't eat consistent amounts of food.

They're not little cars that consume X gallons of gas each day, or eat three equal meals, seven days a week. That eight tablespoons of food a day trans-lates, often, into one decent-size meal every forty-eight hours. And that's where parents get so frustrated: They assume that that one good meal in six is the ideal they should strive for, and they get worried about the five meals where their child just picks at her food. Instead, try to look at the bigger picture, and see the one larger meal and the five or so scanty meals as a perfectly normal, healthy cycle for your preschooler. You'll save yourself a lot of frustration.

Children eat more when they're growing.

Kids grow in spurts, not in a nice, linear fashion—you know, all of a sudden, their pants are too short and all their clothes don't fit. Just before a growth spurt, kids need additional calories, and they'll eat more. Once the growth spurt has finished, they'll eat less—further confusing and frustrating parents who thought, *Finally! My child is eating!* Instead, think, *Oh, the growth spurt must be over, and she's readjusting her food intake.* Kids eat because they grow—they don't grow because they eat.

Most kids are reluctant to taste new foods.

Left to their own devices, kids *will* eat, but it's a rare child who will chow
right down into food he's never before tasted. If parents don't offer new
foods consistently, kids won't take that step on their own. Here's where a bit
of gentle persuasion might be in order: Parents can make it fun for kids to try
new foods by modeling eating a variety of foods, keeping the portions of
new foods small, letting kids try a new food several times before finally
making up their minds on it, letting kids use condiments to season foods the
way they like them, and using a "two-bite" or a "taste of everything" rule
before kids get dessert or other, more familiar foods. (And hey, if you need
to use dessert as an incentive to get your kid to try a new food, so be it!)

But don't get in a fight or a battle of wills with your kids over eating
something new—that's the surest way to make sure that they won't try it.

Oh, yeah—it's also a time to eat. As far as we're concerned, however, dinnertime is primarily a social time for families, and only secondarily about food. Unfortunately, too many families get so focused
on the food—how much their kids eat, whether the kids eat, what
the kids eat, how long it takes them to eat, whether they're eating
enough, and so on—that they lose sight of the broader purposes of
family dinners. Instead of a time to bond and talk, mealtimes
become a battleground over food.

Suffice it to say that if you want to talk about "family values,"
mealtime is one time of day where you can, almost literally, put your
money where your mouth is. If you value being with your family,
prove it by having dinner together. But if you're too worried about
food to actually enjoy dinner, we have a suggestion for you—focus
on making dinnertime pleasant. If you can work on the social skills
around the dining room table, it's likely that the food problems will
be a lot easier to solve.

The One- (or Two-, or Three-) Bite Rule

When Michael arrived at Anna and Cameron's place, they had
just finished whipping up a Mexican feast: chicken fajitas, rice, and

carrots. Sounded good to Michael. Madeline's idea of a great Mexican dinner, however, was a little different from that of her parents: a tortilla with mustard. Period.

"That's it," said Anna, "the house specialty. And I warn you, Michael, she's very hungry, so if you try to make her eat anything else, that's going to be your first battle."

"That's fine," Michael told them. "She can have her tortilla with mustard. But I'm going to introduce what I call the one-bite rule. In order to get that tortilla, Madeline has to have one bite of each of the other dishes you've made: one bite of chicken, one bite of rice, and one bite of carrots. That's where we're Drawing the Line. After those three bites, she can eat what she wants. Beyond that, we're not even going to have a conversation about food tonight."

If Cameron and Anna had a worksheet for dealing with Madeline's food issues, it would look like this:

Drawing the Line: **Madeline**

Priority	Target Behavior	Positive Alternative	When/ Where Does It Occur?	Draw the Line	Drawing the Line: Reward?	Drawing the Line: Penalty?
1	Madeline won't eat anything new. Whines and protests if we try to get her to eat anything but what she likes.	Madeline tries new foods, eats what we make—without whining.	Dinnertime, at the dining room table.	Madeline must taste at least one bite of each dish we make for dinner.	• Madeline can eat whatever parts of dinner she wants (up to a full serving) *after* she's had her tastes of each thing. • Don't reinforce the whining by trying to reason with Madeline or talk about food.	• Withhold fave foods until Madeline tastes each food • Ignore any whining or protests. • If whining escalates, a brief time-out (turning her chair away from the table or sitting on the stairs or in another room for a few seconds).

As we can see, what Michael wanted to do was shift the focus away from quantity—*how much* Madeline ate—to variety: encouraging her to expand her food repertoire beyond a few basic favorites, like chicken fingers or grilled cheese sandwiches.

"The mistake we all tend to make is that we push quantity rather than variety," he told Cameron and Anna. "North American families are trying to get so much food into their kids that they end up serving up all kinds of horrible food because that's all the kids will eat in large quantities. Kids will eat enough to meet their basic energy needs, but they won't try new foods on their own. That's something we have to work on with them. So for starters, if we can get Madeline to taste just a little bit of everything, we're making progress. Once she's had those tastes, I'll trip over my feet to get her anything else she wants."

To get Madeline to taste the chicken, rice, and carrots, Michael used the reward of her tortilla with mustard as an incentive.

"Your mom told me you like mustard fajitas," he told Madeline, seated next to him at the dinner table. The little girl nodded. "So let's go ahead and make one up, just the way Madeline likes it. The mustard fajita—the house specialty!"

Rather than giving Madeline her tortilla, though, Michael put it on his own plate.

"You know what?" he said. "I'm going to hold this over here for a minute."

"I want it," said Madeline.

"I bet you do," said Michael. "Anna, could you please pass Madeline the carrots?"

Anna passed over the serving dish. Michael put a carrot on Madeline's plate.

"So before you eat your fajita, Madeline, what I need you to do is have one of these."

To everyone's surprise, Madeline reached for the carrot, put it in her mouth, chewed, and swallowed. Then she held out her hand for the fajita.

"Thattagirl!" said Michael. "Oh, are you good! This is going to go so fast. Can I have just a teeny bit of chicken and rice for Madeline, please?"

Madeline, in turn, looked horrified. Her lower lip jutted out. "No."

Michael served himself some chicken and rice to go with the tortilla and carrots on his plate. "Wait for me," he said. "First, I'm going to take a little bit for my dinner. Now, Madeline, can you point to a piece that you want?"

"I don't want any chicken . . ."

"You gotta take just one bite, just an itty-bitty taste," Michael replied. "You know what I'm going to do? I'm going to give you this piece right here, because it's so tiny. And then just a little bit of rice." He served up a bite-size portion of each food onto her plate.

"I don't *want* any," Madeline repeated. She began to push the plate away. Michael stopped her hand.

"Okay," said Michael, "that's fine. If you don't want it, you can just leave it on your plate."

Madeline sat in her chair for a moment, considering her dilemma.

"I'm not going to get into arguments or discussions with Madeline about this," Michael explained to Cameron and Anna, who were watching the scene with great interest. "The food's there on her plate, and once she's taken a taste of the chicken and a taste of the rice, then she can go ahead and have her mustard fajita. But if she doesn't want her fajita, she doesn't have to eat the other stuff."

With that, Michael began eating his own dinner. "Man, this is good stuff!" he said, between mouthfuls. "You guys are great cooks! Hey, Anna—why don't you tell us what you did at work today?"

As Anna began to talk about her day, Madeline relented and took a bite of rice.

"Thattagirl!" said Michael. "Oh man, are you the best!"

"Can I have it now?" asked Madeline, pointing to her mustard fajita, still just out of reach on Michael's plate.

Tip: Nix the "How Was School Today?"

We've all been there. You ask, "How was school today?" and your kid says, "Fine." You prod further: "What did you learn?" Your kid says, "Nothing." End of conversation.

Why the silence? Maybe it's because your kids don't really know how to have conversations. Like anything else, dinner conversation is an art that has to be learned. Kids may be so used to the fighting, nagging, and whining over food that they've never actually heard a real dinner conversation.

So show them how! Instead of asking dead-end questions, start modeling conversation skills for your kids. Say, "Do you know what I did at work today?" or "Do you know what happened to me today?" And then tell your family. Talk about what happened at the playgroup, the interesting article you read about robots, the bugs you caught with your child, the three-legged dog you saw on your walk. Ask your partner questions, and show that you're interested in the answers. If you talk about your day first, the kids will be more likely to talk about theirs.

Dinnertime is primarily about being together as a family, and only secondarily about eating and food. And the thing that makes all the difference is communication. So put your money where your mouth is and model great dinnertime talks for your kids.

"You want the mustard fajita?" asked Michael. "Okay, you can have it just as soon as you have that bit of chicken."

"I don't want that," said Madeline, "I want my fajita with mustard!" Michael kept on eating his dinner.

"I don't want it!" Madeline insisted. "Mommy, I don't want it! I don't like it!"

"Okay," said Michael, "but we don't really want to know about it. You don't have to eat your chicken if you don't want your fajita. But we don't want to hear about what you want or don't want right now. Anna, what else happened at work?"

Madeline's mouth opened in the beginnings of a shriek—and Michael instantly turned her chair away from the table. The suddenness of the move stopped her mid-scream. The moment Madeline quieted, Michael turned her chair back to the table.

"Why'd I turn you away?" he asked her. "I turned you away because you were screaming. There's no screaming at the dinner table—we talk in nice voices at dinner. Now, do you want your fajita? Because as soon as you eat that little tiny bit of chicken, it's yours."

After about ten minutes, Madeline finally decided she was hungry enough. She speared the chicken on her fork, popped it in her mouth, chewed, and swallowed.

"That's my girl!" said Michael. "Way to go, Maddie!" And he handed her the prized mustard fajita. Which she ate.

So, Stop Talking About Eating—and Start Having Real Conversations!

Dinnertime is a time for families to come together and reconnect at the end of the day. Instead of having conversations about ideas, current events, or what happened at work or at school, however, many families—parents and kids—fall into the trap of talking about food and eating. And those conversations all too often take the form of complaining, whining, coaxing, nagging, or arguing.

On the one hand, parents pester kids to eat, haggling and negotiating over every little bite:

- "What about chicken, do you want some chicken?"
- "Just take one bite, sweetie, it's yummy."
- "You like broccoli— you ate it yesterday! Look, like little trees! Look!"
- "What about half a piece, then? Okay, what about just this little bit here? What about one bite? No? Come on, just one bite."
- "How do you know you don't like it if you've never tried it?"
- "Eat your roast beef, honey. Come on, eat your rice now. Eat your meat. Okay, eat your rice. Your rice, eat your rice. Come on, open your mouth wide and . . ."
- "Look, look, it's an airplane! Open your mouth wide for the airplane! Open . . ."
- "If you don't eat your beans you don't get any dessert. You want dessert, don't you?"

Do things like this come out of your mouth at dinnertime? If they do, we have one word for you: *Stop*. These kinds of statements aren't dinner conversation, they're nagging.

Kids, on the other hand, often contribute their fair share of inappropriate talk to dinnertime "conversations":

- "Oh, that's gross!"
- "I hate fish!"
- "I'm not eating that!"
- "I want a grilled cheese sandwich!"
- "What's that green thing? I can't eat green things!"
- "Mommy! The potatoes are touching the chicken!"
- "I want to watch TV!"
- "I don't like it."
- "I don't want it."
- "I'm not hungry!"

When kids start up, it's up to parents to squelch the negative talk. Don't engage with kids who are complaining: Paying attention to kids' refusals to eat just reinforces the behavior.

What to do instead?

- First, resolve not to argue about food—at dinner, or any other time. It's never worth it. Instead, set aside a time, away from the table, to talk about kids' likes and dislikes, their bodies and health, and why it's important to eat a variety of food. These are great conversations to have—but not at the table.
- Make one dinner, not a separate meal for every child. You're not a short-order cook, and this is your family's dining room, not a restaurant.
- Emphasize variety and balance over quantity. Rather than trying to get your children to eat a lot, focus on getting them to at least taste everything on their plates. The more kids are exposed to and try new foods, the more likely they are to develop healthy eating habits as adults. Offer a variety of healthy foods,

and let small treats be part of the menu: A serving of ice cream or cake now and then is fine when it's balanced by more nutritious foods.

- Before you sit down to eat, work out the rules with the kids:

    First, they have to sit at the table for dinner. Be flexible: A two-year-old can manage maybe fifteen minutes at the table. A five-year-old can sit a bit longer.

    Second, they have to eat two bites of each dish, or take a taste of everything on their plates, before they get dessert or before they can have a second helping of the foods they like best. Let the kids use low-fat gravies, seasonings, sauces, and condiments if that makes the food more appetizing. Eventually, they'll prefer the food over the sauce.

    Over time, require larger portions. Have the one-bite rule become the two-bite, then the three-bite rule.

- Then, at the dinner table, enforce the rules. If kids protest, you can ignore them. You can say firmly to a child, "I understand, but I don't want to know about it. I don't want to listen to an argument." *And if they don't eat, fine*. A missed meal isn't fatal—your job is to put healthy food in front of them. Theirs is to eat. If, later on in the evening, your child says she's hungry, go back to the two-bite rule: "You can have your dinner once you've tried two bites of the other foods."

- Handle inappropriate behavior and tantrums at the dinner table the way you would at any other time: with brief time-outs. You can abruptly turn your child's chair away from the table, or firmly seat him back down in his chair. If she's really wailing, take her to a brief time-out on the stairs or in another room. When she's ready to join you again, she's welcome at the table.

In short, stop arguing about food! Life's too short. Talk about your day and have some fun instead. Your goal at dinnertime isn't to shovel calories into your child, it's to have a good time with your family.

More Peaceful Mealtimes

When Michael checked back with Anna and Cameron in a month, they reported that Madeline was getting more adventurous about trying new foods, and that dinnertime was much more peaceful.

"We've been worrying less about how much the kids eat and instead are focusing on getting Madeline to branch out and try at least a mouthful of each thing," says Cameron. "We're pretty happy with how it's going. As far as we're concerned, it's a success just to get her to eat anything other than honey, mustard, and bread. Her first reaction, often, is still, 'No, I'm not eating this!' Now we just ignore the protests and enforce the one-taste rule. Some days all we get is one taste, and sometimes she'll try something and it's pure delight."

"The kids know the rules now," says Anna. "There's only one dinner, not separate meals for each kid. You have to try one bite of everything to get dessert or more of your favorite food."

But She Doesn't Eat Anything (Except Chocolate, Cookies, Cake, Chips, Juice, and Milk)!

Like many moms, Lisa's concerned that her daughter, three-year-old Phoebe, doesn't seem to get enough to eat. The little girl just isn't interested in breakfast, lunch, or dinner—she turns away from the exquisite meals that Lisa prepares, and cries and kicks up a fuss if her parents try to insist that she eat "decent" meals.

"I can't guarantee that Phoebe will eat anything," says Lisa. "She just has no appetite. She's really not an eater."

Robert, Phoebe's dad, disagrees with his wife. "Phoebe eats," he says. "It's just that all she eats is junk food."

Robert's got a point. Lisa's so frantic that Phoebe will waste away to nothing that she's resorted to sugar:

"I can't get her to eat breakfast, so I've started giving her cake for breakfast—just a little bit of cake, something sweet, a cookie, a biscotto, just something, so at least I can say she didn't go to school on an empty stomach. And sometimes she doesn't even eat that."

All day long, Lisa cajoles Phoebe to eat. And when she doesn't, Lisa finally offers her candy, cookies, and cake. Phoebe also drinks a lot of bottles—of sugary juice and high-fat milk. Add that to the junk food, and it's not surprising that by the time dinnertime rolls around Phoebe's not hungry: She's already got all the calories she needs for the day. Unfortunately, they're empty calories.

What to do? Two things:

- First, adjust expectations. Lisa needs to realize that Phoebe's getting enough to eat, just of the wrong foods. Startling as it is to believe, a typical three-year-old needs only about eight tablespoons of food a day, or, roughly, one good meal every forty-eight hours. It's very, very easy for kids to get those eight tablespoons from junk, leaving no room for the healthy stuff.
- Second, lose the junk. Lisa needs to steel her nerves and stop offering Phoebe the high-sugar, low-nutrition foods that have become her main source of calories. She also needs to cut out the bottles of milk and juice, which are high-sugar, nutrient-dense sources of energy that compete with "real" food. (In any case, at age three, Phoebe's definitely old enough to drink out of a cup, not a bottle.)

Once the junk's no longer competing with healthy food, Phoebe will have enough room in her stomach for dinner. It might take a couple of days to make the transition, but in the end Phoebe will get most of her calories from healthy sources. And once she's had a few bites of each healthy food on her dinner plate, there's nothing wrong with letting her have a cookie (just one!) at the end of the meal.

"If we say they're not getting dessert, which can even be fruit or yogurt, that's a major downer," says Cameron. "They'll often eat if they know they get dessert after."

"But if they don't want to eat it, that's fine," says Anna. "They still have to sit at the table—or they're on the stairs for time out. This is our time together. This is our time as a family."

OUT OF DIAPERS AND ONTO THE TOILET

Warning: Bad toilet-training pun ahead:

It's a pain in the rear if your old-enough child still won't use the toilet.

First of all, there's the gross-out factor: It ain't pretty, and it ain't fun or easy, to clean up the bowel movements of a two-and-a-half- or three-year-old child.

And that's assuming that your kid doesn't tamper with his diaper. Some parents aren't so lucky. Two-and-a-half-year-old Mitchell, for example, is liable to take off his diaper and use any part of the house—the living room floor, behind the couch, his brother's bed-room, his own bed—as his own personal toilet.

"Is She Ready?"

"Wait till they're ready." That's the tagline one diaper company used in a series of commercials to sell diapers to older children.

Well, forgive us for being skeptical, but we're not convinced that diaper companies are the best judges of when a kid is ready to be toilet trained. The message that parents should wait for kids to take the lead is more about selling diapers than it is about child development.

Frankly, children aren't necessarily the best judges about when it's time to graduate to the potty, either. It's a rare child who will say to her parents, "Hey, Mom! Hey, Dad! I'm ready to be toilet trained now—let's go!"

Parents who wait for their child to announce that she's "ready" will end up waiting a long time. In the meantime, the kid is deprived of the independence and skills she could have had earlier. When parents delay toilet training, the message they inadvertently send to their kids is, *It's okay not to try to learn new things. It's okay to act less mature than you really are.* So don't wait for your child! Instead, pay close attention for the cues that suggest kids are ready, and then create an environment that makes potty training as easy and as fun as possible.

So how can you tell when kids are *really* ready to use the toilet? Here are some hints:

- Generally, by about age two, kids are ready to begin to learn how to use the potty.
- If your daughter is longer than her changing table, she's probably ready to be toilet trained.
- If you can have a six-hundred-word conversation with your son about why he doesn't want to be toilet trained, he's ready to be toilet trained. If he can protest at great length about the fact that he doesn't want to use the toilet, he's—ironically—ready to use it.

- If she can hold in a bowel movement until you put her back into her diaper, she's ready to be toilet trained.
- If he hides—for example, behind the couch or next to the fridge—while having a bowel movement, he's ready to be toilet trained.
- If she can announce when she's about to "make a pee," or says "poo-poo, Mommy," just before she goes, she's ready to be toilet trained.
- If he shows interest in the toilet—for example, putting a doll or teddy bear on the potty, or reading books and talking about the toilet—he's ready to be toilet trained.
- If she's increasingly impatient at diaper changes, fighting you on them and crying, she's ready to be toilet trained.
- If he wants to be changed each time his diaper is slightly soiled, he's ready to be toilet trained.
- If she gives physical cues such as grabbing her crotch or holding her hand to her bottom before peeing or pooping, she's ready to be toilet trained.

Don't wait for your child to tell you he's ready. Ask yourself if *you're* ready to commit to the process of toilet training. Look for the cues that he's ready, and then go.

If that weren't bad enough, Mitchell can be a bit of an artist: "The last time he did it in his crib, he finger-painted everywhere," says his mom, Linda. "He stomped it all over his feet, and took it with his hands and smeared it all over the rails. I walked in there, and it was a complete disaster. It wasn't fun."

We'll say. Add the expense of diapers and pull-ups to the parental-aggravation and gag-me factors, and there's another compelling reason to get kids using the toilet.

The above reasons aside, however, perhaps most important is that kids need to be toilet trained because it's a crucial developmental milestone that gives them a sense of accomplishment and increased independence and opportunities. Most preschools and kids' programs, for example, won't take children who aren't toilet trained. Kids who haven't made that leap are left out of stimulating programs. And parents are stuck waiting until the next session, hoping and praying that by then, potty training will have taken hold.

But trust us: Unless you take it upon yourself to toilet train your child, you're going to wait a long, long time for the process to "just happen" on its own. And if you're worried that pushing your toddler to use the toilet could somehow be psychologically damaging, we have two words for you: *Lighten up!* Toilet training doesn't have to be anything but fun for kids. Teaching your toddler how to take the appropriate developmental step of using the toilet is just one more necessary, healthy task in the repertoire of parenting. Just like with any other task, your approach makes all the difference. There are easy, fun, and healthy ways to get kids out of diapers. All that Freudian mumbo-jumbo about psychological scarring from improper toilet training is pretty much a load of . . . well, you know.

In this section, we'll show you how Linda and her husband, Barry, helped their son Mitchell learn to use the toilet successfully.

Not surprisingly, Linda and Barry were pretty tired of Mitchell's refusals to use the potty—and of his creative "accidents." Working with Michael, they came up with a strategy to get Mitchell out of diapers and using the toilet. Linda and Barry's worksheet for Mitchell looked like this:

Drawing the Line: Mitchell

Priority	Target Behavior	Positive Alternative	When/ Where Does It Occur?	Draw the Line	Drawing the Line: Reward?	Drawing the Line: Penalty?
1	Mitchell refuses to use the toilet—and sometimes uses the entire house as his own personal bathroom.	Having Mitchell use the toilet consistently; get him out of diapers and into "big-boy" underwear.	• Times he's most likely to have a bowel movement: after breakfast; between 3 and 4 PM. • Hides behind couch or crouches next to fridge when he's about to go.	The new world order: no more diapers! Mitchell has to use the toilet to pee and have bowel movements.	• Gummy bears! For any success on the toilet, Mitchell gets a forbidden treat. • Lots of praise and parental excitement whenever he goes.	• A cold wipe to clean up his "accidents." • On the toilet, whining and crying drive parents out—cooperation brings them in.

Over the course of a long weekend, Linda and Barry put their plan into action. Let's take a look at how they helped Mitchell get on board with toilet training.

Tip: It Takes Time and Commitment

The more intense time you can devote to toilet training, the easier the process will be. See if you can set aside a period of time—say, a long weekend, March break, or a week at the cottage in the summer—to devote to the task. And then be ready to commit to the process. It may take a few days or weeks—or, in some stubborn cases, months—but you've got to put in the time and the effort to make your strategy work.

STEP 1: Sleuthing—Track Your Child's Bodily Rhythms

As Sheldon is fond of saying, when it comes to psychology, it often helps to have physiology on your side. Just as you'll have a lot more success at getting your kid to try new foods when she's actually hungry, your kid will have a lot more success on the toilet if you put her there when she actually needs to go.

One of the first steps in the process, therefore, is to familiarize yourself with your child's bodily rhythms. You may already know the times of day when your child is most likely to go. If so, great! If you're not quite sure, keep a log for three or four days—long enough to notice a pattern. Note the times of day when you find her wet, or having a bowel movement.

Also note *where* your child has a bowel movement, and the types of behavior that accompany it. Lots of kids like to sneak off to a quiet, more private part of the house, such as behind the couch or next to the fridge or washing machine. Watch for that telltale *I'm having a poop* expression—you know, that dreamy, confused, concentrated, or faraway look. Look for crotch grabbing or a child holding her hand to her bum, as if to "catch" a bowel movement.

With this information at hand, you'll be able to read the signs that your child's ready to go. When you see the signs, take her to the toilet!

Linda and Barry were fairly familiar with Mitchell's schedule. Three or four days of record keeping confirmed that he was most likely to have a bowel movement after breakfast, or at about 3 or 4 PM. Left to his own devices, he'd get quiet and hide behind the couch to go.

Tip: Getting Them Ready to Go

Before you start, get your kids used to the idea of toilet training, and excited about it. Talk lots about toilet training. Read books about it. And swallow your inhibitions—let your children watch you go to the bathroom as often as you can. Kids imitate our every move, including bathroom behaviors!

STEP 2: Get Your Child Comfortable on the Toilet

In the process of toilet training, kids are going to be sitting on the toilet a lot. One of the reasons why a lot of kids won't go on the toilet, however, is that they feel physically insecure. From a tiny kid's point of view, the toilet seat might as well be twenty feet off the ground. So one of our first steps is to make sure that children feel safe on the toilet. That way, they can relax and do their business.

With Mitchell, Linda and Barry made sure that the kid's toilet seat they were using didn't wobble, and that it was broad enough for him to sit on comfortably and feel supported. They also wanted to make sure that his little legs didn't dangle into nothingness: Linda got a step stool so that Mitchell could climb onto the toilet and then have somewhere to rest his feet while he sat.

Then they looked at posture. They made sure that Mitchell was sitting with his legs spread far apart and so that all his joints—hips, knees, and ankles—were at ninety degrees. To help him sit comfortably, Mitchell's pants and underwear were off completely, as opposed to bunched around his ankles.

"What kids need to learn to do on the toilet most of all is just relax," says Michael. "So have a good seat, a firm foundation, good posture, pants off, and legs far apart. With practice—and some really killer rewards waiting for us—we just may manage to pull this off."

Potty Chair or Toilet? It's Up to Your Kid

Should you use a small potty chair for toilet training, or put your kid directly on the toilet (equipped, of course, with a modified, kid-size seat)? We say, let your kid decide.

If your child likes to go into the bathroom alone and wants some privacy, a potty chair may be a better option. Time is often of the essence when a child has to go, and using a potty chair can make navigating the bathroom easier for a two-year-old.

If, on the other hand, your child seems to want your company in the bathroom, or wants you to take her in and set her up, she's probably better off on the toilet. Since you're going to be in there anyway, you may as well keep things simpler and eliminate the eventual transition from potty chair to toilet.

Letting your child decide where to go—chair or toilet—also gives her some autonomy in the process, which may help make toilet training more fun for her.

STEP 3: Lose the Diaper (In Fact, Lose the Clothes)

Okay, we're in the big leagues now. When you start actively toilet training, it's time—during the day—to get kids out of diapers and into underwear. The message is clear: *You're a big boy or girl now—no more diapers!* (At night, you may very well still need diapers or pull-ups for a while. Some kids become night trained once they're day trained; others take a bit longer to stop having accidents at night.)

During those times of day when you're actively taking your child back and forth to the washroom (see Step 4, below), lose the underwear, too. In fact, if you have the luxury of living in a warm climate or toilet training in the summer months, feel free to let loose your child's inner nudist and have her get naked. Or crank up the heat inside the house to let your kid run around starkers. If it's too cold, or if you or your child is otherwise uncomfortable with nudity, dress

her in only a T-shirt and a pair of big-girl underwear—but take the
underwear off completely while she actually sits on the toilet.

Why the minimal clothing? For a few reasons:

- First, in this age of superabsorbent disposable diapers, it can be
  hard for kids in diapers to know when they're actually wet.
  When they're naked or in underwear, the feeling of wetness—
  or the sound of pee hitting the floor—is a lot more apparent.
- Similarly, having few or no clothes on allows both parent and
  child to follow the child's body cues and get a better sense of
  what's going on.
- Having few or no clothes on makes it that much easier to get on
  the toilet quickly! When parents and kids have to fumble with
  snaps, elastic, and buttons, there's more potential for accidents.
- Finally, without a diaper, or underwear or pants bunched around
  their ankles, kids can sit more comfortably on the toilet, with
  legs spread wide apart.

Yes, we can virtually guarantee that you're going to have to clean up
some accidents during the process. But live through it—in the long
run, it'll help. (We will warn you, though: Once your child gets to like
running around naked, you may have a tough time convincing her
to get back into her clothes. But that's a different behavioral issue.)

STEP 4: Get Them On—and Off—the Toilet Until They Go

It's time to get on the toilet! Now that you know the times of day
your child's most likely to go, zero in on those times to practice.

Right after breakfast, Linda and Barry took Mitchell to sit on the
toilet. They let him sit there for about five minutes at a time, and
then took him off the toilet for a shorter break—about two minutes.
They repeated this seven-minute cycle for about an hour, or until
Mitchell had some success. They did the same thing in the late
afternoon, another time Mitchell usually had a bowel movement.
And if they saw him make a beeline for the back of the couch or

beside the fridge, or get that *I'm gonna go* expression, they immediately took him to the toilet for the on-again-off-again drill.

Why the multiple trips? Because during toilet training, kids need multiple opportunities for success. The constant on-and-off routine multiplies the likelihood that kids will actually use the toilet successfully. And that's important, because toilet training will not happen until kids go on the toilet, and then get reinforced for going.

Which leads to Step 5.

STEP 5: Reward the Successes

Rewarding on the Toilet: Should You Use Food?

In chapter 3, we've discussed the pros and cons of using food as a reward (see page 61). We often use junk food—chocolate chips, M&M's, gummy bears—because it's just such a super treat for most kids. They'd do a lot to get their hands on some candy. And when you're toilet training, you want your rewards to work hard for you.

If you're not comfortable using a small amount of candy during toilet training, however, that's fine. Special stickers or a toy like Play-Doh or Matchbox cars might be in order. Whatever you pick, however, be sure it's something that moves the earth for your kid.

And whatever you pick as your kid's special treat, make absolutely sure that she doesn't get that treat anywhere else or at any other time. If she can get it anytime, then it ceases to be compelling on the toilet.

When Mitchell had any kind of success on the toilet—if he produced even a drop—Linda and Barry rewarded him mightily with one of his favorite treats: gummy bears.

But here's the key: Linda and Barry didn't wait for Mitchell to use the toilet before they showed him the gummy bears. Instead, they used the candy as the proverbial carrot. At the *beginning* of the toilet-training hour, they showed Mitchell the big jar full of candy and said, "Hey buddy—see these? This is what you get when you use the toilet! Do you need to go to use the toilet?"

Bribery? Not really—Mitchell still had to produce results on the toilet to get some gummy bears. Incentive? Definitely. With the candy in clear view, Mitchell had a very compelling reason to use the potty.

In addition to giving him gummy bears, Linda and Barry made a huge fuss every time Mitchell used the toilet successfully—lots of praise, hugs, high fives, and the like. In short, they tried to keep the experience as fun as possible.

Tip: Don't Reward *on* the Toilet

Parents often fall into the trap of paying too much attention to the kids while they're actually on the toilet. They have long conversations with kids, read stories, do puzzles, and turn the whole experience into an hour-long trip to Playland.

But let's face it: The toilet isn't really the place for games, toys, food, or long conversations. We'd prefer kids to go into the bathroom, sit on the toilet, do their business efficiently, and get the heck outta there!

So don't pay too much attention to your child while she's on the toilet. Don't have conversations (and especially don't have conversations when she's complaining, whining, or crying), don't play with toys, and don't give food or other treats. All the attention and fun stuff comes *after* she's used the potty, washed her hands, and come out of the bathroom.

STEP 6: Walk Away from the Crying; Penalize the Uncooperative Behavior

At first, Mitchell kicked up a fuss when Linda and Barry began bringing him to the toilet. In fact, his wails made it sound as though he were being tortured. Rather than engage with him during the histrionics—and positively reinforcing the crying—Linda and Barry simply walked away. When he quieted down a bit, or got downright cheerful, they went back into the bathroom and let him know he was doing a good job. "Hey buddy," Barry would tell his son, "you're being such a good boy! You're being such a good boy! You're sitting like a real gentleman. Let's make a pee-pee now."

In short, Linda and Barry let Mitchell's behavior call the shots. They made their coming and going a function of their son's behavior: The quiet, cooperative behavior drew them closer, while the fussy, whiny, cranky stuff sent them out the door. The message they conveyed to Mitchell was simple: *This is no big deal. If you're going to complain, we're going to turn around and ignore you. As soon as you start to calm a little bit, we'll come back in and talk to you awhile.*

As for Mitchell's accidents, Linda and Barry penalized them in a different way. Despite their best efforts, Mitchell did persist in sneaking off a few times to have a bowel movement in his pants— and once, on the floor. The little boy understood perfectly well the concept of toilet training, and that he wasn't supposed to use the house as his own personal toilet. In response to his on-purpose accidents, Linda and Barry cleaned him up, very mechanically, with a wipe or cloth soaked in very cold water. They also made Mitchell help them clean up the poop from the floor. The quick, unpleasant shock of the cold wipe, plus the unpleasant chore, conveyed the message: *You go in the toilet.*

The Result? One Successful Kid, and Two Very Happy Parents

Linda and Barry spent the better part of four days working hard to get Mitchell out of diapers. By the end of that long weekend, they were miles ahead of the game. And by the end of a week and a half, Mitchell was consistently using the toilet on his own.

"We just persisted with getting him going on the toilet and the positive reinforcement," says Linda. "And then he would get his rewards. We worked out a system where he got one thing if he peed and a choice of three things when he made a bowel movement. At one point he was doing it just to get those rewards, but it worked, he was doing it."

Along the way, Mitchell had a few accidents. Sometimes, despite his best efforts, he didn't quite make it to the toilet. But Linda and

Barry just forged ahead. And when Mitchell deliberately went in his pants, they penalized the behavior.

"I used cold water to wash him," says Linda. "In fact, I put his bottom right into the water. He didn't like it very much. He cried, but he didn't do it again. From then on, he would come up to me and say, 'Mommy, pee-pee,' or 'Mommy, ca-ca, I got to go,' and he has been going. It's amazing. I never thought that little Mitchell was going to be out of diapers at two. I really thought that it was going to be a lot longer. It was amazing. I called my mother. I called the world. I called everybody to tell him that he did it!"

A Really Stubborn Case? Use a Suppository

David is three and a half years old and absolutely refuses to be toilet trained. In fact, he won't even sit on the toilet. His mom, Angela, is a bit desperate. She's the sole parent of David and his two-year-old brother, Matty. Plus, she's expecting another baby in a few months. Her goal is to have at least one kid out of diapers before the baby is born.

Angela knows that David is ready to use the toilet. She's checked with his pediatrician to make sure there aren't any physical or medical reasons preventing him from using the potty. Plus, David's behavior and cues let Angela know that her son is physically ready to use the toilet.

"If I try to put him on the toilet, either I'll get a great big hissy fit, where he cries and whines and says things like 'No, I don't want to go, no, I don't want to go.' Or he'll come up with excuses: The toilet is cold, my legs are cold, the potty is too cold. If I tell him he's a big boy, and that he can't go to school if he's wearing diapers, he'll say, 'I don't want to be a big boy. I want to be a baby.' If I convince him to go in and sit on the toilet, he'll be totally distracted. He'll want to play with this and want to play with that, and won't actually relax to sit down and do what he has to do."

Working with Michael, Angela tried every trick in the book to get David to use the toilet. They did succeed in having him pee in the potty. But this kid had buns of steel from years of practicing holding it in. He absolutely refused to have a bowel movement anywhere but his diapers. He'd hold it in all day and finally go in his diaper during the night.

After six weeks, Angela and Michael decided to cut to the chase and use a suppository to ensure that David would go during the day. When she knew that David was likely to have a bowel movement, Angela asked him if he was able to go on the toilet. If he refused, she told him that she was going to put a pill in his bum to help him out. And it worked—within a week or two, David was finally using the toilet.

Suppositories aren't a parent's first choice, but in really stubborn cases they can make a big difference. The suppository helped David understand the sensation of having to go to the bathroom. It also showed him that it didn't hurt to use the toilet, and that there was nothing to fear. And finally, it allowed him to experience success on the toilet.

Think using a suppository is drastic? "For those of you who think I'm using psychological terror tactics," says Michael, "consider what a psycho-logical nightmare a five-year-old in diapers is. And take a look at David now. He's delighted to be out of his diapers—and guess what? He likes me, he really likes me. He didn't freak out over this. So the grown-ups shouldn't worry too much, either."

And Mitchell?

"He's proud of himself, of the fact that he's wearing underwear like his brother. I think he feels like he's a big boy now. I keep asking, 'Mitchell, who's a big boy now?' And he smiles and says, 'Me.'"

FIGHTS THROUGH THE NIGHT: GETTING KIDS TO SLEEP (IN THEIR OWN BEDS)

"Bedtime is a major problem in my house—major," says Arlene.

This divorced mom of two has been sleep deprived for eight years—since Jacqueline, her older daughter, was born. Whether it's going to bed, getting to sleep, staying asleep, or staying in their own beds, nighttime is far from peaceful for Arlene, Jacqueline, and five-year-old Morgan.

The ordeal begins at bedtime, when the girls, especially Morgan, seem to get more wired and wide awake than sleepy. After a bath and several stories, the whining and crying, clinginess, and temper tantrums begin in earnest.

"The kids want me to lie down and stay with them until they fall asleep," says Arlene. "On a good night, if I lie down with them, they'll eventually go to sleep. On a bad night, they'll just stay awake. If I try to leave, Morgan especially gets very anxious. She'll try to follow me downstairs and say things like, 'Mommy, Mommy, I just want my mommy, I just want to be with my mommy. I need my mommy.' I'll tell her that she's okay, but if I try to put her back into her bed, she'll launch into hysterical temper tantrums that can go on for two, three, or four hours of screaming in the middle of the night. It's awful."

On the nights when the girls *do* fall asleep, they don't stay asleep. "Morgan usually gets up anywhere between 12 and 2 in the morning, and then Jacqueline wakes up anywhere between 3 and 5 AM, and they both want to come sleep in my bed," says Arlene. "So then we have the trips back and forth from my room to theirs, and we have another round of fights and temper tantrums. Sometimes it goes on for hours, and I'm so exhausted I end up letting them sleep with me, because otherwise we'd all be up all night. But I don't sleep well with them in the bed. I have not had a decent amount of sleep in eight years and it has taken a toll on me. It absolutely has."

Does any of this sound familiar? If it does, that's not surprising. Parents ask us constantly about sleep issues. Getting the kids to bed—and getting them to *stay* in bed and sleep through the night—is a huge hassle in many households.

But sleep deprivation is more than a behavior issue: It's a health issue. Anyone with a brand-new baby, or anyone who does shift work, can tell you that sleep deprivation affects both health and well-being. Without a decent night's sleep, it's hard to function or concentrate—and it's harder to be a good parent. Kids also suffer when they don't sleep well: They're more irritable, more likely to get sick, and less able to learn or have fun.

Clearly, sleep deprivation is a bit of a crisis for Arlene's family, and families in general. There are lots of ways that Arlene can help make bedtime peaceful and help her daughters transition from wakefulness to sleep. But in the end, parents can't sleep for their kids, so Morgan and Jacqueline need to learn to go to sleep on their own, and to stay asleep in their own beds.

Timing, Talking, and Proximity at Bedtime

Not surprisingly, when it comes to bedtime for Jacqueline and Morgan, timing, talking, and proximity are all off-kilter.

- **Timing:** It's obvious that the entire going-to-bed process takes far too long. Arlene reads story after story to the girls in a bid to get them to settle. She lies with them in their beds for hours. And on the really bad nights, the bedtime battles never really end, continuing into the wee hours until all three fall into Arlene's bed, exhausted. Over the course of the evening and night, the girls have plenty of opportunity to get worked up. Arlene needs to figure out how to act quickly to nip the bed-time hysterics in the bud—*before* they become hysterics—and make the bedtime routine last a more reasonable amount of time.
- **Talking:** In a nutshell, there's way too much of it going on, from both Mom and kids. In this house, bedtime has become a battle of words, in the form of storytelling, negotiating, futile comforting, crying and complaining, and the like. Most nights, for example, Arlene is drawn into complex negotiations with the girls, especially Morgan, trying to explain to her daughters that they must go to bed, that there's nothing to be scared of, that they have to sleep in their own beds (okay, after just one more story), and so on. Remember, though: Talking is hugely rewarding to kids! By talking to the girls so much, Arlene is—without meaning to—rewarding their refusals to go to bed. She needs to talk less, and act more.
- **Proximity:** Here, a couple of things are happening. The first, obviously, is that the girls aren't where they should be—in their beds, asleep, as opposed to in Arlene's bed or fighting with their mom downstairs. Less obvious is that Arlene, also, is in the wrong place. In fact, her proximity to the girls is the reverse of what it should be: She ends up rewarding or reinforcing their inappropriate behavior (getting out of bed, whininess, clingi-ness) by drawing closer when the girls act up, while penalizing

their appropriate behavior (staying in bed) by keeping farther away (for example, downstairs cleaning up, while the girls are struggling to get to sleep upstairs). Inadvertently, she's telling Morgan and Jacqueline that the best way to get their mom's attention and company is to get out of bed. Although it may seem counterintuitive at first, Arlene has to reverse her proximity to the girls in relation to their behavior: The crying, clinginess, whining, and getting out of bed should move her farther away, while calmly staying in bed draws her closer.

With this in mind, how can Arlene Draw the Line around sleep? Let's take a look at how she worked with Michael to create a plan for getting some shut-eye and making bedtime hassles a thing of the past.

Drawing the Line at Bedtime

If we wrote down a plan for Arlene on paper, it would look something like this:

Drawing the Line: Jacqueline and Morgan

Priority	Target Behavior	Positive Alternative	When/ Where Does It Occur?	Draw the Line	Drawing the Line: Reward?	Drawing the Line: Penalty?
1	Kids won't go to bed!	Having a peaceful bed-time routine; having the kids sleep in their own beds through the night.	At night, in their rooms, my room, throughout the house.	Require that Morgan and Jacqueline stay and sleep in their own beds.	Leave door open and go to them at regular intervals (1–2 minutes at first) as long as they're in their beds.	• If they get out of bed, escort them back and close the door. Open their door when they're quiet. • Lock my bedroom door so they can't come in. Close their door.

Arlene knows her number one priority: to end all the histrionics that go on through the night. She knows what she'd like to replace that behavior with: a peaceful bedtime routine and having Morgan and Jacqueline sleep through the night in their own beds. And obviously, she knows when and where the battles take place: This is a bedtime issue, after all.

Now Arlene needs to figure out how to reinforce the behavior she wants and penalize the inappropriate stuff. When the kids stay in their own beds with a minimum of fuss, she wants to reinforce that behavior with a reward. And she needs to penalize them when they get out. In this case, the reward is simply Arlene's attention and praise. As long as the kids stay in bed, she'll keep coming to check on them, to let them know she's there and that they're doing a great job. But if the girls get out of their beds, then they've crossed the line, and she'll penalize them by robotically escorting them back to bed and closing their bedroom door for a few seconds, until they're quiet. Arlene also decided to lock her own bedroom door at night, and hold tight if either girl tried to come into her room.

In other words, good behavior will now draw Arlene closer to Morgan and Jacqueline, while their crying and getting out of bed gets her farther away.

Arlene is now going to pay close attention to timing, talking, and proximity. As part of her plan, she's going to talk less, act quicker, and get close to Morgan and Jacqueline—both to escort them immediately back to bed, but also to reward them when they stay in bed.

Putting the Plan into Action

Here's how Arlene created a new world order around bedtime for Morgan and Jacqueline.

First, she made sure that the girls had a peaceful, predictable nighttime routine that set the stage for sleep.

"Now I do a lot less talking," says Arlene. "We go upstairs, we have bath time for fifteen or twenty minutes or so, and then they get in their pajamas and brush their teeth. They choose one story now, instead of three or four. One kid per night gets to pick a story, and then we sit together on one of their beds and read.

"At the end of the story, both kids go in their own beds. I say good night to them, I rub their backs, and then I tell them that I'll leave the door open and the light on—they like to have a small night-light on—as long as they're quiet. And I tell them that I'll come in and check on them every couple of minutes. But if there's any kind of a fuss, then we shut the door and turn the light off. That's their choice."

If Morgan or Jacqueline gets out of bed, Arlene's true to her word—she escorts them back without saying a word, and shuts the door for a few seconds to a minute or so, until the girls are quiet. Then she opens the door and asks, "Why did I shut the door? I shut it because you have to stay in bed. Do you want the door open? Then you have to stay in bed. I'll come check on you in a few minutes."

The result? Sleep, finally—peaceful sleep, without hysterics—for the whole family.

Arlene reports: "It's been great! The first two nights took a little bit of trial and error, but now I'm in and out of their bedroom in five minutes. If Morgan scoots out of her room to come looking for me, I just march her back to her room. But because she knows I'm going to check on her, she stays in bed. Now she actually looks forward to me coming in and checking on her every few minutes. She'll even call down to me if I'm downstairs, 'Mom, it's been a few minutes! How come you're not coming up and checking on me? I'm in my room.' If she does get out, I just turn her around, bring her back to her bed, and she goes right back to sleep. There's no fight, no temper tantrums, nothing. For four or five years, Morgan never slept through the night—and now she's sleeping through. I was shocked."

So Your Kids Won't Go to Sleep?

Well, you can't *make* children sleep, but you can establish conditions that make it easier for them to get to sleep—and that make staying in bed more rewarding than getting out of bed.

- First, establish a consistent bedtime routine, and don't rush it. Routine is an essential process that helps kids make the transition from wakefulness to a state of sleep. On the other hand, the bedtime routine shouldn't last forever: a bath, brushing teeth, changing into pajamas, and a story or two plus a kiss and quick cuddle should about do it.

- Second, establish consistent rules about sleep, and be prepared to enforce them. Be absolute about when lights are out, and use only a night-light (good sleep happens in the dark!).

- Let kids know that if they stay in bed, you'll come to check on them every few minutes. And then do it: Until they're fast asleep, every few minutes reward their quiet behavior by standing at the doorway and sticking your head in so that they know you're there. Say nothing, or almost nothing—don't get drawn into a conversation beyond, "You're doing a great job of staying in bed. Good night. I'll come check on you in a couple more minutes." As time goes on, you can allow longer intervals between check-ins. In the early stages, though, err on the side of checking on them more rather than less. The constant check-ins make kids feel secure—and that's our goal.

- If the kids make a big fuss or get out of bed, escort them back to their rooms and into bed without saying anything. Close the door for a few seconds, or until they start to quiet down if they're making a fuss. Then open the door and ask, "Why did I shut the door? I shut it because you got out of your bed. Do you want the door open? Then you have to stay in bed. Okay? I'll come check on you in a few minutes. Good night."

- Finally, be determined, and be persistent. Between checking on the kids and escorting them back to bed, it might feel like you're making five hundred trips back and forth, but they'll eventually see that you mean business. And eventually, they'll sleep.

But Will I Have to Do This Forever?

When you Draw the Line with your kids, the surest—and quickest—path to success is practice. So don't hesitate to set up regular times to practice new skills with your kids.

But you may be wondering, *How long do I need to practice? Do I need to reward my kids forever? And how and when do I stop?*

In the next chapter, we'll walk you through the next step: fading out your support and letting the kids navigate the new world order on their own.

Should You Let Your Baby "Cry It Out"? No Way!

If you're tempted to Draw the Line on sleep with your infant by letting him or her "cry it out," we have one word for you: *Don't!*

We want to make one thing clear as day: *Babies under the age of roughly four to six months should not be left to cry.* On the contrary, we believe that parents and caregivers should respond as quickly as possible to a young baby's cries. If we hear an infant wail, we're on our feet and running to find out what the kid needs: A clean diaper? Food? A pacifier? Attention? Cuddles? Movement? Whatever it is, we'll try to figure that out and give it to them. And when we can't figure it out, we'll at least stay close by.

Why? Because aside from smiling, crying is a young baby's only system of communication. When young infants cry, they're saying, *Hey, I need help over here!* And parents' role is to respond to that need. By responding quickly, moms and dads establish a trusting relationship with their children: Babies learn that their needs will be met and that their voice counts. As they get older, these are the kids who will trust more, and cry less.

Want proof? A landmark study* done by Bell and Ainsworth and published in the journal *Child Development* looked at how quickly parents or caregivers responded to the cries of babies less than six months old. Some parents went to their infants at the first cry, while others let the kids "cry it out" and responded much more slowly. What Bell and Ainsworth found was startling: After six months of age, the kids who had very responsive parents *cried less than the kids who were left to cry.* In other words, young babies who are left to cry become older babies and toddlers who cry more.

In short, when you hear the sound of crying, *get up and comfort your baby.* You simply cannot "spoil" an infant. As children grow older and develop more sophisticated communication skills, you can start to ignore some crying. But for younger babies, get up and act—quickly. In the long run, you'll save everyone a lot of tears.

* Bell, S. M., and M. D. S. Ainsworth. "Infant Crying and Maternal Responsiveness." *Child Development* 43, (1972) 4:1171–1190.

—6—

"Will I Have to Do This Forever?"

Lose the scaffolding: fading out the support.

Imagine you're trying to teach a child to ride a two-wheeled bike. You don't just pop her on, put her hands on the handlebars, push her off, and—*ciao, baby!*—she's riding. That's not the way it works.

For most kids, getting the hang of riding a bike is a repetitive, multistep process. She may start off on a tricycle to get the idea of pushing pedals. From there, she moves to a two-wheeler with training wheels. And from there, you run alongside the bike, putting your hands on the bars to keep her steady, taking them off, putting them back on, taking them off, over and over until, one day, she starts pedaling on her own and takes off solo, without the need for your support. Occasionally, she wipes out, and then you wipe up the tears, kiss the scrapes, and encourage her to get back on. From there, who knows? A paper route, commuting to school, the Tour de France—it's up to her.

The process is the same anytime kids learn to master a new skill. At first, it's all about the external support: the training wheels, the steadying hand on the handlebars.

As we saw in the previous chapters, that external support comes in the form of the rewards or reinforcers that parents use to help kids learn how to behave in the car, get to sleep in their own beds, use the toilet, share, or try new foods at the dinner table. Whether it's sweet stuff like M&M's and gummy bears, fifteen-minute play sessions to model sharing, a parental presence at the bedroom door every few minutes, or regular, specific praise, parents support the emergence of their kids' new skills with these external treats, effectively saying, *Look at the great stuff that comes your way when you behave well or act like a big kid!*

Penalties, likewise, are also an external force that parents use to help kids rise to new standards of behavior. Those quick trips to time out, repeated over and over, send a constant message to children about how to act. *If you get out of bed, the door closes*, is the message Arlene's daughters quickly learned. *If you reach to grab one of your brother's toys without asking, I'll stop your hand*, is what Michael taught Mickey and Aaron. *Fighting in the car? The car stops*. That's the lesson that Rhys, Peter, and Caleb learned on their practice car sessions with Corinne.

But of course, we don't want to rely on external forces to govern our kids' behavior forever. Parents' ultimate goal is for kids to internalize a code of conduct. We want kids to behave appropriately because it's an effective way of being in the world and "the right thing" to do—not because they get M&M's or constant praise, and not because they fear punishment if they don't behave. In other words, we want kids to lose life's training wheels and be able to navigate the world from an inner sense of balance. We want the reward to be the confidence and pleasure kids get from newfound abilities, not the attention and candy.

Think of the near-constant rewards and penalties as a form of *scaffolding*. Like the scaffolding that supports a new building as it takes shape, these tools help support new behavior as it takes shape. As the building is able to support itself, gradually the scaffolding comes down. Finally—assuming, that is, that it's built on a solid foundation—the building stands on its own.

The final step in teaching kids appropriate behaviors, then, is to fade out parental support as children master new skills so that the kids can stand on their own:

STEP 9: Lose the scaffolding. Over time, fade out your support.

How do you dismantle the scaffolding? Let's take a look at how the parents in the previous chapter made the transition.

PEACE IN THE CAR

When Corinne started practicing car trips with the boys, she erred on the side of giving them too much rather than too little positive reinforcement. Every few minutes at first, she rewarded the boys with praise and candy. She kept up that schedule until she noticed a marked improvement in their behavior—for example, the time intervals between fisticuffs in the backseat began to increase: From fighting every few minutes, the boys began to go for longer and longer before melting down.

As Rhys, Peter, and Caleb learned how to behave in the car, Corinne was able to rely less and less on M&M's. As the good behavior increased and the teasing, whining, and fighting decreased, Corinne upped the ante, handing out the chocolate and the praise every ten or fifteen minutes or so. She continued to phase out the candy until the boys sometimes simply got a small treat at the end of a long trip. And eventually, they got no candy at all.

Likewise, Corinne let the boys' behavior dictate how and when to phase out the penalty of stopping. At first, she pulled over, without warning, at the first and slightest sign of any untoward behavior from the backseat. The shock and the immediacy of her reaction got the boys' attention. Over time, Corinne noticed that she was pulling over less and less. She then incorporated a *warning* into the cycle. Instead of pulling over immediately at the first sign of dissent, she let the boys know that they were only a few seconds away from stopping:

"Guys," she'd say, "keep that up and what happens?"

"You'll stop the car" would inevitably be the answer from the backseat. And more often than not, the warning was enough to nip the unwanted behavior in the bud. (Keep in mind that Corinne's warning worked only because Rhys, Caleb, and Peter knew that it wasn't an empty threat: If Corinne said she was going to pull over, she meant it.)

Now car rides are generally a pleasure—or, at the very least, a manageable necessity—for Corinne and the kids.

"It's sometimes still impossible for me to believe that we could have three boys in the car and a nice conversation going on, but that's what happens," she says. "They'll be playing with the toys and conversing with me. I'm still giving lots of verbal praise. I'll tell them, 'You guys are doing a great job! Isn't this nice? We can all talk and have fun.' Sometimes I'll have a CD in for the kids to listen to. It's just been smooth sailing. It's nice."

BROTHERLY LOVE

When Michael set out to help Aaron and Mickey learn how to play together without clobbering each other, he began by setting up daily practice sessions. Every day, for about fifteen or twenty minutes, Michael or the boys' parents, Lily and Jim, made some time to sit down and practice the skills of play—taking turns, sharing, trading, and collaborating—with the boys.

At the outset, an adult modeled the skills of play and monitored the boys closely. Michael, for example, got right down on the floor with Mickey and Aaron and made himself part of the action. If the boys took a turn, Michael took a turn. If the boys traded cars, Michael traded his cars, too. If Aaron or Mickey stepped out of line—grab-bing, hitting, crying, or otherwise being a poor sport—Michael nipped the behavior in the bud with a quick time-out and redirection. Similarly, he praised the boys for their cooperative behavior.

Over time, the boys became more and more adept at fair play. With an adult guiding them, they would take turns, trade cars and LEGO pieces with each other, and play with each other without coming to blows—and even have some fun in the process.

"Now we need to slowly, gradually, factor out the adult support," Michael told Lily and Jim. "We've shown them how to share and we've seen them do it. Now we want them to do it independently, so that the the good play doesn't depend on one of you guys being there."

To back out adult support, the adults set up a practice play session with the two boys, as usual. But then the adults began to get up off the floor and retreat: to sit on the couch for a minute or two, or to go to the kitchen to grab a cup of coffee.

"Tell the kids, 'Hey, it's your turn. I gotta go for a second. I'll be right back.' And then you're off to the kitchen for a couple of minutes," Michael explained. "But then, at least initially, come right back, fairly quickly, to check in with the kids. Let them know you're watching. Ask them how they're doing. Tell them what a fantastic job they're doing at sharing, play for half a minute, tell them you'll be right back, and then take off again—this time for a little longer. Keep up the routine of coming and going, each time staying away a little bit longer. Eventually, you'll factor yourself out of the play altogether."

Keep in mind that factoring yourself out of the kids' play doesn't mean that you can't engage with the kids, both in response to great behavior and to deal with skirmishes. Nothing reinforces your children's behavior like your attention, so make a point of getting down on the floor and playing with your kids just for fun, not necessarily to teach them anything. On the other hand, if a fight does break out, you can intervene—although you may just find that your kids now have the skills to get themselves back on track.

BON APPÉTIT!

When Cameron and Anna tried to get four-year-old Madeline to eat anything beyond a few of her favorite foods, they faced a battle. Working with Michael, Cameron and Anna figured out how to get Madeline to eat more: They used a food she really liked—a tortilla with mustard—as a reward. Once Madeline tasted each food on the dinner menu, she was free to eat her own dinner: up to one full serving of each of the foods she liked best. Beyond that, Cameron and Anna weren't going to nag or argue with their daughter, and they sent her to a brief time-out (by turning her chair away from the table) if she put up a fuss.

As kids get more comfortable with tasting new foods, parents can fade out their support in a few ways:

- First, begin to require more from your kids. Over time, and as they get older and have larger appetites, move from a one-bite to a two-bite, then a three-bite rule. Still, worry less about quantity than variety—forcing a child who isn't hungry to clear his plate is a surefire way to instill some poor eating habits.
- You may have used a sweet dessert as the ultimate reward at the end of each meal. If that's your family's eating style, that's fine. But many families prefer not to give their kids sugar every day. If that's the case, then begin to phase out the sweet rewards, substituting yogurt or fruit for desserts. Or if you'd like, phase out sweet desserts several nights a week. Kids need to learn that eating healthy food is its own reward. (Still, focus on balance: Completely banishing any junk food ensures that kids will want it even more. We suggest you insist on mostly healthy food, and treat the kids to something sweet every so often. In moderation, everything's probably fine.)
- At the same time, focus on having a fun time at family dinners. Require the kids to sit at the table for longer periods of time as they get older. Model conversations and get the kids talking about their days, school, their friends, whatever's going on in their lives.
- If your child doesn't eat dinner for a few nights, don't worry too much about it! She won't starve. If and when she gets hungry later on in the evening, offer her dinner again, with the same two-bite or taste-everything rule.

OUT OF THE DIAPERS AND ONTO THE TOILET

It didn't take Linda and Barry long to potty train their two-year-old son, Mitchell. First, they tracked his bodily rhythms to get a sense of when he needed to go. And then they put him on the toilet during those times. For about an hour at a time, they'd put Mitchell on the toilet for five minutes, take him off for a couple, put him back on again, take him off, and so on, until he had some success.

And Linda and Barry rewarded Mitchell's successes mightily, with tons of praise and gummy bears. As his new skills became entrenched, Linda and Barry began thinning out the rewards. For a few weeks, Mitchell got the gummy bears only when he had a bowel movement on the toilet. And then, eventually, they got rid of the candy altogether, relying only on their praise to reward their son's successes. "I don't get a treat every time I go to the washroom," Linda reasoned. "Why should Mitchell?"

After the initial euphoria of toilet training wore off, the fact that Mitchell used the toilet seemed like no big deal to Linda and Barry. The little boy's bathroom behavior was just one more skill, nothing to comment on. They stopped praising Mitchell so enthusiastically for his toileting success.

Fading Out Too Fast

And then there came trouble in paradise. Mitchell began to regress.

"After about six weeks of no accidents, things started going down the drain," said Linda. "He began peeing in his pants and having bowel movements on the floor, everywhere in the house."

Here's an example of where parents may have backed out their support a little too quickly. Linda and Barry assumed that toilet training had become routine for Mitchell. In fact, the little boy valued his parents' praise and attention more than they realized. By regressing, he was able to bring back their attention.

Linda and Barry realized they had moved too quickly. They

slowed down in their efforts to phase out the scaffolding. Once more, they began to tell Mitchell what a great job he was doing when he used the potty successfully. Linda, a stay-at-home mom, also tried to make sure that she carved out an hour or so of time to hang out with her son for some intense one-on-one time. That way, as she and Barry began to—slowly!—fade out their over-the-top praise for toileting successes, Mitchell got the attention he needed during other parts of the day.

When they began once more to pay more attention to Mitchell's achievements—in and out of the bathroom—his accidents stopped. "A lot of the accidents were in fact because he missed the attention that he was getting. Once I started giving him the attention he needed, the accidents disappeared," said Linda. "We could read a book together, or do a puzzle, or even just sit and play—I'd tickle him and make him laugh. That 'together time' really did him a lot of good."

Sweet Dreams

Single mom Arlene Drew the Line around bedtime with Morgan and Jacqueline by requiring them to stay in their beds. As long as the girls cooperated, their bedroom door remained open, and Arlene checked on them at regular intervals. If the girls got out of bed, Arlene closed the door for a few seconds, opening it only when Morgan and Jacqueline were back in bed and quiet.

At the beginning of each evening, Arlene checked on the girls lots—every minute or two, to start, until they were asleep. Why so often? Because her daughters—Morgan especially—had very little practice and experience around staying in bed and going to sleep on their own. A minute or two was about all they could stand being in bed without some adult support. Arlene recognized the girls' tolerance, and respected it.

For similar reasons, Arlene also stayed close by the girls' bedroom at first. She didn't go downstairs, but remained in the hallway, in her bedroom, or in the bathroom, tidying up from the bath. She wanted Morgan and Jacqueline to feel her presence, to know their mom was close by.

As the evenings progressed and the girls moved closer and closer to sleep—and finally fell asleep—Arlene began to increase the time intervals between her check-ins, from every couple of minutes, to every five minutes, ten minutes, fifteen minutes, and, eventually, to every half an hour. She also allowed herself to get farther away from the girls, moving downstairs to clean up the kitchen, watch the news, or read.

Arlene let Morgan and Jacqueline's behavior guide her as she began to fade out her support. As the weeks progressed, Arlene noticed that it took less and less time for Morgan and Jacqueline to fall asleep, and that Morgan called out for her less and less. She also noticed that their bedroom door remained open most of the time—there was little need to close it to penalize the girls for getting out of bed.

Guided by Morgan and Jacqueline's increasingly sophisticated sleep abilities, Arlene could cut back on her rounds as "night watch-woman" and check on the girls just once or twice per evening. Her daughters knew how to go to sleep on their own, and how to settle themselves back to sleep when they woke up. They knew that they had to stay in their beds—and they knew that their mom would be there if they needed her. And for the first time in years, everyone in the house got a good night's sleep.

THE BALANCING ACT OF FADING OUT SUPPORT

Like learning to ride a bike, fading out the support is a balancing act. Of course parents want to support their kids' independence, and fading out the external supports is part of the process of helping them become independent. But if you fade out too quickly, your child may regress. If you're not sure which direction to take, we suggest you err on the side of fading out too slowly rather than too quickly.

In time, as new habits become entrenched, phase out the material rewards—candy, stickers, toys, money, what have you—almost completely. Use them only as the logical outcome of an action: Dessert comes at the end of the meal. An ice cream cone comes at the end of our drive in the country. A video comes after we've cleaned up the toys from the playroom. A story comes after we're ready for bed. Allowance comes when you've done your chores for the week.

Keep the praise and the attention going longer. Over time, you don't have to jump up and down every time your kid goes to the john or shares with her sister, but it never hurts to thank your kids at regular intervals for being cooperative, to get down on the floor to play with them, or to tell them just how much you love them.

What's Next? The Final Step

STEP 10: What next? Go back to your list and tackle the next item!

Congratulations! You've done a lot of hard work to get to this point, and—if things have gone according to plan—you and your kids have found some intelligent, workable, and fun solutions to old behavior problems. Now it's back to the drawing board. Parents: Go back to that list of Target Behaviors and pick the next most pressing item to work with. But be warned: This process could get easier and easier, as both you and your kids learn to *generalize:* to apply the new skills you've learned in one situation to the next.

While you're at it, remember to go have some fun with your kids as well!

—7—

Beyond the Kids: From Polarized Partners to Parents on the Same Page

Want your kids to listen to you? Then you need to
listen to each other—and develop a joint plan.

Ask any parent who has more than one child, and they'll likely tell you how different each kid is. Take Charles and Denise. He works as a security guard from seven at night until seven in the morning. She works twenty-four hours a day as the full-time parent of four-year-old Keisha and seven-year-old Michaela—and she's expecting their third in a few months. Michaela was a placid, dreamy baby who's grown into an equally laid-back little girl who generally goes along with her mom and dad's requests. And then there's Keisha. A high-energy dynamo of a baby who didn't sleep much, she's now an exuberant, outgoing preschooler with a stubborn streak a mile long. She'll often meet parental requests with a firm "no!" Lately, she's been finding ways to play her parents off each other—if she gets a no from her mom (and Denise says no a lot), then Keisha's likely to go to her dad and see if she can get a yes from him. And often, she can, because Charles tends to say yes to the kids a lot more than his wife does.

Just as the kids in a family can differ in terms of style and temperament, so parents also often come to the table with very different approaches. Charles and Denise are a classic example of parents with different styles. She's tough and no-nonsense, while he's more indulgent and laid-back.

And not surprisingly, when parents have different styles, conflict can often be the result.

Denise wants Charles to help more with child care, and to back her up more as she deals with Keisha. He'd like her to lighten up a bit and not be so hard on their daughters all the time. Charles thinks Denise is too tough. She thinks he's not tough enough. He thinks she's forever saying no to Michaela and Keisha and sending them to time out, while she thinks he lets them get away with murder. And sometimes it feels like they could murder each other.

In this game of parental he-says-she-says, the tougher Denise gets, the more laid-back Charles gets to compensate. And the more passive Charles is, the more Denise feels the need to lay down the law to make up for him. And the angrier they both get at each other. "Relax," Charles will tell his wife—in front of the kids, or in the middle of a heated moment where Denise is trying to send Keisha to time out. "I can't relax when you never do a thing around here!" she'll retort angrily. "I need a vacation from all of you."

Charles needs to understand that he can't undermine Denise in front of the kids. Denise needs to take Charles's perspective into account: He feels that there's just too much tension in the household. And there is. But fighting and undermining each other won't ease the tension. Having a joint approach, an agreed-upon plan, and each other's support will help these partners find a common middle ground. In this chapter, we talk about the importance of parents getting on the same page.

POLARIZED PARENTS

If it's true that opposites attract, it's also true that the same opposing qualities that initially attracted people to each other can often be their downfall as parents. As Sheldon points out, like so many parents, Charles and Denise have *polarized*. She's decided he's a softie, so she plays hardball. He's decided she's the bad cop, so he plays good cop. And the harder Denise gets, the softer Charles gets. In the end, they end up as one-dimensional caricatures of themselves: Denise finds it almost impossible to relax around the kids (even though she'd like to), while Charles ends up letting things go that he knows he shouldn't.

Melanie and Dennis have a similar dynamic when it comes to dealing with their two boys, Aedan and Dylan. When the boys act up—or act out—Melanie's right in there. She thinks she's a hands-on parent. Dennis, on the other hand, thinks she overreacts and micromanages—and that she's too soft on the kids, to boot. As a result, Melanie's *always* reacting to the kids, while Dennis hardly reacts at all—until he does.

"I don't think she's strict enough," Dennis says. "She'll fly off the handle sometimes and punish them, but her idea of punishment is ten seconds of yelling and then everything's fine. And then she feels guilty and sucks up to them. And so the boys just act up again. So I end up just sitting on the couch and letting her do her thing."

Dennis doesn't agree with his wife's parenting style, so when the boys fight or otherwise misbehave, he's conditioned himself to sit back and not get involved or interfere with Melanie—until, that is, he gets so angry that he loses it.

"Yeah, sometimes I get mad," he admits.

And when Dennis gets mad, watch out!

"He takes it too far and he goes overboard," says Melanie. "He'll just lose his temper and yell to the point where I think the boys are scared of him. They'll listen to him, but only because they're scared of what his reaction might be. I don't want to be like that. And I wish he'd help out more if he doesn't like what I'm doing. What am I supposed to do if he's just going to sit on the couch and watch TV?"

You can see how the polarization between Dennis and Melanie has spiraled out of control: The more Melanie does, the less Dennis does. The softer she is, the harder he becomes. He undercuts her authority with the kids. She makes him into bad cop. She feels like she does all the work while he sits like a lump on the couch, channel

surfing and doing nothing. He feels like she won't let him do anything, so why should he bother getting up to help? Both parents get
frustrated—Melanie flies off the handle regularly, while Dennis
stews and stews until he loses it. The result? Not only do the parents
end up angry at each other, but the kids, Aedan and Dylan, end up
lost in the shuffle. No one wins.

A No-Win Situation

When parents polarize, everyone in the household loses out. Instead
of letting their different styles complement each other and strengthen
the relationship, polarized parents allow their differences to come
between them and weaken family dynamics. What happens when
parents polarize? A few things:

- First of all, they fight. Almost every interaction begins to feel
  like a battle, not only between parent and child, but between
  parent and parent as well. Tension permeates the household,
  even when the kids aren't acting up.
- Second, the kids—like Keisha—pick up on the dynamic and
  milk it. They play parents off each other in order to get what
  they want. *Mom won't let me have a cookie? Then I'll go ask Dad.*
- Finally, the kids lose out developmentally. Instead of focusing
  on teaching and modeling appropriate behavior to their kids,
  parents focus on each other's shortcomings—and the kids get
  lost in the shuffle.

Over the longer term, the result is an unhappy household, where
tension is the norm, and where kids don't learn how to *generalize*
good behavior. That is, good behavior becomes arbitrary: Rather
than internalizing a set of consistent, predictable rules about what's
appropriate and what isn't, kids learn instead to behave one way
with Dad (in order to infuriate Mom) and another way with Mom
(so that she'll be too distracted by Dad's reaction to her reaction) in

order to get what they want. Instead of a unified approach to discipline for the family, the rules shift depending on who's in charge at a certain moment.

THE YIN AND YANG OF PARENTING

"I want our kids to feel like they can have fun and play and do what they have to do in their home," says Melanie. "But then again, I want them to understand that they have to respect our needs and wants, and our rules. I want a happy medium, but it just doesn't seem to work that way."

What Melanie wants—what *most* parents want—is the kind of family dynamic that's the result of a consistent, balanced parenting style. In a nutshell, that balance is the balance between two factors: *warmth* and *control*. When parents polarize, however, too often what happens is that one parent (such as Charles or Melanie) becomes the source of most of the warmth, while the other (like Denise) becomes the prime controlling factor or becomes increasingly uninvolved (such as Dennis, most of the time). What parents need is a balance of *both*.

Kids need a balance of strictness and nurturance, of play and no-nonsense, of warmth and control. Control sets limits for kids and teaches them the difference between acceptable and inappropriate behavior. Warmth and affection are equally crucial: They're the foundation of all of kids' future attachments and relationships with other people. We like to talk about the "yin and yang" of parenting: Only in combination do the two styles—different as black and white—make up a complete and effective parenting style.

"Warmth without control—a permissive style of parenting where parents just can't say no—leads to kids who want everything, but can't be satisfied by anything," says Sheldon. "On the other hand, control without warmth—what developmental psychologists refer to as an authoritarian parenting style—leads to a sort of temporary obedience, where children do what they're supposed to do, but only because they're scared of being punished, like Aedan and Dylan with

Dennis. As soon as the control is removed, the behavior reverts, and the kids act up again, as they do when Melanie is around."

Warmth and Control: How Parenting Styles Stack Up

Think back to our discussion of parent types in chapter 1. As you can see from the chart below, an *authoritative* parenting style—the style kids need to become secure, independent, successful adults—combines *high* levels of *both* parental warmth and control. When parents polarize, however, each tends to gravitate toward one of the other styles: One tends toward being more authoritarian or uninvolved, while the other tends toward permissiveness.

Parent Type	Control Level	Warmth Level	Result
Authoritarian	High	Low	Kids who "obey"—but only when a parent's around to enforce the rules. Low levels of independence.
Permissive	Low	High	Kids who are happy—as long as they always get their way. Low levels of independence.
Uninvolved	Low	Low	Kids who don't have a secure relationship to their parents, and who therefore are at risk of forming inappropriate—or no—close relationships.
Authoritative	High	High	Kids who have a secure relationship to their parents, and who internalize and generalize rules of good behavior. High levels of independence.

"What parents need is *both* these qualities," Sheldon continues. An authoritative parenting style combines high levels of warmth with high levels of control. This is the combination that breeds independence, self-esteem, and competence. When we unify those two forces, kids—and parents—get the most bang for the parenting buck."

In other words, Denise needs a dose of Charles's relaxation and flexibility, while he needs a dose of her tough, no-nonsense approach. Melanie needs to learn to lay down the law a little more decisively, à la Dennis, while Dennis needs to temper his temper with some of his wife's nurturance.

The bottom line is this: If you as parents can't listen to and respect each other, it's doubtful that your kids are going to listen to and respect you, consistently. Yes, the authoritarian parent may get obedience through threats, while the permissive one may get it through cajoling and bribery, but neither of these approaches creates kids who will behave well without threat or bribe. Parents, you need to get on the same page and come up with a consistent approach to your relationship with your kids! You'll find your own relationship improves as a result.

In this chapter, we'll show you how to make the most of both parents' strengths by communicating, creating a plan, and backing each other up. In other words, we'll show you how to move beyond polarization and get on the same page.

STEP 1: Recognize You Have a Problem—and It's Not Your Spouse (or Your Kids)!

The first step toward most change is admitting that you have a problem. Fortunately, most parents are quick to admit that something's wrong. Unfortunately, too many parents feel that the problem is their partner. *If he or she would only change*, they think, *then all our problems would be solved.*

Wrong. We hate to tell you this, but the problem isn't your co-parent. And it's not you, either. The problem is that the two of you aren't communicating with each other. Instead of capitalizing on your different parenting strengths to create a solid foundation for your kids, you've stopped listening to each other. You've fallen into the trap of simply reacting to each other and compensating for what you believe are the other's shortcomings.

So sit down. Talk to each other. More important, *listen* to each other, and resist the urge to jump in while your partner talks about what he or she wants. Get both points of view on parenting on the table, and then see if you can put aside the blame long enough to acknowledge that together, you'd make a great team.

Take Caroline and John, yet another set of parents who have polarized along the "too tough–not tough enough" continuum with their kids, two-year-old Shelby and five-year-old Ryan. John, says Caroline, "is loving and caring and sweet. He's not a big nasty guy by any means, but if he has decided that the kids are going to do something, then they are going to do it—end of discussion. Me, I'm a talker. I'll sit down and discuss it."

"But when Caroline asks the kids to do something," says John, "it sounds like she's saying, *Do it—if it's okay with you. Do it, but only if you feel like it.*"

"I wish for him to be more sensitive and discuss things through," says Caroline.

"I wish for her to be stronger with the discipline," says John. "That's where we have a conflict. We want to come together—and get a little more of each other's style."

How do you come together as parents? Well, we won't pretend that what we're suggesting takes the place of intensive soul-searching or couples' therapy. But we can virtually guarantee that coming together starts with getting beyond the blame and thinking of yourselves as—and acting like—a team, a united front toward your kids. With that attitude in mind, you can take the next step: Resolve to come up with a unified *plan* that can turn your differences into strengths, and that focuses on what's best for the kids, not on who's a better parent.

STEP 2: Make a Plan—Together—and Agree to Stick to It

"You know," says Melanie, "I have my plan in my mind. Dennis has his plan in his mind. But we've never sat down and talked about those plans together."

Sound familiar? Too often, polarized parents run on different agendas—agendas that they never discuss with each other. In order to come together, those two agendas need to become one. Parents need to talk about and come up with a set plan for dealing with the kids (and each other).

So what goes into your plan? In a nutshell, it's a document that describes expectations and rules, for both kids and parents. What do you want from your children? What is acceptable behavior and what isn't? Where will you Draw the Line? What are appropriate rewards and penalties? You may also want to go over the family's schedule, both kids' and parents', and decide who's responsible for what.

If this all sounds familiar, that's because throughout this book we've been asking you to fill out this very information in the worksheet on page 18. If you've been filling out worksheets for your kids, you're ahead of the game—you've got your plan. It's time to sit down with your partner and review the information, see whether you both agree on how to proceed, and make any necessary changes. If you haven't yet gotten around to filling out this information, now's the time to start.

And when we say that we want parents to get on the same page, we mean that literally: *You need to write down your plan on paper.* That way, nothing's left to chance. Writing it down increases the likelihood that you'll both take it seriously. With a written plan in place, both parents are much more likely to act according to the rules. Of course, the plan can and will change. It's a dynamic thing, a work in progress. But by writing it down on paper, it becomes real, a more formal contract between you and your partner. You both know what's expected of you and of the kids, and neither of you can arbitrarily change the plan or the rules without consulting the other.

With an agreed-upon plan in place, both parents are more likely to act consistently. Instead of one flying off the handle while the other sits back and stews, now both parents can get involved with a moderate approach. And when both of you act consistently, your kids get the message that you mean business: The household rules will be enforced. Behavior problems and kids' flare-ups can be nipped in the bud, and kids will have a harder time playing parents off each other.

When Melanie and Dennis agreed on how to deal with Aedan and Dylan's sibling battles, for example, the parents noticed an almost immediate change in the dynamics of the household. Before their plan, Melanie intervened in the boys' fights by yelling at them, while Dennis sat back and stewed until he erupted. With a plan in place, both parents quickly put the boys in time out—either by briefly taking away their opportunities to play video games or by hauling the instigator off to his room for a few seconds—the moment a fight began. Melanie could stay calmer, and Dennis could act more quickly. As a result, the boys began to fight less, and, as Dennis put it, "the tension level in the household has been cut in half."

In the past, the boys didn't react to Melanie's discipline because they picked up on the fact that Dennis didn't take Melanie seriously or agree with her.

"They knew that I was just going to sit there and not do anything," admits Dennis. "So they just kept at it. Once I started getting up and taking them to their rooms, they realized that I meant it. We both mean it."

"The big change is that we're both reacting to them," says Melanie. "And we're both doing the same thing. I know Aedan and Dylan are feeling that. They know that they'll get the same reaction, the same time-out, whether it's me or Dennis. So they don't try to push our buttons the same way that they did before, because they know they can't get away with it."

STEP 3: Find a Time Every Day to Review the Plan and See What's Working

Just because your plan is written down, that doesn't mean it's carved in stone. As we pointed out above, your plan is dynamic. That means that it can and should change according to how well it's working. And the only way for both parents to know how well it's working, and to make changes as necessary, is to talk to each other—preferably daily.

Have a daily conversation? Some of you may do this already. Others may wonder when on earth you'll find the time to plan constantly about the kids. But we're not talking about half-hour conversations here. We're talking ninety seconds to five minutes, most days of the week, just to check in and see how things are going, chew the fat on the kids. How is the plan working? Are the rewards and penalties motivating enough? What went on at home or in school today? What's on the agenda for tomorrow? Build in a regular, scheduled time to talk to each other—*in private*—about what's going on in the house. You'll find that it saves you time in the end.

For Melanie and Dennis, that conversation takes place each day sometime after 9 PM, when the kids are in bed. The two review how the day went and what's on the schedule for tomorrow. For example, if the boys have hockey, Melanie and Dennis will go over how they'll handle the transition from home to car to rink, who's driving the boys to practice, and the rewards and penalties they'll get depending on their behavior. The parents also try to identify potential places for explosions: Getting the boys to clean up before leaving the house can sometimes be tricky, for example, so Melanie and Dennis know to be prepared to act quickly during cleanup time to nip any fights—between Aedan and Dylan, but also between parents—in the bud.

And that's a great thing about constant check-ins: They reduce the tension that can build up when things get left unsaid or problems unaddressed day after day. When you *don't* talk to your partner, you know what can happen: You get more and more annoyed as the days go by, and then, by the time a few days or a week has passed, you finally just blow up in the middle of dealing with the kids—kind of like Dennis used to do with Aedan and Dylan.

So stop going to bed angry. Get used to checking in with each other regularly. And get used to opening up your mouth and saying what you think—even if you think your co-parent ought to know it without you having to say anything. We all want to be understood intuitively by our partners. But in reality, most of us aren't that good at mind reading. The only guarantee you have that your partner knows what you want is to come right out and say it, even if that feels uncomfortable at first.

John and Caroline do their check-in by phone during the day. John makes sure that he calls Caroline, who runs a home-based day care, from the office every day just to see how the kids are doing. The check-in, says the couple, gets John up to speed on how the day went and reduces the family's "wait till your father gets home" syndrome. When he walks through the door at the end of the day, John already knows what the kids have been up to all day—and that allows him to mentally prepare for the evening ahead.

Checking in by phone has the added advantage of giving Caroline and John some privacy. They can go over the kids' behavior and discuss any changes to their plan without Ryan and Shelby listening in. If they disagree, they can work out a solution without the kids' input. Which takes us to our next point.

STEP 4: Don't Fight in Front of the Kids

We sometimes hear the argument that it's healthy for children to see their parents fight because fighting in front of the kids shows them a model of conflict resolution.

We couldn't agree less. Disputes aren't generally resolved by fighting. They're resolved by negotiation, discussion, and compromise—and sometimes by people simply agreeing to disagree. Regardless of whether or not the "conflict resolution" theory holds water (and we don't think it does), what is true is that most of the time parents *don't* resolve their conflicts in front of the kids—the kids just see the dispute. And the message kids get is that fighting is the way to approach or solve problems.

Those moments when your kids are acting up and you're trying to figure out how to deal with them aren't the times you need to worry about teaching them conflict resolution skills. Children will have plenty of time to learn about conflict resolution, but in the heat of the moment your first priority should be presenting a consistent, united parental front—the rules are the rules, whether you're with Mom or Dad—and nipping the behavioral problem in the bud.

Agreeing to Disagree

There's a big difference between fighting in front of the kids and disagreeing with your partner. It's perfectly acceptable to say to your children, "I really liked that movie, but Daddy didn't," or to let them know that you have different political leanings, tastes, and preferences. Kids who see that people under the same roof can have different opinions and still get along learn the truly important skills of acceptance, tolerance, and compromise. In this world, *those* are the skills our kids need to see modeled, not fighting.

That's where having a plan is so crucial. With a strategy already in place, parents know in advance how they're going to react to kids' behavioral flare-ups. The potential for fighting is reduced at the outset.

Finish What You Start

Sometimes, however, even the best-laid plans go awry, and one or both parents are left to wing it in the face of a kid's latest misdemeanor. If that's the case, remember this simple bit of advice: Don't undermine each other. If one parent takes charge of a situation, that parent should be able to resolve the situation without being contradicted, belittled, or otherwise undermined by the other parent.

So, for example, when Denise is in the midst of a battle with four-year-old Keisha, that means Charles may need to swallow some of his misgivings about his wife's approach and back her up. Instead of telling Denise—in front of their daughter—"Relax, it's not such a big deal," Charles needs to support his wife and let Keisha know that she's got to listen to her mom. Later on, he and Denise can discuss his misgivings about her approach and plan for the future. (And by the way, part of that plan might just include Charles taking a bit more initiative in responding to the girls, so that Denise doesn't feel that she has to intervene all the time. For her part, Denise may need to find some places to lighten up and let the kids have a bit more freedom and leeway.)

If you feel a fight brewing, if you're not sure how to proceed, or if you absolutely disagree with how your partner's handling something, go to Step 5: Take a time-out.

STEP 5: Take a Parental Time-Out

What if the kids throw you for a loop and you're not sure how to react? Instead of fighting with each other or negotiating about the kids in front of the kids, take a quick *parental* time-out—away from the kids—and have a brief discussion with your partner about how to proceed. You may want to duck into the kitchen or the bedroom for a moment to strategize. John and Caroline have even been known to lock themselves into the bathroom while they come to a quick agreement on what to do next. As Caroline says:

"If John and I don't agree on something that's happening in the house, and Ryan's sitting there watching us, we've learned to leave the room and go and hide in the bathroom and figure out what the answer is. Even if the issue's as small as whether he can have one little candy, yes or no, we're in the bathroom—because we're not going to fight in front of him and he's not going to have anything to

---

Tip: Develop a Signal

If you need a parental time-out, develop a signal or code word or phrase that tells your partner, *Let's get out of here and talk for a minute,* or *Back me up on this one.* You might say something like, "Can you help me out in the kitchen for a moment, dear?" or point to yourself, as if to say, *I'll handle this situation.*

When you get the impulse to talk in front of the kids about their behavior, don't! Use your signal and take time out, or wait and back each other up in the meantime.

---

do with the conversation. And that's really opened it up for us. Instead of John talking to Ryan, and me talking to Ryan, and the three of us trying to decide, it's now just me and John. We, as the parents, are going to decide."

STEP 6: Remember to Have Some Fun!

All parents need a bit of time to themselves, just to relax and enjoy life as an adult, not as only Mommy or Daddy. Again, try to factor in some "me" time for each parent into your weekly plan. In households where one parent works outside the home and one parent stays home with the kids, this is especially important for the stay-at-home parent. Charles and Denise, for example, have built in blocks of time for Charles to play on his employee ball team, and for Denise to have an afternoon to herself once a week while Charles takes the kids out to the driving range or to the park. As well, every few days he'll watch the kids for half an hour or so while Denise walks to the library to choose some books.

As much as "me" time is important, no romantic relationship thrives if the partners can't have some fun together. So as you make your plan, include some fun time for yourselves as a couple, and some downtime for each parent. Plan a weekly date (it doesn't have to be expensive: even renting a DVD or video or going for a walk together counts), arrange child care, and find some time to spend with your partner—and to remember what attracted you to each other in the first place.

— 8 —

Parent Traps

The seven most common parenting errors—and how to avoid them.

In the years we've practiced as child psychologists, we've worked with thousands of kids and hundreds of families, helping parents and children tackle tough developmental and behavior problems. Not surprisingly, we've seen the same issues come up over and over. We've also seen parents—well-meaning, caring, involved, and concerned parents—make the same errors, time and time again. Throughout this book, we've talked about these errors in detail. Here, however, is a quick "cheat sheet" of what we think are the seven least effective parenting "strategies" out there for dealing with kids' problem behavior.

PARENT TRAP 1: "HE'S JUST NOT READY"

Underestimating your children's potential.

I try to feed her fruits and vegetables, but she just won't eat them! I guess she's just not ready to try new foods. She'll grow out of this phase eventually.

My seven-year-old son is hyperactive—we just can't expect him to sit through dinner and have a conversation with us. He eats in front of the TV. When he's older, he'll come back to the table.

My three-year-old is obviously too young to be toilet trained. He's not interested in the potty at all. I guess he'll let us know when he's ready.

One of the toughest parts of raising children is figuring out appropriate expectations. What's appropriate for a two-year-old, a six-year-old, a kid with an ADHD diagnosis? All too often in our work with families, we see parents expect and settle for much less from their children than the kids are actually capable of.

Why do we underestimate our kids' potential? Well, one reason is that parents often assume that *what* their children do is all that they *can* do—and that to expect more would be to force unrealistic standards upon their sons and daughters. So when a two-year-old refuses to use a spoon or sit on the potty, her parents assume that she *can't* do those things. Rather than face a tantrum or risk "traumatizing" their daughter with what they assume must be unreasonable demands, her parents back off. "She's not ready," they say. "She can eat with her hands for now, and we might as well stick with the diapers for a few more months. She'll tell us when she's ready."

Well, here's the thing: When was the last time you heard a two-year-old announce, "Hey, Mom! Hey, Daddy! I'm ready to be toilet trained now! And while I'm at it, I thought I'd like to sit at the table a bit longer, use some cutlery, learn how to swim, and sleep through the night in my own bed."

It does happen, but more often than not, children aren't going to push themselves when it comes to learning and practicing new, necessary developmental skills, such as trying new foods, being toilet trained, speaking clearly, sharing, or sitting at the table. But that doesn't mean they're not ready or able to do these things—or that they'll simply tell us when they are. Our job as parents is to teach kids new skills—and to hold them to increasingly skilled, mature, and sophisticated standards of behavior.

Take toilet training. One of our pet peeves is when diaper companies try to sell more diapers to older kids with the message, "Wait till they're ready." Of course, diaper companies aren't really the best judges of when kids are "ready" to be toilet trained—and neither, often, are kids. Michael has worked with hundreds of children on this very issue, and experience has taught him that a child who can tell you when he has peed or pooped (or has to), who hides behind the couch or in a corner for some privacy—or tells you to "go away"—while he's having a bowel movement, or who holds off on having a bowel movement until he's "safely" in diapers or training pants, is a child who is ready to use the potty—even if he makes it clear that he'd prefer to use diapers rather than try something new and unfamiliar.

So what's the harm in waiting? Well, the most obvious disadvantage is that we could wait a very long time—often much longer than is necessary or good for a kid. (And in some cases, we could wait forever: Imagine a child who was never pushed to share!) The longer we wait, the longer we're depriving our kids of the independence and skills they need for success. Every time a parent says to a reluctant but capable child, "I guess you might as well stay in diapers," that parent is, in effect, telling the child, *It's okay for you to act less mature than you really are*. And that's not a message we want to give our kids.

On the other hand, when we challenge our kids to try a little harder and move a little closer toward more independent, more mature behavior—in other words, when we push them toward meeting their full potential—we're giving them more opportunities to learn and have fun. A child who is toilet trained, for example, can wear more grown-up clothes, can participate in more play and educational programs, has more independence, and has a sense of pride and accomplishment that translates into other aspects of his or her life.

"We'll Do It for Her": Adjusting the Environment to Accommodate a Child's Delays or Disabilities

One of the ways that parents and families underestimate children's potential is by adjusting the environment to compensate for delays or disabilities.

Three-year-old Ariel, for example, doesn't have very many words—but boy, can this little girl scream! Whenever Ariel can't find the words to make herself understood, she expresses her frustration by howling and shrieking.

Understandably, Ariel's parents and her two older sisters find the screams unsettling—who wants to listen to a frustrated, wailing three-year-old? In an effort to keep the little girl's screams to a minimum, her family has learned to minimize her frustration by "talking for her." They try to anticipate Ariel's needs and desires before she has a chance to speak, and creatively interpret the sounds she does make. If Ariel points to the fridge, for example, her older sister will open the door and begin to list the various things inside it. "What do you want, Ariel? Do you want juice? Do you want an apple? Some chicken? An orange?" If Ariel looks at the TV, her dad will rush to turn it on, and then flip the channels until the little girl nods and smiles.

As a result of her family's efforts, Ariel doesn't have to use her words all that much. Language becomes less and less important as her family compensates for her speech delays by talking for her.

Ariel's family has fallen into a pattern of assuming that because she doesn't use words that often, she can't. And while Ariel does have a speech delay that will need work and therapy, she definitely has the ability to learn to use words to communicate. Instead of minimizing the importance of spoken language in the house, Ariel's family needs to emphasize it, working with her speech therapist to find ways to encourage the little girl to use her words, and rewarding her for speaking rather than for staying silent.

Of course, kids with special needs require special care and attention. But families should make sure to use this care and attention to optimize a child's developmental potential, not to reinforce and entrench a delay or disability.

We're not suggesting that parents raise the bar so high that their kids are doomed to fail. What we are suggesting is that parents need to catch themselves when they say their kids "aren't ready" to take the next step toward maturity: It just might be the case that the child has the ability, while *Mom or Dad* isn't quite ready to insist that their offspring live up to their potential.

And why don't parents challenge their kids? Often for the simple reason that they don't want to face the conflict that will inevitably arise when a child doesn't get his or her way—which leads to our second parenting trap.

Parent Trap 2: "I Don't Want to Fight About It"

Avoiding confrontation.

Two-and-a-half-year-old Remy has a hard time containing himself when his parents take him into the grocery store and other public places: He grabs, bolts, and throws tantrums if he can't have everything he wants. His mom, Camille, copes by avoiding taking him to stores whenever possible—thus avoiding having to deal with her son's screaming fits and what she just knows are the disapproving stares of other customers. His dad, Nolan, picks Remy up and holds him firmly, containing the little boy physically so that he *can't* act up.

The problem with both approaches, however, is that neither teaches Remy how to behave out in public. By avoiding confrontations (containing Remy in difficult situations or avoiding them altogether), Remy's parents deprive their son of the ability to learn, not to mention the opportunity to visit interesting places. And when parents avoid situations because they expect their kids to behave inappropriately, ultimately the kids lose out.

When it comes to taking their son out in public, Nolan and Camille need to embrace, rather than avoid, confrontation.

Embrace confrontation? It goes against all instinct. Let's face it: The sound of your own child screaming is probably one of the most painful things in the world. (We're not immune to this, by the way. As child psychologists, we don't bat an eye when other people's children throw temper tantrums or wail when we say no. But when our own kids let loose, it's a whole different register, and it's torture.) Who would voluntarily inflict that pain by provoking conflict with their kids?

Well, we would. Why? Because we know from lots of experience that the pain of addressing a kid's problematic behavior is a short-term discomfort that has long-term rewards. If Camille and Nolan can weather the storms of Remy's tantrums and Draw the Line around appropriate behavior out in public, they—and their son—will reap the benefits. They'll be able to take Remy to a variety of interesting, enjoyable places, and know that the whole family can learn and have fun. (For a detailed description of Drawing the Line, see chapter 2.)

What are the chances that Remy will grow out of his impulsive behavior in the store? Slim to none—unless he can learn new, more appropriate behavior to replace the grabbing, bolting, and tantrums. Kids don't miraculously grow out of problematic behaviors. In fact, the opposite tends to happen: If a child learns that throwing a tantrum in a grocery store is a good way to get what he wants from his weary, embarrassed parents, then he'll start to generalize that behavior, throwing fits in other situations in order to get what he wants. And the more entrenched that behavior becomes, the more difficult it will be to resolve.

Instead of avoiding the mall, Camille and Nolan need to teach Remy appropriate behavior out in public, and be prepared to weather the storms of his tantrums as part of the learning process. But they can do things to make the process easier, such as practicing with Remy when the store isn't busy and when they're not in a rush, planning ahead with motivating rewards and penalties, and setting up times to practice when they have the luxury of being able to leave if they get overwhelmed.

Drawing the Line—by which we mean setting up small periods of controlled conflict with kids—has another important advantage: Because parents can orchestrate the conflict on their own terms, when they're prepared for the challenge, they're less likely to get overwhelmed and lose their cool—or just give up. Which leads us to Parenting Trap 3.

Parent Trap 3: "Okay, Okay, Have It Your Way—I Give Up!"

Giving in to a kid who's more stubborn than you.

Has this ever happened at your house? Your daughter wants ice cream for breakfast. You, quite reasonably, say no. She begins to wheedle, then whine. You hold the line. She starts to cry, then scream, then settles in for a full-on tantrum. After fifteen minutes, you can't take it anymore. "Fine," you hear yourself saying as you walk to the freezer, "you can have some ice cream if you'll just stop that racket! Look, look, here it is!"

Avoiding confrontation is one parenting trap. Another, equally dangerous trap to fall into is letting yourself get into a confrontation with your child, only to give in midway through the experience. By giving in to a child's unreasonable demands, parents essentially reward their kids for inappropriate behavior. When you feed your child ice cream because she throws a tantrum, you're rewarding the tantrum—thus letting her know that her screams and wails are a surefire way to get exactly what she wants in the future. If she just screams long enough, she knows she can get what she wants. Not a lesson you particularly want to teach.

If you're going to get into a battle of wills with your children, make sure of two things: first, that the issue is worth battling about, and, second, that you are prepared to stand your ground, even if it takes all day.

Is It Worth It? Requirements Versus Requests

Parents need to differentiate between what their children *must* do and what parents would simply *like* the kids to do. Some things—no ice cream for breakfast, going to school, no biting, whatever the rules are in your house—are nonnegotiable. With other issues— wearing a plaid shirt with striped pants, watching one more video, eating carrots but not peas—you may feel comfortable with some negotiation or wiggle room.

If it's worth battling about, it's a *requirement*: "We don't have ice cream for breakfast, and that's that." On the other hand, if there's room to negotiate, then it's a *request* ("Would you like to wear your pink sweatshirt?"), and you need to allow your child some input into the discussion.

Here's a tip: If it's a requirement, don't treat it like a request. If it's time to go to school, and school is not negotiable, then don't ask, "Would you like to go to school today?" Asking a yes-or-no question implies that your child has the choice of whether or not to go—and what are you going to do if she says no? Instead, you can say, "It's time to get ready for school. Would you like to wear your blue shirt or your red shirt?"

Standing Your Ground

There's no point in getting into a battle of wills over something negotiable. If it's not negotiable, however, you'd better be prepared to win the battle. If your daughter wants ice cream for breakfast, and you've decided that she can't have it, then you must be able to show her that you mean what you say, no matter how loud she screams. Plug your ears or leave the room if you need to, but this isn't a situation in which to negotiate. (In any case, we only negotiate with reasonable children, and any child in the middle of a tantrum is not being reasonable. Wait till she calms down before suggesting that ice cream comes after she's had two bites of everything on her plate at dinner.)

It all comes down to credibility. When your kids know, from experience, that you mean what you say—tantrum or not—you'll find that confrontations don't last nearly as long. At twenty-three months, Michael's daughter Vanessa still lets out bloodcurdling screams whenever he requires her to end a favorite activity, such as turning off the TV to get ready for bed. Experience, however, has taught Vanessa that her dad is credible: He means what he says and isn't going to let the screaming get in the way of a required activity. So the screams last about five seconds before Vanessa quiets down and gets on with it. And once she's acting quietly and reasonably, Michael can talk to her about a fun activity—like reading a book—that can come after she's had her bath. (For more on credibility, see chapter 4.)

We're not particularly interested in having unnecessary power struggles with kids, which is why we want parents to think hard about the difference between requirements and requests. If it's a request, it's not worth fighting about. But if it's a requirement, well . . . make them do it—and don't cave just because you don't want to hear the yelling.

PARENT TRAP 4: "THIS TIME, I MEAN IT!"

Waiting too long and punishing too much.

"Pick up your toys, please."

"Let your sister have a turn."

"Don't touch Mommy's camera."

"Please turn off the TV and come set the table."

They're all reasonable requests, right? So why don't our kids listen to us the first time we make them? And yet all too often, it feels like they don't. So we ask again, and again, and again, and again, until—sometime around repetition number ten—we finally lose it and start to yell. "I've told you ten times to pick up your toys and you still haven't done it! No TV tonight!"

It's a classic parenting trap: We wait too long, get too worked up, and then we get too angry and punish too much.

There are several problems with this so-called parenting strategy. One is that it sends a mixed message to your kids: Sometimes (that is, the tenth time) you mean what you say, but most of the time you don't. Sometimes you act decisively (for example, turning off the television immediately until your child sets the table), but most of the time you don't, letting the situation drag on. As a result, *you lose credibility with your kids*. If they know from experience that you're not likely to follow through on your requests—or at least, not for a good long time—why should they take you seriously?

Another problem inherent in this parenting trap is that it breeds anger, resentment, and tears—and other negative emotions that seem out of all proportion to the situation. By the time your kid ignores you for the tenth time, you lose it, and impose an entire evening of punishment over a task that would have taken five minutes. The punishment is so big because you're really punishing the nine times your child ignored you before you finally lost it. Often, because the punishment seems (and is) out of proportion, kids resent it—and you: "I was going to set the table once the show was over! I hate you!" And your credibility is undermined further: Not only do your words count for little in the eyes of your kids, but you're unfair to boot. So why should they listen?

It's a vicious cycle. But it's easy to break. Think timing, less talking, and proximity. First, timing: If you ask your daughter to do something, and she doesn't listen, you have to react *immediately*, while you're still calm. How do you react? Well, often the solution is about proximity: Get closer. Walk into the room where she is, get close to her, make eye contact, and repeat the request, calmly and politely. And, finally, keep talk to a minimum: Your actions speak louder than words. By getting up, getting closer, and making eye contact, you're already sending a strong message to your daughter that you mean business. If you need to, you can take further actions, such as turning off the TV or walking a reluctant child through the motions. (And remember, if you're calm, you'll also have the presence of mind to be reasonable. So if your daughter politely suggests that she'll set the table once her television program is over, you may feel that that's an acceptable deal.)

In a nutshell: If you find yourself continually repeating requests or instructions, and getting angrier and angrier with your child in the process, *stop*. You've already let the situation get out of control. Stop talking, get close, and act. That way, you'll avoid losing your cool, which leads to Parent Trap 5.

Parent Trap 5: "You'll Pay for That!"

Using penalty as retribution instead of as information.

As the previous parent trap illustrates, when parents wait too long to react to their kids' inappropriate behavior, tempers can flare and the situation can quickly escalate. When Mom or Dad finally does react, the reaction is often out of all proportion to the kids' original transgression. In the process, the purpose of penalty—"No TV tonight!"—shifts. Instead of using penalty as a teaching opportunity, the frustrated parent now punishes out of revenge—to "get back" at a misbehaving, annoying child.

The purpose of penalty is to *teach kids how to behave,* not to hurt a child's feelings or as retribution for bratty behavior. The whole point of penalty is to guide children to more appropriate forms of behavior. That's why we advocate penalties that are swift, short, and—if necessary—relentlessly repetitive: A five-second time-out, repeated ten or fifteen times, provides ten or fifteen opportunities for a child to learn. On the other hand, an entire evening's punishment for a momentary act of inappropriate behavior is so out of proportion that it's pretty much useless as a teaching opportunity. Instead of teaching a child to respond to a parent's request, at most it's likely to teach a child that her parents are unfair and mean, and that she should feel resentful and ashamed of herself. (For more on penalties, see chapter 3.)

Let's look at a different situation. Take our friend Jonathan. At four years old, he's learning to share his parents' attention with his year-old baby brother, Ryan. Jonathan's parents, Jason and Marla, have noticed that he's acting up a lot more these days, engaging in a lot of so-called attention-getting behaviors. Sometimes it seems as though the little boy knows exactly which buttons to push to get a rise out of his parents. A classic example? One night, after being tucked into bed and while waiting for his story, Jonathan picks up the glass of water on his night table and slowly pours it onto his mattress. "Mommy," he calls to Marla, busy with Ryan in the other room, "my bed's all wet." Marla, exhausted from a day of work and the demands of parenting two young children, appears in the doorway. Seeing what Jonathan's done, she loses it. "That's it!" she yells. "You're sleeping in that bed tonight! That'll teach you!"

Now, on the one hand, Marla's reaction seems like a logical one: You made your bed, now lie in it. If a child does something inappropriate, he's got to learn to live with the logical consequences of his actions, right? Fair enough.

But what does sleeping in a cold, uncomfortable bed actually *teach* Jonathan? True, it well may teach him not to pull the same stunt again. But as he lies in his soaked sheets, unable to sleep, his mother fuming at him, he may also learn to feel pretty bad about himself. The message his mom has given him is that he deserves to spend an entire night in discomfort because of a moment of acting out. (And when Jonathan's cranky all the next day because he didn't get enough sleep, everyone will pay for it.) What's more, the more Jonathan internalizes the image of himself as a "bad kid," the more he'll act like one.

There are more appropriate, equally "logical" consequences to Jonathan's actions. Marla or Jason could take a deep breath, ask Jonathan to get out of bed, and have him help remake the bed with dry sheets. Further, the extra time it takes to deal with the bed might mean that Jonathan won't get a story that night—just a hug and a kiss good night. The penalty is still logical, but now the scale and the intent are more appropriate. Jonathan (and, hopefully, his parents) can sleep through the night, and start fresh the next day.

The next time you find yourself in a difficult parenting situation, react swiftly, get up close to your kid, and keep talk to a minimum (remember: timing, less talking, and proximity!). That'll help keep you from losing your cool and punishing out of anger and revenge. Then ask yourself, *What do I want to teach my child? And what do my actions actually teach him?*

Of course, penalty is only half of the equation. Often kids act up precisely because they're not getting enough attention or positive reinforcement for their good behavior. Which leads to our sixth parent trap.

Parent Trap 6: "But She's *Supposed* to Do That!"

Waiting too long and rewarding too little, too much, or not at all.

Rewarding a child for a specific behavior is like adding fuel to fire—as a result, the behavior increases. Rewards go hand in hand with penalties: While penalizing your child for misbehaving will show him what *not* to do, rewarding actually shows kids *what* to do. For this reason, it's incredibly important to reward, or reinforce, kids' appropriate behavior. And parents should aim to reward much more often than they penalize.

Very few parents would disagree with those last statements. The problem is that the vast majority of parents don't know how to reward effectively. Just as parents often wait too long and punish too much, they tend to wait too long and then reward too little, too much, or not at all.

Take a child, like Remy, who has trouble behaving in stores. What parents will often say is, "If you're good in the store, I'll get you a chocolate bar after we're done shopping." It sounds good in theory, but in fact, the scale is way off: A two-year-old learning how to act appropriately in the store probably can't wait a full hour for his reward. And he may not associate his chocolate bar with his behavior during the entire previous hour. What's more, this is an all-or-nothing strategy: What if Remy behaves well about half the time? Does he get half a chocolate bar? Nothing at all? The whole thing? It just gets too complicated.

A much more effective strategy would be to break down both the size of the reward and the time increments: Instead of a chocolate bar as a reward for an hour of good behavior, what about half an M&M for *every five minutes or so* of good behavior? In the end, Remy probably gets a little less chocolate, but he's rewarded ten or twelve more times—which means that his good behavior is reinforced at least tenfold (and he doesn't eat as much sugar, to boot). What's more, the scale is more appropriate to a two-year-old's worldview. Remy may have a hard time associating a chocolate bar with his behavior during the previous hour. But when his cooperative behavior is rewarded as it occurs, it's much easier for him to make the connection between the M&M's and staying close by his mom. As a result, he's much more likely to learn what it means to behave well out in public. It also means that his parents can alternate swiftly between reward and penalty—discouraging inappropriate behavior with a quick time-out one moment, and rewarding appropriate stuff with an M&M the next.

To be effective, rewards, like penalties, need to be short, swift, small—and specific. Instead of going out for dinner "because you had a good day," a parent is better off giving a child a hug or praising him for small instances of good behavior: "I really like how nicely you're playing with your brother. Great job!" "What a beautiful job you did of setting the table! Thank you for doing it when I asked."

Parents also make the mistake of rewarding too little or not at all. For the most part, it's not that they don't think they should reward their kids, but rather that rewarding is one of the hardest things for parents to learn how to do well. Why? For a number of reasons:

- **It's easier to spot "bad" behavior than it is to notice the "good" stuff:** While inappropriate behavior is often very noticeable, appropriate behavior often slips under our radar.
- **Who has time—or energy?** Slipping a child half an M&M every five minutes is a lot more work than buying him a chocolate bar at the checkout counter. Similarly, getting up out of your chair and crossing the room to praise a quiet child at ten-minute intervals can be a pain.
- **But she's playing quietly: I don't want to interrupt her!** This is a classic. Parents can under-reward because they don't want to rock the boat. If a "difficult" child is finally playing by herself or is quiet, why on earth should we disturb her? In fact, however, noticing and rewarding your child for playing quietly is likely to *prolong* her quiet play in the longer term.
- **Why should I reward my kid for sleeping at night, eating his vegetables, or playing nicely? Isn't he *supposed* to do that?**

Yes, he's supposed to do that. Unfortunately, without positive reinforcement or reward, he often *won't know* he's supposed to do that—just as, without penalty, he won't know what he shouldn't do.

- **It's really hard to praise her when she's been getting on my nerves all day.** Even when parents do notice good behavior, many can't help but hold grudges against their child's recent bad behavior. This is especially true in situations where a kid's been acting up all day. In these cases, parents understandably resent their kids, and may not feel like praising their small acts of cooperation. Hard as it sometimes is, though, we've got to put aside grudges, switch gears, and let kids know when they're doing okay.

In sum, rewarding is one of the most valuable tools in your parenting toolbox. Even though it can sometimes be difficult to reward your kids, it's always worth the extra effort.

Parent Trap 7: "Who's in Charge Here?"

Taking control away from kids.

Ask any parent for a wish list of personality traits they'd like to see in their children, and you'll hear some strikingly similar answers. Among other things, parents want their children to be creative, independent beings who can think and do for themselves, who have high levels of self-esteem, and who can meet, overcome—and enjoy!—challenges.

Often, however, parents feel torn between these desires for their kids and their wishes for appropriate behavior. They want their kids to act appropriately, but they don't want to squelch their children's personality. When we make seemingly outlandish suggestions—such as asking parents to embrace conflict or insist upon appropriate behavior—parents often assume that we're interested in controlling kids, in or creating compliant little robots who simply do what they're told.

Nothing could be farther from the truth. As developmental psychologists, we're not interested in controlling children's behavior or thinking for them. Rather, we're interested in teaching children *how to control themselves*. When kids are able to control themselves and the situations around them, a world of possibility and opportunity opens up to them.

Think of any creative person, from a kindergartner drawing at a table to a famous musician, and you'll find someone with a more or less well developed sense of self-direction and self-control. These are learned skills, and they begin—if we're lucky—in early childhood. From self-organization ("Where do you put things? Where do you sit? How do you behave?"), kids become progressively more self-aware ("Oh, my stuff goes over there, and here's how I'm expected to behave at school, in the car, at the playground, during dinner"). Out of self-awareness comes self-reliance ("I know how! Don't worry, Mom, I can do that myself!"), and with self-reliance come a sense of accomplishment and self-esteem ("I did it. I can do it!"). Kids whose self-esteem is based in a real sense of accomplishment are well prepared to meet life's challenges head-on.

Too often, though, parents make the mistake of taking control away from their kids. One more time, take a look at Remy in the grocery store. When the little boy bolts, his dad, Nolan, has gotten into the habit of just picking him up and holding him tight so that he can't run away or flop to the ground in a fit of tears. Imprisoned in his father's arms, however, Remy has very little control over the situation. He's not learning how to control himself in public. Instead, Nolan's taken all control—a strategy that will work only as long as Remy's small enough to be tucked under one arm.

To teach their son more about self-control, Remy's parents decide on a new approach: those constant, consistent rewards and penalties. As long as Remy walks quietly beside her, Camille, his mom, praises him and gives him little treats at regular intervals. At the first sign of bolting or a tantrum, she sends him to time out by pulling him back to her or sitting him down gently but firmly on the floor and telling him, "Stay by me. Do you want to keep going? Yes? Then you have to stay by me." When Remy's ready to move again, off they go.

Every time Camille takes her son to the store, she's providing him with an opportunity to learn self-control. In essence, she's telling him, "You're in charge, buddy. You decide how this will play out. If you walk nicely beside me, you'll get treats, and we'll have time and energy to go to the park afterward. If you want to bolt and scream and throw tantrums, it's time out." Because Camille's utterly consistent and predictable, Remy figures out—fairly quickly—how to control the situation to get what he wants: bits of chocolate, a trip to the park, and, most important, his mom's praise. Now he's on the way to becoming a self-aware, self-reliant kid with a healthy sense of self-esteem.

In the short term, it's often easier to prevent a child from misbehaving than it is to teach him how to behave appropriately. But when parents take control away from kids, they also take away the opportunity for kids to learn how to control themselves.

— 9 —

Parent Triumphs

Ten not-so-secret tips for creating cooperative—and happy!—kids.

If parents are capable of making mistakes when it comes to managing children's behavior, they're also more than capable of developing effective parenting strategies. In this chapter, we sum up the most important rules of the parenting road.

PARENT TRIUMPH 1: "GO AHEAD, MANIPULATE ME!"

Let your kids' behavior dictate your response.

We laugh when we hear well-meaning parents say, "I don't want my child to manipulate me."

Why do we laugh? Because our kids manipulate us all the time, whether or not we recognize it. What's important isn't *whether* the kids manipulate us. What's crucial is *how* they do it.

As both parents and child psychologists, we want kids to manipulate us. But here's the catch: We want them to learn to manipulate us with their *good* behavior. In other words, we want kids to learn that they can wrap us around their little fingers—with polite, cooperative, empathetic, cheerful, and other pro-social behaviors.

Take Violet. She's two and a half years old and has a stubborn streak. As her dad, Andrew, puts it, "Violet's been two since she was one and a half." Like a lot of so-called terrible twos, Violet wants her own way in pretty much all situations. When things don't work out precisely according to her specifications, she drops to the floor and screams. And when Violet screams, Andrew and his wife, Nima, come running—and pour on the attention in an effort to get her to stop.

"What's wrong, sweetie?" they ask. "Come on, Violet, it's okay. Why all the fuss? Look, your bunny's right here. Or what about the blue frog? Do you want to sit on Daddy's lap? Come on, baby, use your words, use your words." And so on.

Violet's no fool. She knows that the best way to get her parents to pay lots and lots of attention to her—to trip over backward to please her—is to sit down and scream. How does she know this? Through experience. Whenever she screams, Andrew and Nima fall all over themselves to make her stop. So of course she does it.

Manipulative? You bet. But what if Violet learned that an opposite set of strategies could get her the attention she craves? What if Nima and Andrew decided to ignore the screams and respond to Violet only when she quieted down, used her words, and generally behaved in a more mature, appropriate fashion?

In fact, that's exactly what Violet's exasperated parents finally decided to do. They reversed their reactions to their daughter's screams: The louder and more intractable Violet got, the farther away and less responsive her parents got. The quieter and more cooperative Violet became, the more attention they gave her.

"It's like Violet's got a fishing line, and she's hooked you," explains Michael to Andrew and Nima. "Her appropriate behavior reels you in. The difficult behavior? It drives you out to sea. You're gone. She controls the situation with her actions."

It took a few weeks to erase old habits and learn new ones, but it worked. As Violet began to realize that her inappropriate behavior pushed her parents' attention away rather than pulling it in, the "sit-down-and-scream" tactics began to fade away. In their place,

Violet started using new tactics, such as talking and cooperating, to get the attention she craved.

Manipulation? You bet. But it's a positive kind of manipulation: In the long run, it shows kids that appropriate behavior yields them power, authority, influence, and pleasurable experiences. It's teaching Violet to get what she needs using socially acceptable tactics.

Kids have the skills to manipulate their parents and other adults with inappropriate behavior—which means they have the skills to learn how to manipulate with good behavior, too. So don't worry about *whether* your kids are manipulating you, because they are. Worry about *how* you let them manipulate you. Instead of trying to control your kids' behavior, let their behavior control—or manipulate—you. Their appropriate behavior should draw you closer and attract your attention and praise, while the whining, fighting, rudeness, stubbornness, noncompliance, tantrums, and other negative behavior pushes you farther away and invites penalties.

In short, let your actions tell your kids, *Go ahead, manipulate me— with your fantastic behavior!*

Parent Triumph 2: "Yes, No, Maybe So"

Respond to your kids—even when you're ignoring them.

One of the most important things parents can do is to respond to their children. Responding starts when the kids are tiny babies. When they coo and gurgle, we coo and gurgle back at them. And when they cry, we come running—even if we have to come running in the middle of the night. When a baby cries, he's in some kind of distress, and crying is his only way of communicating that. Our job as parents is to respond to that communication. In so doing, we let our very young children know that their needs will be met, and that the world is a safe, secure place for them to explore.

Responding continues past infancy into childhood. Little kids have a repertoire of communication skills beyond gurgling and crying.

They can talk (or scream), hug (or hit), smile (or cry), cooperate (or let you know they're not interested in your agenda by flat-out refusing to do anything you ask).

Of course, it's easy to respond when your child communicates in socially acceptable ways. If she says, "Mommy, can I please have a cookie?" the answer is right there: some version of "Yes, you may," or "Yes, but not until after dinner," or "No, sweetie, you can't. You already had two cookies, and that's enough." If she says, "I love you, Daddy," the appropriate response is, "I love you, too—more than the highest mountain in the whole world!"

But what if your child demands your attention by acting inappropriately—say, by throwing a tantrum, interrupting, whining, grabbing, or defying you? Well, you still must respond, whether or not you agree with your kid's communication strategies. Kids are no different from anyone else: They scream to be heard. If they're yelling or whining, it's because we aren't listening and responding—or because, over time, they've discovered that the best and fastest way to get us to respond is by using these annoying tactics.

Even when you've actively decided to ignore a certain behavior as a form of penalty—like Violet's parents, above, who decided to ignore their daughter's screaming and just walk away—you still need to respond to your child. When Nima and Andrew started to penalize the screaming, they told their daughter at the outset, "You're screaming, Violet. Use your words and we'll listen. If you scream, we're not going to talk to you until your use your nice words." Only then did they turn their backs and leave Violet to scream by herself.

When your child asks for your attention, give it to him. When he calls for you, respond. That doesn't mean dropping whatever you're doing to kowtow to your kids. And it doesn't mean always saying yes. It means always acknowledging their bids for attention—even if the response is "No," or "Not now," or "I'm talking to Grandma right now, so I can't talk to you. I'll talk to you in about five minutes."

Parent Triumph 3: Think Small

Scale down your responses to the kids.

If we had to sum up our strategies for Drawing the Line, or dealing with kids' inappropriate behavior, in one word, that word would be *minimal*: small requirements, small units of time, small rewards, small penalties, short distances, few words, low voice, and so on. In short (pun intended), think small.

- **Small requirements:** When Michael Drew the Line with four-year-old Aedan over manners, he simply set up a situation (painting) that Aedan found irresistible. Then Michael kept the requirements minimal: If Aedan wanted to paint, all he had to do was say "please." That was it. No big deal. Similarly, when Michael Drew the Line with the Kleins, a family of finicky eaters, he again kept the requirements simple: He didn't dictate that each child had to clean his or her plate to get dessert. All he stipulated was that each kid needed to take two bites of each food.
- **Small units of time:** When Corinne set out to show her three boys how to behave well in the car, she wanted to reward them for their appropriate behavior. At the outset, she kept those requirements for quiet, peaceful, cooperative behavior quite small: For every five minutes of peace (and yes, she timed those minutes by the car's clock), Corinne rewarded the boys.
- **Small rewards:** Corinne rewarded her sons with chocolate. She didn't hand out entire chocolate bars every five minutes. She didn't hand out individual chocolate kisses. She didn't even give each boy a single M&M. In fact, Corinne gave each child *one-quarter of an M&M*.
- **Small penalties:** Amanda and Ashleigh are two- and three-year-old sisters who can throw *Titanic*-size tantrums. Despite their outsize behavior, when Michael Drew the Line with them, the penalties were minimal. The moment either girl began to

shriek, wail, or scream, he put her in her high chair for a quick time-out—often no more than ten or fifteen seconds. (Similarly, the very moment either girl quieted, Michael was quick to reward her with praise and by taking her out of the high chair and back to play.)

- **Short distances:** You can't Draw the Line from the other room. If your child isn't listening to you, get up, get close, and act. For example, when five-year-old Kevin ignores Lori, his mom's, requests, Lori needs to shorten the distance between her and Kevin. Instead of yelling from the top of the stairs, Lori needs to go to her son in the basement, get down to his level, look him in the eye, and repeat her request. If he still doesn't comply, she needs to walk him through the action.
- **Few words and low voice:** In the heat of the moment (as you'll read below), act, don't yak! Don't talk to (or at) your kids when they're acting up. Instead, keep your words to a minimum—for example, "No biting"—as you take your kid to time out. As well, keep your voice flat and low: If you're close to your kid (short distances), you won't need to shout. And if you respond immediately (short units of time), you won't find yourself getting angry and yelling.

PARENT TRIUMPH 4: NIP IT IN THE BUD

React immediately to kids' inappropriate behaviors.

Let's face it: As parents, we all get tired. And when we're tired, we're often tempted to just sit on the couch and hope that, kid-wise, whatever storm is brewing will just pass.

You know what we mean. For example, your older son is starting to antagonize his younger sister, maybe just by getting into her space a little—poking her, or imitating her. She's starting to complain, just a little—"Don't!" she tells her brother in that telltale whiny tone.

Maybe this won't go anywhere, you think. *Maybe, if I just ignore it, it'll pass.*

Yeah, sure it will.

Despite parents' wishful thinking, it's a rare behavioral storm that actually passes if ignored. What's much more likely to happen is that the situation will *escalate.* Once he's gotten a rise out of his sister, your son will likely keep going in his bid to pester her. And once she starts whining about it, she'll likely keep whining about it, until, eventually, she's crying and screaming about it. Think of Newton's first law of motion: An object at rest will stay at rest, while an object in motion will stay in motion—unless an opposing force intervenes.

As parents, we are that opposing force. And the quicker we act to squelch kids' inappropriate behavior, the greater the likelihood that we'll be able to avert, or at least minimize, that behavior.

We're forever telling parents to "nip it in the bud." When you're Drawing the Line, at the *first sign* of inappropriate behavior, intervene! Haul yourself up off the couch, get close to your son, physically move him a couple of feet away from your daughter, and tell him, "Why did I move you? Because you were bothering your sister. Don't bother her. If you want to play with her, ask her nicely." To your daughter, you can say, "If your brother is bothering you, you can tell him to please stop—but you don't need to whine." Keep intervening, if you have to, each time the kids act up.

When you're dealing with kids' inappropriate behavior, timing is everything. By nipping the behavior in the bud, you prevent the situation from escalating, and save yourself—and the kids—a lot of aggravation. And when you intervene quickly, you won't have to intervene as forcefully: It's much easier to give your kids a quick, stern time-out than it is to tear them apart when they're fighting like wildcats.

So the next time you're tempted to see if "it'll pass," resist the temptation. Get up, get close to your kids, and nip the situation in the bud. You'll thank yourself later.

Parent Triumph 5: In the Heat of the Moment, Act, Don't Yak!

When it comes to dealing with problematic behavior, actions speak louder than words. Don't yell or talk—get up and deal with it.

So you've resolved to nip inappropriate behavior in the bud and react immediately when kids act up. That's great.

Unfortunately, for too many parents, reacting takes the form of talking. In our efforts to get the kids to stop acting up and behave appropriately, many of us parents try to "use our words" when action would be much more effective. We yell and shout. We cajole and coax. We count to three. We explain, ad nauseam, why certain behavior is unacceptable. We wheedle and negotiate, reason and pontificate.

Forgive us for being crude, but what we need to do is *shut up, get up, and act.* Whether the boys are fighting, your two-year-old daughter is throwing a monster tantrum, or your five-year-old son won't pick up his toys and come to dinner, you need to stop talking and show the kids you mean business. Get up and separate the boys, and take each to his room for a brief time-out. Go to your son and walk him through the act of putting away the toys. Then march him to the dinner table if he won't come himself. Ignore the tantrum by walking away. If it persists, put your daughter in her room (or in her high chair) for a few moments until the histrionics subside.

To the extent that you use words in these encounters, keep them to a minimum: "No fighting." "Where does this piece go? It goes here. And this piece? It goes here. And this piece goes here." "No screaming."

Why shouldn't you talk? First, because talking to kids, even yelling at them, is a form of paying attention. And when we pay attention to negative behavior, we reinforce it, even when we don't mean to. Second, kids who are actively fighting, defying you, screaming, or otherwise engaging in inappropriate behavior aren't in the right frame of mind to listen to you. They're not being reasonable, so reasoning with them will get you nowhere. And, frankly, in that state, they don't care what you have to say.

When the fighting, defiance, and hysterics have subsided—and only then—use your words. Which leads to our next parent triumph.

Parent Triumph 6: And When You Do Yak . . .

. . . be specific, informative, and brief.

Five-year-old Ryan can be a bit of a bully. At school or at day care, he's always making a pest of himself by grabbing toys other kids are playing with, or inserting himself into their play by shoving, pinching, hitting, or biting. Ryan hasn't learned more appropriate social skills for getting kids to play with him. And unless he does, he's going to wind up with some heavy-duty social problems once he hits elementary and high school. Ryan's parents, Caroline and John, recognize that they've got to stop the bullying behaviors and teach their son more socially appropriate alternatives.

Caroline and John Draw the Line around Ryan's bullying behavior by sending him to a brief time-out whenever he gets aggressive. The *moment* Caroline or John notices Ryan's hands straying where they shouldn't be, or that he's otherwise bullying his peers or his sister, they pounce. "Not appropriate, Ryan," Caroline will say, as she takes his arm and leads him upstairs to his room. "Come down when you're ready to play nice and keep your hands to yourself."

Only *after* Ryan comes out of his room (and, generally, it takes him less than a minute to regroup) does Caroline or John talk to him.

"Why did I send you to time out?" they'll ask. If Ryan answers, great. If not, they answer for him: "I sent you to time out because you were pushing Colin. That's bullying, and that's not allowed. Would you like it if Colin pushed you? No. So don't push him. Are you ready to go outside? Great—go tell Colin you're sorry you pushed him, and keep your hands to yourself."

When it comes to discussing his behavior, Caroline and John keep their conversations with their son specific, informative, and brief:

- **Specific:** Caroline and John don't say, "I sent you to time out because you were being bad," or "I sent you to time out because I didn't like your behavior." They tell Ryan exactly what he did—pushing Colin—to get busted, and they tell him what he needs to do—keep his hands to himself—to stay out of time out. When you talk to your kids, try to be as specific as possible. Instead of vague statements such as, "I don't like the way you treat your brother," or "I really wish you wouldn't do that," say, "No hitting your brother," or "Please do not interrupt me when I'm on the telephone." *You* may know what you mean, but your child may not get it.
- **Informative:** Kids deserve to know why they're being penalized (and rewarded). When Caroline and John explain how other kids feel when he takes away their toys or threatens them, they help Ryan understand and internalize appropriate conduct.
- **Brief:** An explanation doesn't have to take more than a few sentences. "Colin doesn't like it when you hit him, and you wouldn't like it if he hit you. If you guys want to have fun with each other, you can't hit. Use your words instead." That just about covers it.

We love talking to kids, and we can have conversations with them that last for hours. But long conversations aren't appropriate in the heat of the moment. When the kids are misbehaving, act first, and talk later—and then keep your conversations short, specific, and informative.

PARENT TRIUMPH 7: GET A LITTLE CLOSER

Get down to kid level—and while you're there,
hug, kiss, and play with your kids.

Four-year-old Aedan and seven-year-old Dylan fight. A lot. Whenever they're left to their own devices, it's a fairly sure bet that these brothers will end up battling it out. Their parents, Melanie and Dennis, have to wade into the fray in order to break it up.

Melanie and Dennis want to Draw the Line around Aedan and Dylan's fights. But it's not enough to simply penalize the boys with a time-out whenever they start to bicker. Melanie and Dennis also need to teach their sons how to play together—to share, take turns, and resolve disputes. To do that, the parents need to get down on the playroom floor with the kids, join in the action, and model the skills of cooperative play for their sons. (And if the boys do begin to fight, their parents' close proximity means that Mom and Dad can nip any conflicts in the bud.)

But we don't advocate getting close to your kids only in the service of Drawing the Line. It's important to get close and join in on your kids' play simply because it's good for you and the kids! Their parents' physical closeness is extremely rewarding to Aedan and Dylan, who relish the time they get to spend with Mom and Dad. Melanie and Dennis, in turn, get to actually enjoy their sons, as opposed to managing their fights from far away.

As often as possible, join in when your kids are playing—even if it's only for a few minutes here and there. Get on the floor with them, get messy with them, wrestle, play chase, paint, bake a cake—whatever makes them giggle. And while you're in close proximity, remember to hug and kiss them lots. Kids whose parents demonstrate their love and affection—and who also demand high standards of behavior—are at an advantage when it comes to social and academic success later in life.

Parent Triumph 8: Pick Your Battles Carefully . . .

Don't try to tackle every problem behavior at once—
you'll only make yourself (and your kid) crazy,
and make your kid feel like a failure.

So you've got this new book with all these snazzy worksheets, and you've filled them in—and now you have a big list of all those problematic behaviors that drive you crazy about your kid. You've read about Drawing the Line, about rewards, ignoring, and penalties, and about timing, talking, and proximity, and it all makes perfect sense. You know just what to do in each situation with your child. And you're raring to go, to nip each and every problematic behavior in the bud and establish a new world order with your kids.

Yes, we're being sarcastic. But we want to drive home an important point: Prioritize! Draw the Line around only one behavior at a time. Don't attempt to cure your kids of all their behavioral problems at once. You'll drive yourself—and your offspring—crazy. And you'll risk making the kids feel picked on and as though they can't do anything right or have a moment's peace.

Narrow your focus. Zero in on just one or two target behaviors, or one specific time of day. For example, you might focus on getting your child to hang up her coat in the back hall instead of throwing it on the floor. For the time being, commit only to that one issue. You can address other areas later.

Too often, parents want to cure in fifteen minutes a behavioral problem that took months or years to establish. It's not going to happen, so do everyone a favor and slow down. Expect change—expect even profound change—but don't expect everything to change overnight. We promise: If you Draw the Line consistently (and realistically), you'll see real, lasting results with your kids, but it'll take a bit of time. And once you've tackled the first issue on your list, you'll find that tackling the second, third, and fourth items gets progressively easier.

Parent Triumph 9: . . . and Be Prepared to Win Those Battles

Be vigilant, consistent, persistent, and predictable. Even if it means playing out a situation 101 times, prove to your kids that you're sticking to your guns on the new world order.

Once you've picked your target behavior, and once you've decided to Draw the Line around it, commit! For example, if you've decided that your daughter must hang up her coat in the back hall, then *every time you hear that coat hit the floor,* you have to commit to ensuring that she hangs it up. In short, be vigilant, consistent, persistent, and predictable.

Be Vigilant

Watch for the behavior you're targeting (dropping the coat on the floor), and penalize it (for example, by making your daughter hang up her coat, and walking her through the action if necessary).

Be equally vigilant when it comes to catching your child's appropriate behavior. At first, every time she hangs up her coat, reward her. Thank her, praise her, tell her you appreciate it. Often we're so caught up in looking for the negative that we fail to recognize or acknowledge the positive stuff. See if you can reverse this cycle: Look for and pay attention to your child's cooperative behavior, and try not to let the negative stuff command too much of your attention. We like to tell parents to try to reward ten times more than they punish.

Be Consistent and Predictable

When it comes to penalties, consistency is key. *Every time* your daughter drops her coat on the floor, react in the same way—you might say, "Please hang up your coat." If she doesn't, get up, get close to her, and walk her through the actions.

Inconsistency is your archenemy when it comes to Drawing the Line. When you're inconsistent, you send the message that the rules change from day to day, depending on your mood or the weather. If you sometimes respond when your daughter drops her coat on the floor, but sometimes you let the issue go, then she has no reason to hang up her coat. *Sometimes Mom or Dad lets me get away with this,* she'll think. *I wonder if I can get away with it this time.*

By responding the same way, every time, you become predictable: Your children should be able to anticipate your response. *If I drop my jacket on the floor, Mom's just going to make me come back and hang it up,* your daughter will eventually think. *I might as well hang it up the first time.*

While you want to respond with absolute consistency each time your child crosses the line (and drops her coat on the floor), you have more wiggle room when it comes to rewards. At the outset, when your daughter does hang up her coat, reward her by letting her know that you appreciate how helpful she's being. But kids should do things like hang up their coats simply because it's required behavior, not because they get rewarded for it. Over time, therefore, thin the rewards—thank your daughter only every third or fourth time she hangs up her coat, and eventually not at all.

Be Persistent

Once you've decided to Draw the Line on a certain behavior, commit—full force! When it comes to that behavior, never get into a battle with your kids that you're not prepared to win. Your daughter *will* hang up her coat, even if you have to walk her through the actions a dozen times, or more. If it takes three weeks, so be it. In the new world order, coats get hung up, not dropped on the floor—period.

When it comes to Drawing the Line, we want kids to see that we'll no longer tolerate a problem behavior, and that we'll persist as long as necessary to make it go away. Why do we need to be so determined? Well, if you don't kill it, you make it stronger: If you lose in your battle of wills with your child, you actually reinforce the bad habit. You send the message that if she just holds out that little bit longer than you, she can drop her coat on the floor any old time she wants.

PARENT TRIUMPH 10: LET KIDS BE KIDS!

And go have some fun with them while you're at it!

We'll leave you with one parting thought about Drawing the Line: Let kids be kids.

Kids aren't little adults. They're people with their own likes, dislikes, capabilities, temperament, priorities, and personalities. For the most part, they don't care about the same things that you care about: They don't wonder whether they should switch mortgages, worry that the house needs a new roof, or sigh at those extra five pounds that arrived on your hips over the holidays. They tend to prefer chicken nuggets over filet mignon, fart jokes over Woody Allen films, and playing in the park as opposed to a really great Pilates class. They *will* ask for candy when they see the candy store, for toys at the toy store, and to play when you drive past the park. Generally, they don't want to wait in line at the bank with you or sit quietly while you have a long, boring conversation with your great-aunt—and no behavior management technique in the book will make them want to, any more than it will make you find fart jokes funny or want to play Captain Underpants for six hours straight.

Sometimes we encounter a parent who sees problem behaviors where we see kids just being kids. Take Denise and her daughter Keisha. Keisha's got a big personality and a lot of energy. She's funny, smart, loud, and creative. And she's got a mind of her own. Of course, Denise wants Keisha to respect her and behave appropriately. But Denise's idea of appropriate behavior—that Keisha should be quiet, demure, and utterly cooperative, even when she's bored—doesn't leave a lot of room for Keisha's big personality or for her to blow off steam and just be a kid. Not surprisingly, Denise and Keisha are in conflict a lot of the time, as Denise picks on and tries to micromanage every aspect of her daughter's behavior, telling her what to do and how to do it.

Denise needs to lighten up, to make room for her daughter's high-energy personality and for the fact that Keisha's four years old, not forty-four. For Denise, that means stopping and taking a deep breath before she intervenes in Keisha's behavior and asking herself some questions:

- **Is the behavior unsafe?** If Keisha's playing with matches or playing barefoot in a woodlot full of rusty nails, by all means Denise should redirect her play. But if Keisha's running and jumping and doing cartwheels in the backyard, or hanging off the monkey bars in the park while yelling like a banshee, she's fine. Kids will always risk falling and hurting themselves, but that doesn't mean that parents should shield them from all risks.
- **Does it harm anyone?** Kids shouldn't hit, bite, scratch, or otherwise harm themselves, other kids, adults, or property— particularly other people's stuff. Beyond that, maybe parents need to butt out.
- **Is it disrespectful?** Kids shouldn't be allowed to be rude or mean to adults or to their peers, and parents and caregivers should intervene when they are. But don't confuse a child's having her own agenda with disrespect. Kids should be allowed to have, and to voice, their opinions, likes, and dislikes. If those opinions, likes, and dislikes differ from parents', that's fine, as long as both kids and parents make room for each other and learn to compromise as necessary.
- **If I don't intervene, will she suffer in the long run?** This one's tricky. Denise sees her micromanagement techniques as essential for Keisha's future well-being. But we see a mom who risks harming her child by squelching her personality and making every decision for her. Yes, kids need to learn to share and

compromise, to take care of their bodies, to use respectful language, to delay gratification, to eat healthy foods and sleep at night. But they also need to make their own decisions and mistakes.

- **Is it really a problem, or does it just bug me?** Be honest: Sometimes we want our kids to want what we want. We want them to wear the red shirt with the blue pants, to like green beans, to choose to sit and draw quietly. They want to wear the plaid shirt with the striped pants, dislike green beans, and run around playing Captain Underpants. So be it.

Keep the rules simple and minimal: Stay safe, don't hurt other people, help adults when they ask, and try to treat other people like you'd want to be treated. And then butt out. We're here to tell parents to lighten up and leave room for kids to be themselves—their loud, obnoxious, silly, outrageous, and sometimes "immature" selves. Give children structure and feedback, but let them take the lead. Let them do it the way they want to do it. Let them make what you think are mistakes and learn their own lessons. Let them have the freedom to explore the world unchecked by a thousand petty rules. The more you let kids make their own decisions (including good ones and not-so-good ones), the more they'll be able to think for themselves. And the more fun they have, the happier they'll be.

Parting Thoughts from
Dr. Michael Weiss

At the time of this writing, I have a two-and-half-year-old daughter, with another baby on the way. When people come over to my house, and they hear my toddler screaming, they often look surprised. Some people even look a bit smug. "But I thought you were the *expert* on child rearing," they'll say, one eyebrow raised.

"I may be an expert," I answer, "but I'm not a magician."

My daughter, like all two-year-olds, wants all kinds of things—more candy, more cartoons, all the toys at the toy store, her parents' absolute and undivided attention 24/7—that she can't have. We want her to do things—go to bed, eat vegetables, use the potty, use her words, wait three minutes—that she doesn't want to do. And when Vanessa doesn't get what she wants, or doesn't want to do what we want her to do, she screams.

Kids scream because they're frustrated because they can't have what they want, when they want it. My daughter—the daughter of a so-called expert—is no different.

Perhaps the difference is that I don't care if she screams. It doesn't bug me. Why? For two reasons.

First, because I know that, as a parent, it's my responsibility to ensure that Vanessa doesn't live on a steady diet of candy and cartoons while remaining in diapers until the age of five. When my wife and I set limits and insist that our daughter live up to age-appropriate standards of behavior, we're paving the way for her to become a successful adult. Vanessa's learning self-regulation and self-control, crucial skills for her future. (If we have anything to do with it, she *won't* be one of those kids who can't wait fifteen minutes for two marshmallows.)

Second, Vanessa's screams don't bug me because they last a nanosecond. When she doesn't get what she wants, she lets out half a howl, looks at me and at her mother, and realizes that we're sticking to our guns. And then it's over. We've been as consistent as we can be with her around our limits and our expectations, and, as a result, her protests—mostly—tend to be microscopic. Mid-scream, she realizes that she's not going to get what she wants, and then, with our encouragement, she stops and goes on to the next thing.

You'll notice in the above paragraph I said that my wife and I have been as consistent *as we can be* with our daughter. But we're human. We're fallible. And like all parents, we're tired and overworked. There have been plenty of times when we've said one thing and done another, and there will be plenty more. Vanessa's ended up in our bed more times than we can count because we were just too bloody tired to do anything else. We've aborted toilet-training missions. We've let her eat food that wasn't healthy for her. We've been convinced of one more story, one more cartoon, one more cookie, more times than we've cared to admit. And we've both walked out of the room in anger and frustration, ready to scream ourselves at the trials of child rearing.

So, I'm an expert. My colleague and dear friend and fellow parent Dr. Sheldon Wagner is also an expert. Over a combined total of sixty years in the field of children's developmental psychology, we've worked with thousands of kids and some of the foremost experts in the field. We think we can say that our approach and perspectives are often unique, and we hope that this book has adequately described many of our techniques. We've worked with hundreds of schools, hospitals, and families. We've helped a lot of parents and teachers overcome some very persistent problems with their kids—including many, many kids with significant developmental delays and behavior problems. Hell, we've even had our own TV show—

and if that doesn't make us experts in this media-saturated world, what does?

But "experts" (and maybe especially experts on television shows) are an illusion. They live in the world of ninety-second sound bytes, hour-long talk shows, airbrushed magazine articles, and books—like this one—that lay out exactly what to do at just the right time in just the right way. Parenting experts talk about how to raise kids. But talk is cheap to those of us who live life in real time, with real kids. We manage our relationships, including those with our children, in real time, moment to moment. And no one is perfect in each moment.

The ideas in this book are sound. We've tested them, again and again, with real kids and in real families, even under the unflinching eye of the television cameras. They work, and, if you choose to use them and apply them consistently, we can virtually guarantee that they will work for you, too.

But if our professional and personal experience dealing with children has taught us anything, it's that, as parents, we need to forgive ourselves our human frailties. Perhaps the most important message of this book, the wisest piece of parental advice we can give is this: Give yourself a break.

At the end of the day, I firmly believe that the "acorn" theory of child development probably trumps all others: In the end, kids will turn out to be like us, their parents. We are our children's role models. They will notice and imitate how we live our lives, how we do our work, how we treat other people and ourselves. Our conduct is the best predictor of our kids' behavior today and their future success as adults. Yes, sometimes we need to manage our kids' behavior, but we *always* need to manage our own, to give our kids the best models we can.

You *will* let the television be a babysitter. You *will* feed your kids chicken nuggets and trans fats. You *will* pull them into bed with you at night. You *will* misjudge your timing. You *will* keep them in diapers too long. You *will* lose it occasionally and yell. And when you do those things, give yourself a break. We're not suggesting that you give up completely. We're saying, be as consistent as you possibly can be. Enforce the rules to the best of your abilities, as often as possible. And then, lighten up. Give yourself a break when you fall down just like every other parent in the world, including us, falls down. And then get up, dust yourself off, laugh, and keep going. Oh, and go hug and kiss your kid.

XOXOX
Dr. Michael Weiss

Acknowledgments

MICHAEL J. WEISS

This book is both a culmination and a starting point for my understanding of children, families, and relationships. Many people have contributed both directly and indirectly to what I have come to understand.

My wife, Debbie, and our daughters, Vanessa and Nina, are my daily tutors, who routinely show me what I do and do not understand about being a family. I love them with every cell in my body. Likewise, the family I grew up with—Gary, Jack, and Sarah Weiss, Norman Weiss, and Beverly and Norman Schuminsky—have been my supporters and teachers. I would be lost without them. My cousin Paul Willis and I have spent many hours talking about all things related to this book, but most of all he has been my working model of a true *mensch*. I also owe a great debt to another of my wonderful cousins, Joel Madison, who encouraged me and gave true feedback, and never once told me I was crazy for wanting to develop these ideas for documentary television. (He works in TV and knows a thing or two about crazy.)

I also have a unique relationship with my in-laws: Herb, Christine, Ryan, Herb Jr., Skyler Kemp, and Summer Sowers, at whose kitchen tables I wrote much of the content that ended up in this book. How many times do you find a son-in-law who *wants* to move in with his wife's mother and father? Also, my friends David Moore, Joshua Stillman (in fact, the whole Stillman/Taube family), and

Dale Nordenberg have been my brothers. Their souls, thoughts, and unconditional friendship have buoyed me all of these years.

Sheldon Wagner and I produced the television show *Real Families*, which portrays the ideas represented in this book. Both the television show and this book were born from four people who saw in our work something worth sharing with others. Irina and Tom O'Hara and Jay and Jean Kaiser put their money and encouragement where their mouths were and made these projects a reality. I try to emulate them as examples of how to live a meaningful life. Our business partner Rob Schneider has been a catalyst who has forced me to think about the ideas behind these projects. He has been a devoted friend. The two people who took big risks to bring our television show to air were Jim Erickson and Barbara Williams. Both were at Alliance-Atlantis in 1998 when I, a non-TV shrink who knew nothing about their business, showed up with a hare-brained idea to do a "reality TV" show about ho-hum everyday child rearing. They loved the idea and supported our show, and together we invented the genre of reality TV (but don't blame us for all those other nutty shows that followed). In the making of *Real Families*, I have become deeply connected to our director of photography, Larry Carey, our location soundman, Chris Newton, and our film editor, Fred Beaulieu. Over the many years of sharing dingy hotel rooms, spending days in dark editing suites, and holding late-night conversations, they became dear friends and collaborators. The stories in this book are a part of what we all shared, and I deeply appreciate their handprints on these projects. My other on-camera collaborators, Drs. Ellen Moss and Brian Goldman, also gave ideas, heart, and a language to these projects. Their input gave Sheldon and me new insights into our work.

The sun still hasn't set on *Real Families*. Thank you to Roselyne Brouillet, Sari Buksner, and Jacques Bouchard at The Multimedia Group of Canada, who syndicated the show around the world. Also, the show was given a great forum in the United States by the Oxygen Network and the thoughtful support of Gerry and Kit Laybourne and Geoffrey Darby. Kit and I developed "shorts" of *Real*

Families for Time Warner Cable together. His feedback was precious, and spending time with yet another *mensch* was a pleasure.

Our academic and clinical colleagues have been another source of lifetime teachers. Starting at Tufts and later at McGill Universities, my mentor and his wife, Philip and Nancy Zelazo, gave birth to my professional life. Few students can say that they are still writing with their graduate school adviser twenty-eight years after they met. Also from back in my Tufts days, I have Emily Bushnell, Rich Chechile, Joe DeBold, Rachel Keen (at the University of Massachusetts), and Jackie Ellis to thank for putting so much effort into such a rough diamond. They were in the delivery room when I was professionally born.

From my days at Harvard and the Children's Hospital in Boston, I had the great fortune of working with Drs. Margaret Bauman, Ron Steingard, Tim Buie (thanks to Kathy Roberts for introducing me to Tim), Leslie Rubin, and Allan Crocker. These people help give Harvard the wonderful reputation it deserves. They have been my role models for how to be thoughtful, rigorous, and human as a clinician and researcher. Dr. Anne Donnellan, now at San Diego University, is also one of my role models. She is always sitting on my shoulder to remind me that, whether we're talking about children, relationships, or empirical research, acceptance and compassion matter first and most. Over the years, I have had relationships with many talented developmental psychologists, all of whom are dear to me. We are lucky to see each other for about four days a year—which is so little time—at the meetings of the Society for Research in Child Development and the International Society of Infant Studies. Yet seeing them even for just a few days leaves me with a renewed sense of curiosity, and questions about what we do. Some of them include David Moore (again), Gerry Turkewitz, Jerry Kagan, Philippe Rochat, Bob Lickliter, Lorraine Bahrick, David Lewkowicz, Robin Cooper (who introduced me to Sheldon Wagner!), Bernie Karmel, and Judy Gardner. I have such a sense of pride in knowing them, and a responsibility to teach others what they have taught me. Thank you to all of you. Finally, my return to academia at Fairfield

University is the product of John McCarthy, Betsy Gardner, Tim Heitzman, Joan Patrick, Billy Davidson, and Glenn Newman. Thank you for letting me into your worlds. I can't wait to see what awaits us.

I have worked with some outstanding special-needs teachers, who have taught me so much about children. Lynne Guilmette and Marcia Dudley are two of the very best. Thank you for the long hours, patience, and love that you invested in our work together. I have always cherished our friendship. Also among the great teachers and therapists I have worked with are Kathy Roberts, Pat Hiles, and my friends and colleagues at Giant Steps School–Connecticut. There are too many of you to list here, but together you have all created a true learning environment not only for our students, but also for all of us who work there.

I also owe a great debt of gratitude to Penny Bowen and friends for introducing me to Carl Kingston. Carl has become a dear colleague and has shown me how to make the information in this book available to many who may not be able to afford the cost of books or tapes of TV shows. Together we have established the not-for-profit Institute for Child and Family Development to help disseminate these materials. His thoughtful considerations are most appreciated.

This book exists thanks to my literary agent, Rick Broadhead. Rick saw our television show, called me up, and asked, "Why no book?" When I couldn't come up with an answer, he brought us to writer Susan Goldberg and, eventually, to our new best friends at Warner Books: Amy Einhorn, Jim Schiff, Frances Jalet-Miller, and Laura Jorstad. Thank you all for allowing this project to happen and for your great sensitivities in letting it become what it is.

I cannot do justice to the thank-yous I owe to the forty-seven families that bared their souls on camera in *Real Families*, or the hundreds and hundreds of families I have worked with over the years. You have taught me to see each person as an individual, to recognize that there are always several paths to peace, and that the most important ingredients in family happiness are forgiveness and acceptance. For all this and more, thank you.

Finally, Sheldon and Susan. Every time I have had anything resembling a good idea, it's had to pass the "Sheldon test" first. You have forged my thinking and held me accountable to my own ideas. But most of all, you are my dear friend, and my life is better because of you. Susan, you gave me the gift of my own words that I could not find before. How can I thank you? Having you live in my head has resulted in having you reside in my heart. My enduring hope is that this is just the beginning.

To all of you, thanks for blessing my life.

Michael J. Weiss, PhD
June 2005

SHELDON WAGNER

> *"Beggar that I am, I am even poor in thanks."*
> —HAMLET

It is one of the great fortunes of my life that I have been privileged to be the student of so many of the psychological giants of the twentieth century. The five years I spent in Geneva as a research assistant to Jean Piaget and his great collaborator, Barbel Inhelder, have marked me profoundly. Piaget was the first psychologist to truly take children seriously. He was the first to take developmental psychology "out into the field"—out onto the playgrounds: shooting marbles with kids, asking questions about where rules came from and what they believed and why they believed it; giving them dilemmas, fascinated by their "misconceptions" that for him were actually rule-governed conceptions. He was also the first to bring experimental psychology into the world of infancy—the field where Michael and I got our stripes. Piaget's *méthode clinique* and analytical approach to development suffuse all that I do.

Near the end of his life, Piaget became interested in what he used to derisively call the "American question"—the most common reaction to his talks in America: how to "accelerate" the immutable developmental stages that he had so elegantly characterized. In other words, "How can I make my five-year-old think like a seven-year-old?" The great lesson I learned was that for effective developmental change to occur, we have to first see the world through the child's eyes and mind. Only then can we make effective developmental change that would be "owned" by the child.

Later, I crossed paths with B. F. Skinner and his colleagues, who taught me techniques that were manifestly effective and elegantly "ballistic." Michael and I are able to accomplish most of what we do because we look at family dynamics through a "behavioral lens," filtering out the extraneous and zeroing in on "the true signal."

At Harvard, I became interested in education. At Piaget's urging, I worked with Seymour Papert in the Artificial Intelligence Laboratory at MIT. Papert felt that computers could change the lives of developmentally disabled students. I believe, still, that there is an enormous capacity to learn in almost all children if we are clever enough to find a way to speak in their language.

At Harvard, I was also fortunate enough to work with Howard Gardner, who was applying Piagetian research methods to children's development in many areas ignored by developmental psychology. The years I spent with him and Dennie Wolff and Ellen Winner at Project Zero honed my acuity for development in other domains that were as rich as the traditional domains of interest such as language and cognition.

The final intellectual legacy I must credit comes from Dante Cicchetti and Jerome Kagan, who convinced me that childhood psychopathology and developmental disabilities were an area where developmental psychology could advance our understanding of the brain and accomplish something useful for the children. Dante used to say, "Sheldon, don't look at the behaviors, look at the *organization* of the behaviors."

After Harvard, I went to teach and do research in the psychology department of the University of Rochester, a terrific academic home that I miss to this day. But I began to realize that my work in the academy wasn't addressing the issues that parents and children needed help with. As fate would have it, I met an applied developmental psychologist named Michael Weiss. I knew of Michael from his publications on infants and through mutual friends. What I didn't know was the true value of working directly with parents and children in real-time, real-life—and sometimes real intense—interactions with children. Michael knew the value of making developmental psychology "useful"—and truly, no one does it better! Certainly, it is the most difficult thing that I have ever done. I am deeply indebted to Drs. Lawrence Finnerty and William Marginson of New Bedford Public Schools for having given me so many opportunities to practice.

Michael's acknowledgments above resonate tremendously with me. I credit all those he credits. In particular, Lynne Guilmette and Marcia Dudley are among the greatest educational and behavioral practitioners I have had the privilege to know.

To Rob Schneider and the "TJB Triumvirate": You were there for us many years before *Supernanny*. You saw the value of bringing our techniques into the home and helping to change the developmental trajectories of all the wonderful children and families with whom we have had the privilege to work. They and I thank you.

To Susan, our collaborator, who has been so instrumental to this project, I thank you for your deft fluency with word and thought. Without you, Michael and I would still be locked into an "oral history model." You spearheaded and shepherded this project, and I am sure that at times it felt like herding cats. Thank you.

Finally, I must acknowledge my wonderful family: my wife, Denisa (the most psychologically healthy person I have ever known), and my treasured children, Manon and Alexei, without whom life would not be worth living. Many of the techniques discussed in this book were field-tested in my home. All the nighttime intrusions, eating resistances, toilet-training protocols, and "behavioral field trips" were tweaked and tuned in real time. But still, I never got it *exactly* right. I still remember my daughter Manon reminding me as I escorted her to time out: "Daddy, remember what you told Michael, short time-outs, short ones!"

God bless all you parents!

Sheldon Wagner, PhD
June 2005

SUSAN GOLDBERG

Thanks to Rick Broadhead for conceiving of this project, introducing me to Michael and Sheldon, and championing *Drawing the Line* to its completion. Many people have mentored me and encouraged this and other writing projects, including Jennifer Glossop, Ward McBurney, Susan Lightstone, and past and current Stern Writing Mistresses. At Warner Books, Amy Einhorn, Jim Schiff, Frances Jalet-Miller, and Laura Jorstad shepherded this book along admirably. *Baby Whisperer* co-author Melinda Blau generously offered professional advice and the "ghost's" perspective. Thank you all.

Rachel Warburton spent hours watching *Real Families* videotapes with me, and put up with my constant refrain of "Michael says . . ." She has nurtured and fiercely defended my life as a writer, and has worked hard to create space in our homes and our lives for me to do my work. She also reminds me of the importance of play. Thank you always for your constant love and support.

Thanks to Michael Weiss and Sheldon Wagner for creating and distilling such clear, compelling, and compassionate ways of relating to kids. Even after watching sixty episodes of *Real Families*, I was (and am) still intrigued by their approach and amazed at its success and consistency—intrigued enough to write a book on it. Sheldon's insights crystallized many key concepts for me, and his dry wit shaped the tone of this book. Throughout countless hours of phone conversations and our all-too-rare meetings, Michael's enthusiasm and generosity made this work both possible and enjoyable. Thank you for your friendship, for starting nearly every conversation over the past six months with "How's Rhys sleeping?" and for listening patiently to the answer to that question.

Over the course of writing this book, I both became a parent for the first time and lost a parent. Both experiences have shaped my life and this work indelibly. My mother, Ruth Goldberg, will forever be my role model for how to live life with grace, integrity, courage, and humor. She and my father, Morley Goldberg, have instilled in me the importance of family and the foundations of what it means to be a good parent. I hope to honor them both by living up to their example. My son, Rhys Isaac, teaches me every day about myself and the world, and I thank him for refreshing my perspective.

Susan Goldberg
June 2005

Drawing the Line
Worksheets

Drawing the Line: _____

Priority	Target Behavior	Positive Alternative	When/ Where Does It Occur?	Draw the Line	Drawing the Line: Reward?	Drawing the Line: Penalty?
1						
2						
3						
4						
5						
6						
7						
8						
9						
10						

Drawing the Line: _____

Priority	Target Behavior	Positive Alternative	When/ Where Does It Occur?	Draw the Line	Drawing the Line: Reward?	Drawing the Line: Penalty?
1						
2						
3						
4						
5						
6						
7						
8						
9						
10						

Drawing the Line: _____

Priority	Target Behavior	Positive Alternative	When/ Where Does It Occur?	Draw the Line	Drawing the Line: Reward?	Drawing the Line: Penalty?
1						
2						
3						
4						
5						
6						
7						
8						
9						
10						

Drawing the Line: _____

Priority	Target Behavior	Positive Alternative	When/ Where Does It Occur?	Draw the Line	Drawing the Line: Reward?	Drawing the Line: Penalty?
1						
2						
3						
4						
5						
6						
7						
8						
9						
10						

Index

About the Authors

Dr. Michael J. Weiss, PhD, received a doctorate in psychology from Tufts University and later honed his understanding of children and parents as a lecturer at McGill University, as a staff psychologist at the Montreal Children's and the Jewish General Hospitals, as a clinical fellow in psychiatry at Harvard University, and then as a staff psychologist at the prestigious Children's Hospital in Boston.

Frustrated with the "establishment" billion-dollar industry of testing and labeling kids, however, he eventually quit the Children's Hospital to found Behavioral Pediatrics and Family Development with Dr. Sheldon Wagner—a consulting group working with developmentally disabled children and their families and schools.

As a testament to the success of Dr. Weiss's commonsense, hands-on approach, all the families he worked with at the hospital came with him—because he was the only doctor who made a difference with their kids. Other doctors could rate children's cognitive functioning, but Dr. Michael Weiss could toilet train an autistic, nonverbal, violent twelve-year-old. (In fact, he may hold the world record for "Most Children Toilet Trained.")

Dr. Weiss is also the executive producer and central character of the Gemini-nominated *Real Families* television series, a show on child development and parenting that has aired in the United States, Canada, the UK, and several other countries worldwide and that is currently in syndication. His documentary, *Inside Autism*, is currently in production.

Dr. Weiss was the senior editor of *Newborn Attention: Biological Constraints and the Influence of Experience* (1991, co-edited with

Philip R. Zelazo, PhD) and has published numerous articles, chapters, and abstracts related to infant and child development. Dr. Weiss is the developmental psychologist at Giant Steps School in Connecticut and an adjunct professor of psychology at Fairfield University.

Sheldon Wagner, PhD, studied at the University of Geneva with renowned developmental psychologist Dr. Jean Piaget. He then completed his doctoral work in psychology at Harvard University, where he researched children's normal and atypical development. Dr. Wagner also worked with Seymour Papert at the Massachusetts Institute of Technology (MIT) Artificial Intelligence Laboratory, and continued his postdoctoral training with Dr. Howard Gardner at Harvard University's Graduate School of Education.

Dr. Wagner was previously assistant professor of psychology and education at the University of Rochester, and has published numerous articles, chapters, and abstracts related to infant and child development. He has lectured internationally on a variety of topics related to infant and child development and developmental disabilities. He lives in Massachusetts with his family.

Susan L. Goldberg, MA, is an Ontario-based writer and editor. She is the co-author, with Paul Grimes, of *The Facts of Life: How to Build Wealth and Protect Your Assets with Life Insurance*, now in its second edition (Wiley, 2003). Susan honed her editorial skills at Ryerson Polytechnical University's publishing program, where she won the Stephen J. Mills Memorial Award. She is the winner of the 2002 Tom Fairley Award for Editorial Excellence, presented by the Editors' Association of Canada. She lives in Toronto and Thunder Bay with her partner and their son.

About Dr. Michael Weiss and
Dr. Sheldon Wagner and *Real Families* TV

You can also see Drs. Weiss and Wagner as they're featured in *Real Families*, a unique, field-documentary-style television show about the most important—and most difficult—job in the world: parenting.

Real Families is a window into the private lives of families from all walks of life. Candid interviews and family scenes taped with hidden cameras allow the viewer to be a fly on the wall, watching as Dr. Weiss and the families collaborate on how to solve common but troubling child-rearing issues. With persistence, intelligence, compassion, and common sense, Michael helps families find manageable solutions to difficult family problems. Viewers follow both the progress and setbacks typical in any real-life family dynamic. In fact, it's seeing both what works and what doesn't that makes *Real Families* so "real."

While Michael works directly with families in the heat of the moment, Dr. Sheldon Wagner steps back to consider the wider theoretical implications of the family dynamic. The audience listens in on conversations between the two psychologists as they break down the situation and analyze it in plain language.

In its first year, *Real Families* was nominated for a Gemini, the highest award in Canadian television programming. It has been broadcast in twelve countries around the world, from the UK to Israel, China, and Japan. This TV series is original and heartwarming, upbeat yet profound and intelligent. Viewers walk away with useful, practical information about raising kids and being in a family. Viewers are enchanted by these real stories and the show's down-to-earth hosts.

Real Families . . . it's about real life. For more information, call 1-877-PARENT-911, or go to www.realfamilies.net.